BULLET IN THE HEART

Four brothers ride to war,
1899-1902

BEVERLEY ROOS-MULLER

Jonathan Ball Publishers
Johannesburg • Cape Town

Photographs and illustrations courtesy of the author, the Muller and Diederichs families,
the War Museum of the Boer Republics and the Simon's Town Museum.

Originally published in South Africa in 2023 by
JONATHAN BALL PUBLISHERS
A division of Media24 (Pty) Ltd
PO Box 33977
Jeppestown
2043

ISBN 978-1-77619-274-8
ebook ISBN 978-1-77619-275-5

www.jonathanball.co.za
www.twitter.com/JonathanBallPub
www.facebook.com/JonathanBallPublishers

Cover by Sean Robertson
Design and typesetting by Nazli Jacobs
Map by Jan Booysen
Set in Minion

BULLET IN THE HEART

Four brothers ride to war, 1899-1902

This book is dedicated to

Ampie (Adriaan Diederichs Muller)
(in memoriam)

and
Nandi Roos and Anneke Muller

Contents

The Muller Family

Names in bold: writers of the Muller war diaries

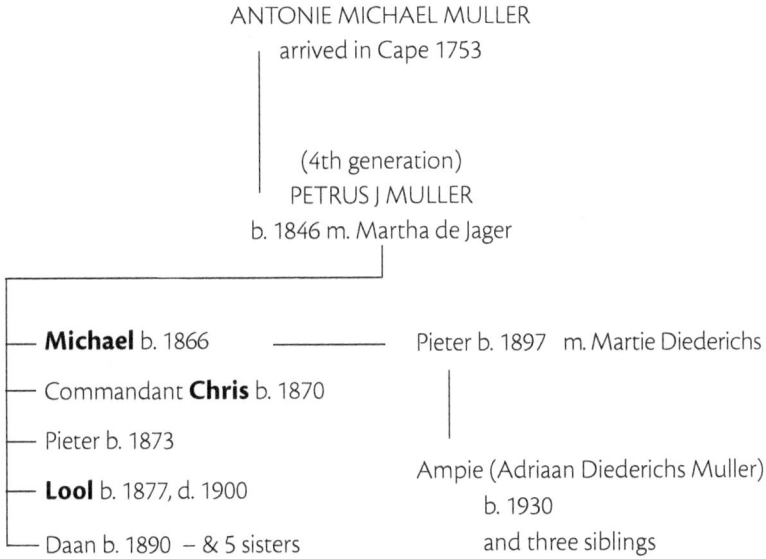

ANTONIE MICHAEL MULLER
arrived in Cape 1753

(4th generation)
PETRUS J MULLER
b. 1846 m. Martha de Jager

— **Michael** b. 1866 ——————— Pieter b. 1897 m. Martie Diederichs

— Commandant **Chris** b. 1870

— Pieter b. 1873

— **Lool** b. 1877, d. 1900   Ampie (Adriaan Diederichs Muller)
                                   b. 1930

— Daan b. 1890 − & 5 sisters   and three siblings

The Muller Brothers

Chris

Michael

Lool

Pieter

Introduction

FOUR BOER BROTHERS, all young adults, readied themselves late in 1899 to defend their sovereign country, the Free State, against the invading British Empire. Three of them kept diaries, the only known instance that this happened in this war. Their powerful and often painfully honest daily entries disclose their remarkable voices within the context of the great and awful circumstances that had suddenly overtaken them.

The gradual discovery of these fraternal diaries, and their other war documents, was particularly significant in that it offered a unique opportunity to examine and contrast how very differently each brother responded to the challenges of war, capture and exile. It is also possible to see their family's struggle to survive as a close reflection of the war's effect on the small Boer population.

This band of brothers from the eastern Free State were Michael Muller, the eldest, then Chris (both of them already married, with very young children), Pieter, and Lodewyk (Lool), the youngest, aged 22 when the war began.

And what remarkably literate, expressive brothers those Mullers were! Full of need to capture their experiences (all written in Afrikaans-Nederlands), sometimes in the thick of battle: the scrawled notes of Chris on the evening after the Magersfontein battle in December 1899, and in the days thereafter, under fire; the rain-dashed pages written by the youngest brother, Lool, at Colesberg; the angry, tightly written diatribe penned by Michael about the insults of his treatment at Surrender Hill – these have the urgency of men determined to go on record. All fought bravely, and all were captured as prisoners of war (POWs). One of them did not survive.

Michael, a gentle, pious man, was not a natural soldier, though he was a stoic one. The war would shake him to the core and ruin him; his grandchildren said that he never really recovered from it.

Chris, then 28, the second son, was a natural leader, confident and handsome. A brave soldier, he rose rapidly through the ranks – unlike in the British army, officers were chosen by their men, for they would not follow someone they did not trust. He quickly became a veldkornet (equivalent to the British rank of captain), and then commandant (similar to lieutenant-colonel) of the Ladybrand commando, a rank his elder, Commandant APJ Diederichs, had held at the time he was killed at Magersfontein. These two families not only fought together, but later became even closer, through marriage.

We know less about Pieter, who did not keep a diary, although his brothers wrote about him, and he was mentioned in their war letters. It seems he was a sturdy and reliable man.

The cheerful, much-loved youngest, Lool, rode off to war in high spirits, as do many young men, thinking this might be his great adventure. It was, for a short while; then the critical loss of his horse and his ensuing capture woke him to harsh reality. His last months in captivity were a heartbreak for him, and a reflection of how the effects of war can bring low the strongest spirit.

Famous war diaries are frequently written in grandiose terms by the well connected or those with an agenda. When written by those less important, less well known, such as the Muller brothers, they give an unabridged view of *exactly* what the writers experienced. These are the authentic, unedited voices of what happened and when it happened.

It is arresting to see how often they differ from the formal histories. Their authenticity is, on the whole, implicit, for they are writing without the benefit of hindsight, and there is no foreknowledge of the outcome of the battles and the prisons and the exiles, and the final victories or defeats. All that exists is in the present, and that is all they record.

When captured in 1900, as all four brothers were, their diaries gave them the only agency they had left. They did not shy away from detailing all the large and little events, the many curiosities, the indignities they experienced; they honestly recorded their intimate thoughts and turbulent emotions.

The Commissiepoort Debating and Sharp-shooting Society, 1898. Lool, with a moustache and bow tie, is seated in the front row, between two of his sisters, Martha and Hannie. Chris is confidently in the centre, also in a bow tie. Eldest brother Michael is to his left, wearing the bowler hat. Pieter is next to Michael. Directly behind the three brothers, in the centre, is paterfamilias Petrus Johannes Muller, in hat and dark glasses.

Their witness forms part of that endless human chain of yearning to be heard, on parchment or paper scraps, cut into concreted walls, hidden in attics or under the floorboards of ghettos: the sounds of the silenced, made visible.

Of the three brothers who left diaries, by far the most fulsome was Chris, who left eight surviving diaries from the beginning of his war to its end in 1902, including his return from exile. An additional diary of his, written in mid-1900, was lost, perhaps mislaid in the post, for as he completed each one, he sent it to his parents for safekeeping (on the whole, the postal service functioned with impressive efficiency). Fortunately, a memoir of Chris's close friend, Andries Meyer, helped complete his record.

Colleen Muller Loesch, the granddaughter of Chris Muller, inherited all his war material. These boxes of mementos included souvenirs, letters and photographs from Chris's POW days in Ceylon (today's Sri Lanka), and even the bandana, flecked with blood, that he used to bind up his wounded leg in 1900. She granted me the right to use the contents of all eight of his diaries, covering the full two and a half years of his war, including his baptism of fire at the legendary battle of Magersfontein, a famous victory by the Boers in December 1899.

The pages of Lool's single diary, a sturdy notebook, are filled halfway, from the beginning of his war in January 1900 until his early and tragic death in Green Point camp in mid-1900. During his active service it is written in calm, measured script, much as if he were sitting in a classroom: this seems remarkable under such dangerous circumstances. After his capture in March 1900, however, his handwriting becomes quite uneven, and never quite returns to his earlier, smooth cursive style.

A quality notebook, Lool's is the smartest of all the Muller diaries. The inside is well preserved. His entries are clear and well formed under the circumstances, easier to read than the diaries of his elder brothers, Michael and Chris.

After his death, Lool's partially filled diary was cared for by a fellow POW, who took it with him to the POW camp on St Helena. When the war ended, Lool's friend, Dawid Kriel, who had been with him on commando, wrote down the details of his death and funeral, and returned the diary and Lool's few belongings to his parents. Such acts of duty and kindness, performed so often by surviving comrades-in-arms after wars have ended, are of extraordinary value to bereaved families. Often they provide the only direct information and connection to those loved ones severed forever, in sad circumstances. The grateful Muller family would certainly have noted that Lool's last coherent thoughts, in his diary, were of longing for home. Despite its great value to his parents, his diary was later mislaid for decades, and rediscovered by chance only while preparing this book – so easily does such precious material vanish.

Michael began his diary at the end of July 1900, when he was captured. From that moment, he kept a complete record of his captivity until he was shipped off as a POW to Bermuda nearly a year later, from Cape Town. He recorded the date and day of the week, the weather (as a farmer, this was a natural obsession), the view, anything that struck him as either important or curious, and his deepest feelings.

It is remarkable he was able to capture so much, for his cloth-covered diary is surprisingly slim. Smaller than his hand (it measures 13,5 x 8 cm), it would have fitted into a shirt pocket (which would have helped to conceal and conserve it), and so slender that it seems barely possible it contains more than a hundred pages of writing in his carefully formed though not especially skilled hand.

After he had filled the entire notebook, Michael began to use a few tiny sheets of almost transparent paper, gleaned from somewhere (paper was at a premium in the camps), carefully folded into tiny double pages, tucked inside the back of the cloth book. Hardly robust; how it survived is a mystery. A magnifying glass is needed to read it, and some words are so close to the eroded edges of the pages that they can no longer easily be deciphered.

After the war, Michael wrote over his original entries in ink, to 'fix' the words on the page – diaries were usually written in pencil, which was less likely to run during wet weather; also, carrying ink and a pen was difficult on the move. The rewrite was quite a labour for him, and it is clear that his handwriting had either improved by the time he inked it, or that the roughness of his earlier hand reflected the roughness of his POW days.

During my research, a missing page of Michael's diary – a frail, minute scrap of paper – was found squashed at the bottom of a box sent from Bloemfontein. I remember the exact moment I pulled it out, without too much interest, and then instantly realised what it was. I had spent years poring over Michael's original diary (inherited by his eldest son Pieter, born in 1897, then passed on to Pieter's son, Ampie, my husband) and was intimately familiar with its size and his handwriting; I had known that there was a missing page because of his meticulously kept dates.

Those tiny, fragile pages, half the size of a playing card, when placed together with the other loose pages tucked inside his diary's back cover, fitted together absolutely precisely, as if they had never been parted. Where this small single sheet, folded over, had been, and why it had been parted from the original diary, is unfathomable. These are the moments a writer of history lives for, and a prickly reminder of how fragile our stories are if they are not preserved.

Another discovered treasure was a thin journal belonging to Nelie, Michael's devoted wife. She had written it many years after the war, when she was widowed, and much of it is domestic. But there are some crucial pages about her war experience, on the run with her two tiny boys between enemy lines, starving and frightened. It is especially precious, for it is the only direct example of a Muller woman's voice in this war.

There are, too, letters between the brothers, and to Nelie from her husband Michael in his POW camp, and other documents and photographs, that amplify all their stories.

These are the brothers who wrote about the war, those brave and unforgiving years now made present in their words.

The diaries: Michael's, top left (his name written on the back); one of Chris's, written in Ceylon (bottom left); and Lool's (bottom right), with the 1898 Debating Society photograph. This is the only time the diaries written by the three Muller brothers came together, more than a century later. (Photo by author.)

*

When asked why I wrote this book about these four Boer brothers, there are two answers, one quite grand, the other practical: I was gently handed the task.

The first, grander reason was drawn from something that Archbishop Desmond Tutu once told me, as he has so many others: that unless we understand each other's stories, we will never understand each other. His wise perception is ingrained into this book: to provide new insight into an old war, one that so deeply affected so many, with long-lasting consequences.

Most English-language books written in the decades after the Boer War of 1899-1902 reflect the Anglophile position, partly because the Empire eventually won, and also because English historians were unable to read the language of the Boers or were reluctant to access their stories. So a one-sided and often deeply inaccurate view of them was offered, even in the best histories. There was an almost entire lack of understanding of Boer culture, how their army operated, and even, earlier on, how super-skilled they were in the saddle and with a rifle – a misjudgement that was soon painfully discovered.

The Boers were far from the 'wild and woolly' figures so parodied in British newspapers, easy propaganda that ridiculed their enemy – even though it then raises the question of why it was so difficult to conquer them! The Boer army was a citizens' army that also included volunteers from other countries and the Cape Colony, and had no mighty Empire to resupply them. After months on commando in the veld, they were indeed in rags. Yet photographs of the Mullers, even while in captivity, show their pride in who they were, their sense of dignity.

The four Muller brothers had been 'properly brought up'; decent living was important – manners, education, the correct outfits for church and out-ings. The Free State was, in the late 1800s, a pious and ordered community with mutually beneficial relationships with its Sotho neighbours, who were trading partners and provided vital seasonal workers. The Free State also had good relations with the Cape Colony, and especially welcomed the many incomers who were of Scottish descent, with similar religious back-ground; some of those Scottish families fought on the Boer side.

The agricultural, settled Free Staters considered themselves very dif-ferent from their northern neighbour, the richer Transvaal, with its local prospectors, gold-hunting foreigners and mining towns that were typical of wilder, frontier societies. These two nations, among the smallest in the world, were separate and sovereign and, on the whole, didn't always much care for each other.

The British had assumed that the Free State would not support the Transvaal in the war; in this, they vastly underestimated the value that the Boers placed on loyalty to their own allies.

My second and more direct reason for writing this book is because my husband, Ampie (Professor Adriaan Diederichs Muller), was the grandson of Michael, eldest of the four Muller brothers. Soon after we met in Cape Town in 1997, he showed me a tiny booklet – the war diary of his grandfather. Naturally, I ignored it: the cramped, spidery writing looked indecipherable, and we were both deeply involved in our work, and each other.

Yet, while preparing to write about another freedom struggle, it occurred to me to look within this little diary's covers, and I began to appreciate Michael's engaging war story. His diary, and a group photograph of a debating society pasted to a ragged mount, were the only two documents with which I began this complex journey of tracking and sourcing information, after more than a century had passed. The discovery of Lool's diary, and then those of Chris, and Nelie Muller's little journal, all lay ahead, along with so much more material. Luckily, extended families often have someone whose task it is to be 'the rememberer', and families everywhere tend to cache war material, those mementos that connect them to a greater history beyond their own, individually lived experiences.

Ampie, who was born in 1930, had known some of that war generation, including both his Boer grandfathers – Michael Muller and Jan Diederichs, his maternal grandfather – both of whom had fought and both of whom he adored. He also remembered Chris Muller, and had attended his funeral. This war was not distant history to Ampie, and was part of the reason he devoted his life to human rights, becoming a co-founder of the South African Centre for Conflict Resolution.

He relished taking me to meet his enormous family of Mullers and Diederichs scattered throughout the country – I teased him that he seemed to be related to just about everyone we met, as so many Afrikaners are. We visited battlefields and graveyards, sites of POW camps, archives in South Africa and in the UK, former family farms, and ports from which the brothers had sailed into exile. Many of Ampie's wonderful elderly aunts (alas, no longer alive), of whom he was so proud, generously provided insight and detail – for they had known the survivors. I took many notes while talking to them, and also requested that, where possible, they write down their recollections.

As the recorder of the Muller war stories, I was not perhaps the most obvious candidate despite my being a writer, and having married into the family. I come from an Irish family, so could not speak a word of Afrikaans until I was sent, at the age of 12, to an Afrikaans boarding school in the Boland. On my arrival at the school, some (by no means all) boarders accused me of being responsible for the Boer War. This was awkward: I had no idea what they were talking about. We learned nothing at school about this war[1] although we heard plenty, during long, dull sessions in history, about the Great Trek, which we all wished had been much shorter.

This now recovered story of the four Muller brothers is offered as part of what Irish philosopher Richard Kearney called 'a hospitality of narratives': different and informed perspectives of shared events. For those who would like to more fully understand the Boer War, their diaries offer an unprecedented opportunity.

And it is worth wondering about their parents, and what sort of people they were, to have raised sons who, in the middle of the most chaotic and life-threatening moments of their lives, could keep their heads for long enough to record, daily, their experiences, thoughts and emotions.

Diaries can be both fascinating and boring. Battles are full of excitement and vigour but war is a long affair. The endless days of waiting for 'the next thing' to happen as soldiers, followed by the brothers' drawn-out months as POWs in South Africa and then in exile, were static by definition. Many entries are as dull as 'Today it is raining' or 'Nothing happened'. Unpacking them demanded much dexterity, to penetrate the *core* of the brothers' stories: their hopes and dreams, their loves, their challenges and courage, and their grief.

Their own experiences were forged in a particular war; yet on a broader, more universal level, these remarkable Muller brothers well reflect the agonies of war anywhere, at any time.

Dr Beverley Roos-Muller
2023

Some explanatory notes

ALTHOUGH THE WAR of 1899-1902 affected most of South Africa, it was and is referred to as the 'Boer War', a term that is historic and widely recognised. This book is *particularly* about the Boers' war, and not a British version of events, of which plenty exist.

I have, wherever possible, included information about the disastrous impact of the war on black South Africans; they certainly paid a terrible price, then and later.

I use the term *English*, in italics, to describe the British, for that is how the Boers referred to them (*die Engelse*). They would often refer separately to the Scots, whom they admired as a fighting force.

The Orange Free State was one of two Boer republics invaded by the British (the other being the Transvaal), and was so referred to in official discourse; but it was more generally referred to simply as the *Vrystaat* (Free State), the term all the Mullers used throughout their diaries.

The imperial measurements of the day – miles, yards and so on – as well as currency have been retained. So too have place names such as Basutoland (today Lesotho).

Very occasionally there are terms included that are considered pejorative and/or racist today but were at the time officially, and widely, used. Where essential for accuracy, they have been kept in the body of this story, marked with the caveat [sic]. The author appreciates the offensiveness of such terms and identifies with the sensitivity with which they need to be addressed and contextualised.

Map of the Orange Free State and surrounding region prior to and during the war

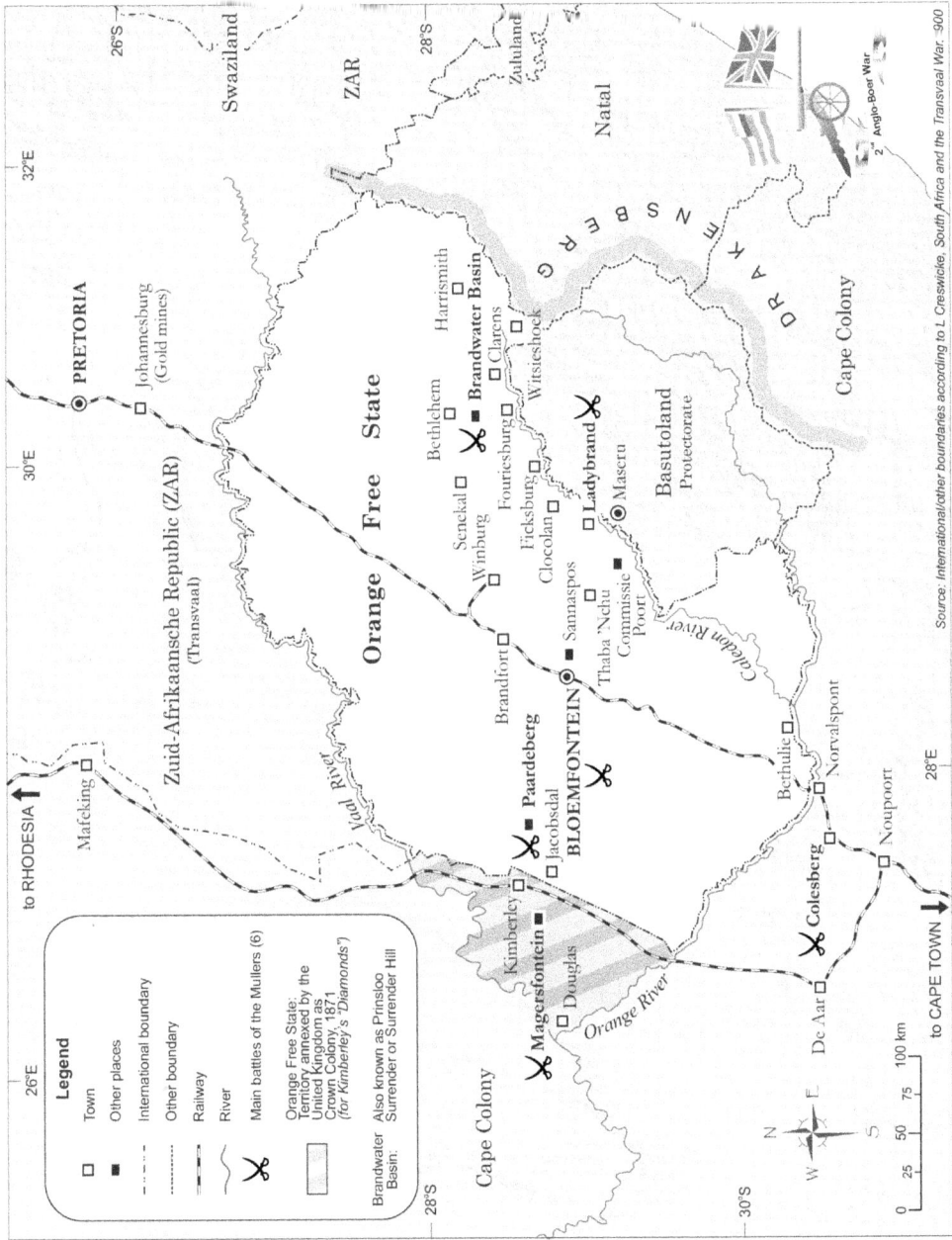

Source: International/other boundaries according to L Creswicke, South Africa and the Transvaal War: 1900

The natural boundaries of the Orange Free State, founded and recognised in 1854, met at the confluence of the Vaal and Orange rivers. After Kimberley's diamonds had been discovered in 1871, that area was 'annexed' by the UK as a Crown Colony. The land between the newer frontier and the earlier one is therefore shown as contested, running to very slightly east of Kimberley and Magersfontein. There was no rail line between Kimberley and Bloemfontein as a result of the disputed annexation: the sole rail route from the Cape to Johannesburg's gold lay through Bloemfontein.

PART I

WAR BEGINS

1899

1

A perfect shot

AT THE EXACT MOMENT that his commander is killed in the early morning of 11 December 1899, Chris Muller is crouched on the ridge of the Magersfontein koppie, ducking under a hail of bullets. This big battleground is 19 miles south of Kimberley, and is now a frontline of the war.

Chris sees the old man drop onto the flat veld before him: the bullet has torn straight through his heart. Streaking through the noise, dust and heat, the men caught on barbed wire, the wounded mules bellowing, the huge cannons thundering, the lyddite smashing, it is a perfect shot.

Commandant APJ Diederichs senses at once that his wound is fatal. It thuds into the centre of his chest, spreading his rich arterial blood across his white shirt and the lower whiskers of his white beard. He has been in war before, and has seen men and beasts killed often enough to sense this is a mortal shot: he has no more time.

The veteran Ladybrander slips to the ground and releases his old rifle, a Martini Henry as familiar to him as his own hand. The long barrel hits the veld. With his final breath he turns to his friend, Veldkornet Jan de Wet, and says, '*Buurman, ek het 'n doodskoot.*' Neighbour, I have been mortally shot.

He is 58 years old, a father and grandfather. He looks older.

Under ceaseless fire, Chris sees the dreadful sequel. Jan de Wet, brother of the famous General Christiaan de Wet, falls too.

On that day the two men die together as they have lived: neighbours, kinsmen and close friends, with adjoining farms in the distant, lovely eastern Free State. They breathe their last at one another's side on this deathfield.

It is a hard beginning of a long day of blood, heat, and victory for the Boers.

Commandant APJ Diederichs of the Ladybrand commando, 1897.

The young soldier on the ridge, Chris, is also seeing his destiny. In the coming months he will be baptised in the field, first as Ladybrand veldkornet, then as trusted commandant, replacing Diederichs. Still in his 20s, he is relatively young for such a heavy responsibility. Boer leaders are usually selected from older, battle-bruised men. But this is not a usual time.

As Chris digs in, he sees (and later records) their wounded:

> A Liebenberg also, J Taljaard was wounded by a rock that was thrown up by a shell. G Lourenz was rendered unconscious with a shell. The rest of our burgers go to the south side, where the fighting was the heaviest. We get the news that many known to us have fallen.

Neither he nor his younger brother, Pieter, can rescue their own men yet; the barrage is too great. Like the British army, they will have to wait and see, for no outcome of this battle can be predicted, though it will be legendary, unprecedented – a mighty upset for the *English,* their greatest loss since the Crimean War of 1853-1856.

Meanwhile, Chris is too busy to think about history. He writes later,

> At the foot of our ridge are many horses, shot dead in heaps. From where we sat, we had a good view of the battlefield. In our vicinity, where the battle started and is still continuing, the enemy's dead and wounded are still lying and those who behave as if they are dead are spread all over the ground. Some of them are trying to stop the bleeding with handkerchiefs. Others cry from the pain.

His 'good view' is that of the notorious wide-open natural gap at Magersfontein, prepared beforehand with small stone walls and trenches by the Boers to cut off their enemy, a neat and necessary ruse laid for them by the cunning of *veggeneraal* (combat general) Koos de la Rey. He had plotted to lure the *English* into a traditional game trap here: leave open a narrowing space and the hunted animals will head for it. There, you wait. And it had worked.

It is still early morning, a hot day after a cold night. The Boer Ladybranders – including Chris and Pieter – are already tired, having ridden back in the early, sodden hours to the farm nearby to secure their horses and fodder, after the Enslin Siding Skirmish many miles south (closer to Hopetown than Kimberley), hard fought on both sides. They had been weary but content, chattering and watering their horses and readying for rest, before the great booming of guns had reached them. They had had to remount and ride rapidly towards the distinctive koppie of nearby Magersfontein in the dawning light.

Rain, which had fallen heavily, had now stopped; the wet earth looked red, like blood, and smelled fresh.

When they arrived at the battlefield it was already rancid with the spilt odours of war. Commandant Diederichs, a calm, experienced man, now led a group of his Ladybranders forward to the gap.

Boer officers do not sit at the back of a battle. They lead their men, ride or run with them, for these commandos are family: son and brother, uncle and father, grandfather and nephew; neighbour, friend. They have known each other from childhood, and ride out regularly with horses and guns, warming themselves at fires at night on the open veld of the wide Free State. Ladybranders had placed their trust in Diederichs, a *vrederegter* (justice of the peace), and a kinsman and intimate of their esteemed young Free State president, Marthinus Steyn.

It is hard for them to grasp that their commandant is dead; yet in the months to come, his men will place their trust in Chris Muller as he leads them through other, fiercely contested fights.

The night before had been dark with lashing rain, but now the African sun glowers down on the battered hats of the Boers, on the tender skin of the panicking, pink British (the backs of the knees of the Highlanders, wearing kilts, are badly blistered). The worst, the Boers say afterwards, are the screams of frightened, dying men. Lying on the wide field of Magersfontein, these foreigners are pinned down by the Boers, skilled beyond imagining at sharpshooting, for they do not miss a speck of movement.

Their enemy is trapped, hiding behind the thigh-high anthills that are their only cover, crying out for their mothers. They call for water.

The Boers, who are family men, are horrified. This is intolerable.

At dusk, Chris and his men are ordered to climb down from the ridge of the koppie and take up positions in and around the trenches, where they will spend an exhausted, jumpy night, for it is not yet clear who the victor is.

As night falls – late, because it is almost the midsummer solstice – the Boers cannot bear the suffering they hear. Take your men, they say, we will give you safety.

Some of the British troops break that trust, or misunderstand, and, advancing close to the Boer trenches, they open fire. They are shot.

Stop that, says the Boer messenger, and there is another lull filled with the noise of agony, before the dying and wounded can be moved back to their own lines. Many remain.

Later, Captain Fichardt will note in his telegram to President Steyn, sent from Jacobsdal at 10.25 pm, that he had personally counted 24 ambulances lumbering back to the *English* camp. In his diary, Chris Muller noted them too: 'The ambulances from both sides are continually busy.'

The Boers have lost about a hundred men, Fichardt tells the president, mainly on the distant side of the gap from the Magersfontein koppie. Here, the Scandinavians,[2] a unit of Boer supporters who took up an exposed position on a flattened knoll, have paid a terrible price. They fought until the last of them was overrun; a handful of their survivors were wounded and taken prisoner.

But the English have lost many hundreds more. The famous Black Watch is almost destroyed, Fichardt reports. It is terribly true: the Scotsmen have paid a shocking price for the blunders of the senior English officer on this bad, sad day, and there are traumatised towns in Scotland gradually receiving news of the disaster. The bodies of Scottish soldiers lie in their hundreds on the sandy open veld, far from their green glens.[3] The Boers have deep respect for the courage of these Scottish foes.

On the field lies the flaccid, heavy body of the *English* observation balloon. The Boer men had fretted about it – 'above it all, is a [hot]-air balloon to spy on us,' Chris observed – yet it was sent up far too late to be of benefit. It is only one of many costly mistakes the English foes have made.

The corpse of a falcon, shot in the melee, lies bleeding on the field. It is remarked on by those who saw it fall, as not fair game; yet none of this is. Mules that carried the ordnance to the trenches and had no protection lie blasted on the field of death: behind the koppie, hundreds of Boer horses have been killed.

The body of Commandant Diederichs has lain, lifeless, throughout all of this fierce day. When respite comes in the cooling evening, his son, Jan, the young husband and father alongside whom Chris had ridden at Enslin, must bury his father. Men open the ruddy ground with spades and place him carefully alongside the bodies of his comrades.

Jan is a strong man, a quick thinker. He looks around for a marker. He cannot use the stock of his father's rifle, for that will be needed. He takes a long *murgbeen* (marrow bone), the strongest bone from an animal carcass, for there are plenty of those. He drives this into the ground next to his father's shoulder. It will act as a memory marker, and years later he and his siblings will return for their father and carry him home to his eastern Free State farm, where he will be reburied in the soft, receiving soil of his fields at Haltwhistle farm. This long bone will prove to a sceptical Kimberley magistrate (who tries to refuse the reclamation) that this body, is, indeed, that of the most senior Boer to die at Magersfontein.

Telegrams are sent and despatches written in the aftermath, in the lengthening night. Some of them are accurate. President Steyn hears of the great success at Magersfontein, vindicating his controversial choice of the junior combat general De la Rey's tactical planning over that of the more senior general Piet Cronjé. But along with it comes also the grievous news of the death of his Diederichs kinsman, to whom he has personally made a solemn promise, just two days previously, that he will never sign his hand to a surrender. He keeps the promise, never forgetting the dead veteran to whom he made it.[4]

The president writes telegrams that, as a soldier and friend, he hoped he would never have to send: among them to the newly widowed MMM Diederichs[5] on the farm Haltwhistle, near present-day Hobhouse, and to the family of Jan de Wet on the neighbouring farm, Juistzoo. It is a hard thing to have sent men you know and respect to their execution.

The farmhouses of both families will soon be burned to the ground by the enemy. Both will lose children; the De Wets will lose almost everyone.

This day, this epic battle at Magersfontein, left long stains, of both success and slaughter. Chris Muller, newly blooded in battle though not yet wounded, recorded the events in flowing detail that night in his fast, scrawling hand, the first of his war diaries. In his later years, he will write an heroic yet conciliatory poem about this battle, that is also a praise-song to Diederichs.

Meanwhile, it begins. It is almost the end of 1899 and this war inflicted on the Boers is under way. Shots have been fired, widows have already begun to grieve.

Four Muller brothers ride to war from the eastern Free State. Three will survive, though they will be POWs for longer than they were ever in the saddle.

This is a war that nobody wanted, except for the already very rich.

2

Four Free State brothers ride to war

WHEN THE FOUR elder Muller brothers saddled up to defend their country, the Free State, they believed that God and justice were on their side, that a win was inevitable. It was an opinion shared by those around them.

In less than a year, all of them had been captured.

That grim fate was not, of course, in the forefront of their minds in 1899. The certitudes of war – death, separation, long hardship – are seldom in the minds of the still-youthful. Quite the opposite: for them, war may be regarded as an adventure, a chance for new experiences and a proving of their mettle.

At least three of the four brothers shared something of this view. Only the eldest, Michael, dreaded what lay ahead. The energetic yet quietly spoken farmer found it unbearably hard to leave his young family behind, not only because of his affectionate nature but also because they were so vulnerable.

Michael was 33 years old at the end of 1899. Slender and mild mannered, he was the father of a toddler and a new baby – Pieter (Petrus Johannes), born on 2 November 1897, and Chrisjan, born on 13 December 1899. His wife, Nelie (Cornelia Christina, nee Van den Heever) was 21 years old at the time, barely 16 when she had married; it would be a long and loving union, but never prosperous.

The second brother of five, Chris, was in his late 20s. Handsome and a born leader with a charismatic flair, he was also married, with a daughter, Joey (Johanna), and an infant son, who died in the first months of the war, early in 1900.

Then there was Pieter, 26, the middle brother, a responsible and serious-minded soldier who was sight-impaired.

The fourth was cheery, lively Lool, 22, full of the nervous energy of a young man keen for excitement.

The fifth and youngest brother, Daan, was aged 9.

There were also five sisters: Non, Hannie, Minnie, Mart and Ellie, most of them married.

The Muller brothers joined, at different times, about 20 000 fit-for-service Free State burgers and about 30 000 more from the Transvaal, as well as some foreign Boer-supporting troops – far more than the British War Office's estimates had guessed at, which would prove one of many costly misjudgements for them.

Chris and Pieter were the first to leave, both dressed in semi-uniform (Boers had no 'official' uniform; as civilian soldiers they wore their own clothes into battle), riding off together to the muster at Hexrivier farm in the Ladybrand district.

Battle ready, November 1899: Chris is at the far right, standing, with Pieter on his right. The others are (according to Chris's diary) Johnny Brink, Z and J Joubert, G Delport, E Kriel and G Laurenz. (Photograph: The War Museum of the Boer Republics, Bloemfontein)

From there, Chris left with Pieter and his commando on 26 November 1899 for the western front of the Free State war; soon they would take part in the triumphant but bloody battle of Magersfontein.

Lool, the youngest, left on 15 January 1900 for Colesberg, raring to get stuck into the enemy.

These Mullers had been residents of the eastern Free State for a single generation. The father of the ten Muller children, Petrus Johannes Muller, born on 7 May 1844, was a direct descendant of the original Muller *stamvader* (founding father), Antonie Michael Muller, who had arrived in the Cape in 1753, and some of whose descendants were still living on their original Riversdale farm, Zeekoegat, in the Cape Colony.[6]

In 1876, along with one of his brothers, Frikkie (George Frederick), Petrus moved with his wife Martha (nee De Jager) and other family members to the fertile Ladybrand district of the Free State, where he bought the farm Palmyra.

By the time the many children of this large Muller family had reached adulthood, their branch of the family was settled in the Commissiepoort region of the Ladybrand district, with a well ordered way of living. They were literate, devout, hard-working and agricultural-middle-class, well off by farming standards. They and their neighbours were very far from the witless peasants described in the British press and, less forgivably, by British officials who, had they read their colonial reports more carefully, should have known better.

The home of these Mullers lay in the lovely borderlands of the eastern Free State, alongside a seam of the Maluti mountains that divided them from the high kingdom of then-Basutoland (today Lesotho) along the Caledon River. This border had always been porous, and that would prove useful to the Boers during the coming months and years of war.

The great Sotho king Moshoeshoe, after decades of strife and sometimes bloody battles with local tribes and Boers but never having been vanquished, had established his permanent 'mountain kingdom', though ruling over less land than his ancestors had controlled. It was now a British Protectorate and outside the reach of any further invasion.

The local Boers had settled into a working relationship with Basutoland, often with good trading, farming and political connections – in the eastern section, most Boers spoke Sotho from childhood.

The entire area is dotted with the caves of the long-dead and the valleys of ancestors so hidden that few outsiders have ever seen them – though anyone is welcome there, to pay respects. Boer women and children hid in them during the war. Drums calling the ancestors sometimes thunder off the golden buffers of the sandstone cliffs. Everything is larded in meaning.

Above all else, the land is extraordinarily, perfectly beautiful. The light is clear and unpolluted and soft. In the early morning, the wide plateaus open up to the horizons and small koppies float on them as if sailing over the plains. In summer, huge thunderhead clouds stampede across the deepening blue skies and unleash life-giving rain, filling the rivers and dams and waterfalls. In winter, the peaks whiten with snow, and in kraals the livestock huddle together to fight off the freeze. Eagles soar over the Golden Gate buttresses, and within overhangs and crevices, if you know where to look, are the marks of the small hunters who once roamed this rich ground before it was fought over and fenced and farmed. It is lush territory, and desirable. It is contested territory, and its history has often been deadly.

The name 'Free State' represented what these Boers had chosen to become but it would not help them avoid the war. The Free State Boers were an agriculturally grounded, pious people with no desire for more expansion – they *especially* did not want the war. But their attractive geography, though perfect for farming, would be their downfall, because *they were in the way.*

Cecil Rhodes had again lost office as the prime minister of the Cape Colony after a second corruption scandal (more recently because of the Jameson Raid and his lying about it afterwards). Despite this, he and his wealthy cohorts in Britain still fixed their eyes on the Transvaal and its gold, hoping it would springboard them to an even bigger prize – the hinterland of the north, where they believed, inaccurately, lay fabled riches. The Free State is in the very centre of South Africa, landlocked, in the crosshairs of travellers north or south, east or west. By its very locality, it was caught up in this unwanted strife.

The Free State's fate lay in that it was inconvenient, a large island of land plonk in the middle of the most efficient, direct and only train route between Cape Town and Johannesburg via its capital, Bloemfontein. Its greatest treasure, diamond-rich Kimberley in the west, had been silkily siphoned off by the British Crown on 27 October 1871 with an annexation that placed it under direct British rule as the Crown Colony of Griqua-land West.

This annoyed the Cape Colony, which desired Kimberley itself (and incorporated it nine years later), almost as much as it upset the Free State within whose natural boundaries it had belonged.

This dry area had been largely ignored until 1869, when a rich diamond-digging site later known as the 'Big Hole' was revealed. Ownership became a huge prize. British officials who masterminded the 1871 land grab claimed they did so because of the Boers' propensity to grab land. Apparently they were unable to see the irony in this. No one was fooled: it would become the richest diamond dig in the world.

The British government eventually, in 1876, payed 'compensation' of £90 000 to the Free State for Kimberley, an overt admission of their culpability, and also one of the most valuable finesses the Crown ever made.

By the time of the Boer War, British investment in Kimberley was worth a colossal (for the time) £40 million sterling, and this fact, linked to Rhodes's protective zeal for his wealth there, would have a significant effect on the route the war took in those early months, and therefore on the Mullers and their companions.

The choice for Free Staters was to either provide free passage to the north-bound British, or support President Kruger's forces in what they believed, in their heart of hearts, would be an impossible war to win. The latter also meant joining the Transvalers, a citizenry that many sober Free Staters despised for their wild ways.

It is important to recognise that these Boer republics were two tiny separate countries with quite different views of how to live. It was not a given that Britain would wage war on *both* of them: in fact, quite the opposite. There was no appetite in Britain for drawing President Steyn and his small Free State republic into the conflict. The young, well-educated head of state, who had been called to the bar at the Inner Temple in London in 1882, was well thought of in British circles of influence. Also, fighting two Boer republics, rather than just one, would double the effort needed to conquer their sole objective – the gold-rich Transvaal.

Steyn, under agonising pressure, upheld his loyalty to the Transvaal despite his honest assessment that the war could not be won. But he also knew that any appeasement to the Cape colonials and imperialists would be shortlived, and come with too high a price-tag: if Kimberley could be casually annexed, so too could the entire Free State at any future date. Neutrality was therefore not a viable option, though it might have been one that many Free Staters longed for. There was little enmity against the *English* in the Free State, unlike in the Transvaal; many Free State *dominees* (ministers) and landed families were of Scottish descent.

War happens, goes the saying, when diplomacy fails. Steyn struggled to find the 'anything but war' route, including at his Bloemfontein peace conference from 31 May to 5 June 1899. There, Kruger was persuaded to agree to compromises demanded by Britain's high commissioner in South Africa, Sir Alfred Milner, who was present under the false pretence of possibly agreeing to a peaceful solution – therefore, Kruger's offer was rejected as too little, too late. In fact, the decision by the UK to go to war with the Transvaal was already a done deal. Kruger had not been wrong when, at the end of this failed conference, he bluntly told Milner that it was not their land he wanted, but their gold.[7]

Steyn battled to avert conflict until the first fatal shots were fired in October 1899, unaware that the decision to take the Transvaal had already been fixed in the early months of 1899 by Rhodes, using cohorts such as Jameson as go-betweens. Proof of this was exposed during the post-war Royal Commission of 1902-1903; presented to the Commission were the private 'hurry up' telegrams sent by Miss Fiona Shaw to politician Dr Leander Starr Jameson early in 1899 on behalf of the Colonial Office, urging him and Rhodes to double down on inciting war.[8]

Late in March 1900, when Michael's firstborn, Pieter, was 3 years old, he came around the corner of their farmhouse on his stick horse – and there was a *kakie* (khaki, or British soldier). He ran, fell, got up and ran, fell again, and rushed inside bawling. He just couldn't make sense of it. He had seen men in *rokke* (dresses). He had seen women with beards!

These startling creatures, burly men in skirts, were Scottish troops in kilts which are not useful for fighting under a burning sun, and certainly odd-looking enough to give the youngster his first major fright – one that, years later, he would tell his own children about.

The khakis began to appear in the Ladybrand district where the Mullers lived around March 1900, but the finale in the eastern Free State did not come quickly. The town of Ladybrand, named after their former president's wife, Lady Brand, had been taken for one day at the end of March by the British, who were forced to retreat immediately. The town was besieged and retaken by both sides until September 1900, when it was occupied finally by the British, months after the fall of Bloemfontein in mid-March (Pretoria had surrendered in June).

Despite their losses, the Free State commandos had fought on towards their easternmost territory, increasingly with their backs to the river border of high Basutoland. By then, the *English* had invaded and burned their farms and homes, crops, cattle and other livestock, and destroyed or stolen tools and machinery. (Canadian forces, fighting for the first time abroad for the British side, noted that some 3 600 000 sheep were slaughtered by British soldiers and left to rot on the veld to make sure they didn't fall back into the hands of the Boers. This carnage baffled not only the Boers but also some of their foes.)

Britain had stipulated beforehand that this war would not impact on civilian life. Nothing could have been less true. Thousands of women and children were either frightened into concentration camps, or forcibly taken there. But this was certainly not because of passivity in Boer women. They were left destitute and starving, along with their children, after their homes, food, livestock, crops and all their belongings had been burned and destroyed. It was either the camps, or die in the veld, which in fact some of them chose to do. Others fled where they could, sometimes into neighbouring countries as refugees. By the end of the war, at least 10 000 women and children were living in perilous circumstances in the veld; the bodies of those who died there were not counted among the enormous number of civilian casualties in this war.

The Free State Boer women remembered stories of the fierce battles around Fouriesburg, and how, after the Boers had defeated the *English* there, they gathered up the wounded and nursed the young men, with their blue eyes and rosy cheeks (so similar to many of their own lads), in their own homes. The war had become domestic; they carefully buried the enemy's dead sons and wrote to their mothers, sometimes continuing the correspondence for years. The men may have fought against each other, but it was possible for women to mourn collectively, for they, too, had sons and husbands and brothers they might lose.

The end of their active war for the three older Muller brothers came in July 1900 at Slaapkrans near the Golden Gate area. Lool had been captured earlier, during the siege of Ladybrand. Their forced capitulation transformed them from hardy soldiers into captive POWs, and the shock of surrender would remain with them for the rest of their lives.

All were sent to Cape Town by train; from there, the three surviving brothers were shipped in exile to camps across the seas. The next two years would be a living misery for them, although they would survive their ordeals (in Chris's case, barely). They would have to draw on as much endurance while prisoners as they had done in their saddles – life as a POW demands a different kind of heroism, a struggle to conserve self-respect. Very little of what they experienced fulfilled any dreams of a glorious war, or of their hopes as proud victors, if indeed they nurtured those notions. Lool, the youngest, seemed to be the only one with that bent of enthusiasm, and he was not destined to see either victory or defeat.

What is of absolute significance is that this war on the Boers would have incredibly long repercussions. They never forgot what happened to their dead women and children, their soldiers and POWs, their burned farms and livestock and crops, their livelihoods, their independence and sovereignty. After the war, many of them would be, for generations, poor whites, having to turn inwards for help and rely on *helpmekaar* (mutual aid) to rebuild their culture, language and prosperity – at the inevitable expense of other cultures and languages that were also directly victims of this destructive war.

Black and brown South Africans had their own history of dispossession to deal with: they had not forgotten territories that had once been under their own dominion, and had been taken with guns and broken promises, over and again, by colonials, by Boers, by functionary and foe, and, most recently and infuriatingly, by those representing the Crown who had promised to be their friends and yet had already waged eleven wars on them over sixty years. After the war they were still bereft of their lands, dignity and independence, but also of any realistic hope for a better future.

And before them were the almost-lost traces, painted in caves, of the light-limbed brown people from a time when these lands had been contested only by the animals they hunted. Many had genetic links with the Boers – bloodlines forgotten or suppressed. Once, Boers and the first people had had progeny, many from legal marriages at the time, and were traders and even allies. These included the Mullers, who were descended from the ancient line of Krotoa as well as other indigenous and slave ancestors. Former relatives became bitter rivals in the struggle to rebuild after the war, their ancestral lines by then disconnected.

It left an ugly legacy and set in motion another freedom struggle, in this same bruised and contested land.

3

Magersfontein's big victory –
Chris and Pieter

WHEN THE MIDDLE BROTHERS, Chris and Pieter Muller, left home near Commissiepoort for the war's front near Kimberley in November 1899, they were two strong young men in their twenties, looking forward to stretching their muscles in what they believed was a righteous war, lucky enough to have had loving homes to leave behind them. Off they went, shoulders squared, scanning the horizon long before any enemy was in sight.

They rode past familiar farms and small settlements until they reached Thaba'Nchu, halfway between Ladybrand and Bloemfontein. Here they were greeted with cheers and tears, the ubiquitous cake and coffee, some speechifying, and a little solemn singing. They arrived at Bloemfontein the next day and again were filled with food, drink and friendly greetings – many turned out to encourage them. It was a rather jolly start.

In line with Boer military tradition, there was an election the next day, 29 November 1899, for they needed more officers to lead the large numbers of burgers who had turned out to fight. Chris noted in his diary that Jan de Wet (soon to die at Magersfontein) was chosen as veldkornet. Several corporals were chosen for the Ladybrand district, among them Chris himself. Though relatively young, he was confident and self-reflective, ready to speak his mind on decisions he felt mattered.

The Ladybrand commando began to move westwards to the battlefields early on 30 November 1899. On the way they stopped at a farm to rest their horses and buy fodder for them, and Chris commented that their hosts seemed depressed by the news from the front. But their first priority was the care of their mounts, for the veld had been utterly plundered by locusts – it was quite bare – and it was very hot and there was no water.

Boers were entirely dependent on being mounted and most were excellent horsemen, having been brought up not only to ride, but also to shoot accurately from the saddle for the pot. They knew their sturdy local mounts, well trained in what was expected of them, and more able to survive the hardy veld than the hundreds of thousands of doomed horses that were being shipped in for British use from milder lands across the ocean.

Passing troops gave them some fodder, then they pressed on until they found water. They arrived at the town of Petrusburg at 5 pm.

The next day, Friday 1 December 1899, they arrived at Modderrivier in the aftermath of a fierce battle in which General Koos de la Rey had lost his young son Adriaan, 'Adaan', aged 19, to enemy bullets. They slaughtered 16 sheep for a braai, then rode on 'over the Nek' – Scholtznek – to join the stalwart De la Rey, already a legend in the making.

At some stage during the next days, Pieter bagged a steenbok. The shooting of the *wildsbokken* was sometimes careless, and two men were given five cuts each with a whip because they recklessly shot at animals that were 'between the burgers'.

On 6 December they arrived in Jacobsdal with a thousand men under General Jacobus Prinsloo. The horses were fed, as were the men. Chris visited the hospital to see if anyone he knew was there, and if he could give or receive messages.

The men's rest that night was disrupted by swarming locusts, and they had to hide under their sleeping bags.

The real action began for Chris the next day, Thursday 7 December. Before sunrise, he joined a group that included Irish volunteers who were busy blowing up part of the railway line to Kimberley in what would become known as the Enslin Skirmish, a bigger event than the term might suggest. The men made do for tools, breaking off a post and clipping its wires while the enemy shot at them, dust flying from nearby bullets as they worked. They shot back at the enemy 'and we got a few good hits on them'.

They managed to set up a cannon to give them cover, then broke up the railway line and derailed a locomotive. At about noon Chris and his fellow burgers advanced, took possession of a koppie, and chased the enemy through the trees, shooting at the retreating lancers.

The Ladybranders were then ordered by their commandant, Diederichs, to withdraw. The retreat was under a barrage of heavy cannon fire, and a burger from Ficksburg was killed and several others wounded, including E Kriel, one of the eight subjects of the pre-war photograph, who was hit in the hand.

They unsaddled at a plundered house where the farmers had been captured by the enemy. Chris recorded that they slept little that night. Their first 'blooding' in the war had been dangerous and exhausting.

The following morning, 8 December, they found 'lovely water' at a dam where there were trees. Chris and some of the others decided to go back to the battlefield to draw out the enemy, as 'it had to be done', part of the endless back and forth tactics of mounted warfare.

That evening, after gathering in prayer, the men slept in a long line. This was the pattern of the next few days, while preparing themselves for the next big thing: Magersfontein.

> 11 December: At half past three we are already in the saddle, and we can hear the shooting and we saw the searchlights, and as soon as it was light enough to see, we also heard the cannons thundering.

Shortly before dawn, the men had arrived at Bisset's farm just north of Magersfontein, wet and hoping for some rest. They now quickly resaddled and continued towards the Magersfontein koppie, which they climbed after hiding their horses in a little kloof nearby.

The wide, flat battlefield lay below.

> Immediately, the cannon started shooting at us. A section of us spread out along the ridge where a rain of bullets comes down on us. Then we take shelter in the ridge while the shells burst around us. J van Rooyen died, Commandant Diedriks [APJ Diederichs], also J [Jan] de Wet is wounded . . . The rest of our burgers go to the south side, where the fighting was the heaviest. We get the news that many known to us have fallen.

Chris had a clear view of the battlefield, of the great number of dead and dying enemy. Some were trying to stop their bleeding with handkerchiefs, as others cried from pain.

A small group of us go to the foremost point of the [Magersfontein] ridge, where our cannons stand; we take positions here. The cannon shoots continuously until seven o'clock. At half past seven, the battle stops.

. . .

During the night, the sentries came to tell us it sounds as if the enemy is coming again. One, two, three, all of us are back in the trench. Later in the night, the same thing happens again. Someone came to look for me and found me sleeping in a sitting position, and he said, quite loudly, 'Here he is!' I got a fright, jumped up, grabbed my weapon – I thought that the enemy was on us: so the night goes on.

Chris's vivid eyewitness account of the battle of Magersfontein was thorough as well as composed, given what they had all just been through. Yet what is also apparent was that by the end of that notable day, his fellow Boers had no idea they had won a famous victory. All they knew was that they had been under heavy fire all day long, had lost some of their own, and had seen many of their enemy's dead or wounded on the flat battlefield in front of them, of which Chris had an excellent view. Also, they needed to be alert for the next attack. What they did not know then, nor in the weeks ahead, was that there would be no 'next attack'.

The *English* were, however, bitterly aware of their defeat, as were the mourning Scots, whose brigades had been torn apart in this fierce, formal battle. It was the Highlanders who had paid the highest price. More than a thousand men died or were wounded at Magersfontein, most of them Scots, and more than 300 from the fabled Black Watch alone.

The Boers counted 87 dead burgers. They had won against insuperable odds, facing a force double their own strength – about 15 000 British troops under Lieutenant-General Lord Methuen, to the Boers' 8 500. In a set-piece battle between an experienced British army and a Boer force that had no training in this type of warfare, the Boers had been victorious, due chiefly to the tactical genius of De la Rey, and the discipline of the Boers who had waited patiently, in the unfamiliar trenches, throughout the drenching night. These Boers had brought the mighty British fighting machine to a halt, and there it remained, in stasis, for months.

At dawn on 12 December, Chris rose from his trench and saw that the British were searching the battlefield for dead and wounded, of which there were very many.

There was by now a truce of sorts, and Boer soldiers raided the field for needed equipment – rifles, bayonets, water canisters.

> Many of the objects they took were covered in blood.
>
> At eight o'clock, the ambulance wagons of the enemy approach. Myself and a friend go to visit the battlefield. It was a terrible scene. We spoke to some of the wounded and gave them water.
>
> At eleven o'clock the cannons begin to bombard one another, until two o'clock. And then the troops returned to their camps. Then some of the Ladybranders went back to the horses to find food.
>
> In the evening at seven o'clock we go back to take up our positions on the ridge. We sleep in the fortified area, on stones, without anything underneath us. And this evening, and also in the morning, singing of songs and psalms echo around the ridges.

This singing was the signifier that the Boer army had finally grasped their extraordinary success. They let themselves go, their voices floating through the dark, connecting and communicating between them.

Those clumsy war balloons, so difficult to inflate, were a complete flop. Eleven of them were shipped to South Africa. They could fly to a maximum of around 3 000 feet – at sea level. There was a running joke among the Boers that by the time the war balloons reached Johannesburg (it is not called the Highveld for nothing), the only place they would be able to fly was at the bottom of the mines! They were soon abandoned.

And the one that had so annoyed Chris at Magersfontein claimed an unexpected own-goal. The fifteenth Marquess of Winchester was sitting way back with other officers during the battle; he stood up to have a good look at this interesting object and was immediately shot dead by a Boer marksman – those skilled sharpshooters were accurate at an almost-unheard-of range of at least 1 200 yards.

The bodies of the two most senior foes who died at Magersfontein, Commandant Diederichs and the Scottish Major-General Sir Andrew

Wauchope, were both buried nearby, according to military tradition and also for sheer practicality, due to the heat. Neither lies there now. Wauchope's body was exhumed within a week for a grand funeral at the large remount station, Matjiesfontein, hundreds of miles from the battlefield – a mis-understanding stemming from the similarity of the two names.[9]

A brave soldier, Wauchope was described by his fellows as the unluckiest man in the military – he was wounded in every battle he fought. At Magers-fontein, he had summoned the courage to confront the inept Lord Methuen over serious flaws in his battle orders the night before. Wauchope's sensible solution had been that Magersfontein should simply be avoided altogether, and the longer route around Jacobsdal to Kimberley taken, but Methuen had shouted this suggestion down. Having lost the argument, Wauchope bravely marched to what he knew would likely be his death.

In the broader sense, Magersfontein *should* have been avoided altogether; if the British army had made directly for Bloemfontein, as was the original war plan, events would have gone very differently. Rhodes's insistence on rushing up to Kimberley as the war began, to protect the vast British invest-ment there, left their army no choice but to 'relieve' the city, for Rhodes had a powerful network of rich associates and did not hesitate to use them. It was literally a sideshow, but with deadly consequences.

Afterwards, the British faced a long, exhausting trek to Bloemfontein, resuming the very route they had needed to be on in the first place.

The great advantage to the British of a war as far away as South Africa was that such distance bought time in tweaking official narratives.

Having safely viewed the doomed battle from some miles back, on Head-quarter Hill, Methuen's first, unblushing despatch proclaimed, 'From now until dark I held my own, face to face with the enemy's entrenchments.' Extraordinarily, no mention of the huge British death toll was included but it is clear from the terse tone of the first despatches of the other sur-viving Magersfontein officers that they regarded the battle as a stuff-up of quite amazing proportions.

When these first dismaying despatches arrived in Britain, along with reports of the frightful number of fatalities, the War Office swung into action – they could not afford public opinion turning against them so soon in the war, which, after all, had been falsely prophesied to be over 'by

Christmas'. The grim despatches, written in the hours after the fateful fight, and marked with blood and grime, were returned with an order to 'revise'.

Methuen, now holed up in the hotel at Modderrivier, waiting for reinforcements, reworded history; it is handy to blame a dead man. 'I would have asked Major-General Wauchope why bayonets were not fixed earlier, and the deployment was made so near the enemy. But he died at the head of the Brigade amongst whom his name must always remain respected and beloved. His high military reputation, his grand character forbid any criticisms on my part . . .' His last few words regarding criticism is an especially neat touch, for, of course, it invites exactly the opposite.

And what did Methuen's soldiers think, those who had survived? You cannot silence everyone: Battie Gray of the Black Watch was forthright. He wrote a poem, 'The Black Watch at Magersfontein – by one who was there', while recuperating from his wounds at the convalescent station at De Aar. His anger seethes off the pages: he and his comrades had not been told of the trenches nor of the barbed wire, though we know that Methuen and his senior staff were aware of them. Who did he feel was to blame? Here is his answer: 'Dearly we paid for the blunder, / A drawingroom General's mistake.'

The well-known comment by Aeschylus, that the first casualty of war is the truth, needs an addendum: in starting a war, the truth has to have been sacrificed a long time in advance. The British public had been lied to about the *real* reason behind this war (which was profit), and continued to be misled. Propaganda in wartime is not unusual, and is condoned as necessary, to keep up public morale.

It is harder, however, to excuse history writers who have ignored or overlooked the original documents in Britain's National Archives, alongside those marked 'Revised'. The revised documents claim that they did not know that De la Rey had entrenched his forces at the foot of the hills, and that the trench, which followed the course of a dry stream and a barbed-wire fence, was reinforced with a further barbed-wire entanglement.

But they *did* know. Methuen's despatch dated the day before the battle includes the phrase 'the trenches at the foot of the kopje'. The trenches had taken a fortnight to dig, and all ten miles of them had been dug directly in front of him, in an area the British knew well as they had briefly occupied the Magersfontein koppie on December 4.[10]

Every excuse that Methuen and his officers made in the later, fluffed-up revised versions is contradicted in their own earlier records, before and immediately after the great battle.

Methuen's command, to attack anyway, meant that the Highland Brigade was used up like blotting paper. Scotland paid the price he had exacted.

The gruesome big battle of Magersfontein was over, but curiously little changed afterwards for the soldiers there.

'Dingaan's Day', 16 December, arrived, a significant day in South Africa's contested history. It originated from the battle of Blood River (Ncome) of 61 years before, when more than 400 Voortrekkers had made a vow to God that if he gave them victory against the approximately 20 000 Zulu warriors they were facing, they would ever after observe the day as holy. Despite the Boers at Magersfontein anticipating another pitched battle, all was quiet, and they spent the holiday in the pious manner they would have at home. They dug another trench to sleep in.

On 17 December, another terribly hot day, they again spotted the air balloon 'standing over the camp of the enemy' sent up to observe them. To the Boers, the balloon was a giant flag saying, 'Here we are!' At the sight of it, they knew to leap back into their trenches, as the shelling was about to begin – it had become a useful signal for them.

The Boers remained jumpy: several times a loose shot went off in their camp, giving them all a fright.

At one o'clock, two food wagons arrived and then *askoek* (hard bread rolls baked in hot ashes) was the order of the day. Over the next few days, food wagons arrived regularly, as did the post, although Chris was sad not to have heard yet from his 'little wife', Dorie. The men began to notice rats infesting the trenches.

Every now and then, both armies sent out a foray to keep the opposition on their toes.

Their ambulance arrived on 21 December, with Dominee Fourie; he hoisted a Red Cross flag onto a vacated home that was close to the battlefield.

Chris's last entry, on 22 December, in this, his first diary, was written in a dashing scrawl. The post had arrived again, and finally he had received longed-for news from home.

[As] the post was given out, the burgers streamed towards it, everywhere, you see people standing with their letters.

The burgers harass me to get leave to go to [a nearby] camp.
One wants a pair of trousers, the other a shirt, and to fetch other
things.

While I was standing with my mug of coffee . . . the enemy moved
out. Our men grab their rifles and leap towards the trench. Soon
they return; false alarm. During this time, we could still hear the
cannons booming in the direction of Kimberley.

   . . .

Before sending his first diary to his father, Chris included this note to him
in the last entry:

Today I received a letter from December 18, and another one from
the 7th, and also one from Pa. I will answer this later.

Don't be sad. I am cheerful and have not felt any discomfort. It is
good that [your] letters found me. The *kêrels* [chaps] do not feel
the difficulties . . .

Hearty greetings and love from CM.

4

Digging in: the cannons say
good morning

CHRIS DID NOT begin his second diary until after New Year of 1900, when he was still dug in at Magersfontein, baking in the same hot trenches.

At this stage, each day had begun to run into the next. 'At six o'clock we hear the thundering of our cannon and those of the enemy. They say good morning to one another!' Chris wrote in an early entry.

This went on for weeks and weeks.

Many Boers who had been in the frontlines during the prior, fierce weeks fell back for rest over the holidays. Chris and Pieter spent the first Christmas of the war on a break in Douglas, a small hamlet not far from Kimberley. They returned to Magersfontein at the end of the first week of January 1900.

The bloody nose the Boers had given the *English* in those first three months of the war had come as a profound shock to Britain. Public predictions had been that a 'small band' of Boers would run away at the first sign of a real fight. This had proved absurdly inaccurate. Partly because of such unfounded optimism, based on no discernible evidence, British preparations had been deeply inadequate. That had cost lives.

Lieutenant-General Sir William Butler, the acting British high commissioner in South Africa before the war, had had the bad luck to be right at the wrong time. He had disagreed with British Imperialists who had urged him to get on with the quest of conquering the lucrative Boer republics, something he felt would be 'quite suicidal'. He had written a series of increasingly urgent letters home, entreating them not to go ahead with a 'war between the races' (meaning Brit versus Boer), for they had no idea 'how inadequate their conception [was] of what war in South Africa would mean . . . and how dangerous'.

Butler himself *did* know what it would mean, for he had taken the trouble to make a 3 000-mile personal inspection of the frontier along the large Cape Colony, and the two republics, after which he again had struggled, in a despatch dated 21 June 1899, to explain to his superiors in Westminster that a war 'might commit the white races of South Africa to a possible internecine struggle wherein about one million men and women, scattered over an area nearly as large as Europe, might be involved'. He had added that there was, entirely inaccurately, an 'infatuated conviction prevalent at home, that the display of "a resolute attitude" would speedily cow the Dutch-speaking population'.

For his pains, Butler had been smacked down by his political masters.[11] He had then gone straight to Sir Alfred (later Lord) Milner, who had been sent to South Africa as a fixer specifically to ensure support for the war, and asked him, pointedly, 'Have I been a hindrance to you, sir, in the prosecution of your designs or plans?'

Milner had said yes, as a matter of fact, he had been. Butler had written his letter of resignation that same night and it had been speedily accepted.

Britain and South Africa had just lost one of few balanced voices – the whistleblower had been silenced.

Butler was soon proved awfully right. The end of 1899 produced 'Black Week' of mid-December, with its serious defeats for the British at Magersfontein, as well as at Stormberg (in the Eastern Cape, just south of the Free State) on 10 December, and Colenso on 15 December (the British disastrous first attempt to cross the Tugela River in Natal and relieve Ladysmith).

Now the British War Office had a fiasco on their hands that not even Butler had predicted. If sanity had prevailed at this point, a solution could have been found. Influential Cape polititian John X Merriman, who was personally opposed to the war, wrote in his own diary on 29 January 1900 that if the Boers were confident that their independence was safe 'they would abandon the war, which has cost us so heavily in every way'.

But a solution was the last thing secretary of state for the colonies Joseph Chamberlain, Cecil Rhodes and their cronies wanted. So the war went on, with a cost to life, human and animal, that was truly horrifying. It would take two and a half more years, and more than half a million British and colonial troops (their greatest-ever overseas force), not to mention a gigantic, growing war debt, to salvage Britian's war. And these figures do not include the deaths of nearly half a million horses (including some mules), nor do they factor in the terrible toll on the civilian Boer and black populations, let alone the impact on the country's future.

The Boers, fortunately, did not know what lay ahead as they entered the new year of 1900. A fight for freedom is not intimidated by overwhelming odds: although the Boers had not sought the war, they had no intention of giving up.

The Ladybranders began their first Sunday of 1900, 7 January, with devotions. During this quiet day, they prepared to resettle themselves back along the frontline.

The next day, Chris took a step up in rank. He reported that all the officers went to a meeting and he was sworn in as an 'acting assistant veldkornet', so he could vote too (as all elected officers could) for a new 'commander-in-chief'. They picked a Ladybrander, Pieter Ferreira.

There had been about thirty senior officers present, and Chris wryly remarked that 'if the enemy could capture our group, it would be a good catch!'

The next few days, punctuated by the cannons bawling at each other every morning, were busy with the bits and bobs of entrenched warfare. Chris ordered tents for his men, which were nicked by other commandos – he had to resign himself to this.

They chopped through limestone to prepare and extend their trenches, and also built fortifications to house their cannons, which was difficult work. Then he was told that the forts weren't up to scratch, so he went out to correct the problem.

Provisions were summoned, regular *braaivleise* were held, and seven wagons were sent to Bloemfontein for clothes, coffee and sugar, milk, fresh bread and post . . . The men made lists of things they wanted.

On 12 January, Chris watched Johnny Brink (one of the eight Ladybranders in the pre-battle photograph) 'cleaning his horse. He seems to be very clumsy, but as cheerful as a bird and satisfied with his work'.

Chris mentioned that, at this stage, the men were going through the motions but that not much was happening, and in the hot, boring days ahead, they increasingly turned to pranks and games to keep occupied. He recorded one 'good joke'. A young man had casually passed on a letter with his father's home address on it, to an older man – it was common-place for them to quickly share news from home, for they all knew each other, or were related. On reading it later himself, he realised to his hor-ror that it was a personal letter from his sweetheart – and the man he had handed it to was her father!

While writing about his colleague's awkward gaffe, his men were sleep-ing under the trees in the heat, smoking or eating, and others baking *askoek*. He visited other *laagers* (camps) to see how they were getting on, wrote his reports, and caught up on news.

When he returned, the forts were not yet satisfactory, so he and his burgers had to work on them until midnight.

On 15 January, Chris informed CC Froneman that he had been chosen as their commandant (as successor to the dead Diederichs), a result heartily welcomed by the Ladybranders.

Finally, on 16 January, came the first rumblings of change. Chris at-tended a council of war at 10 am to lay down rules of engagement 'and so on'. These councils, serious in intent, were often held in informal settings; generals and senior officers would hunker down in a circle on the veld, or under a tree for shelter.

On his return, Chris ate a 'lovely' pot of meat and *pap* (stiff porridge), then lay down under a tree to sleep.

A veldkornet arrived with some newspapers and made them all laugh so much that it gave Chris a headache, to which he seemed to be prone.

At about 4 pm the war balloon was floated and the British lancers pulled out in a westerly direction, while from the east, shots were fired at their fort and a few scouts could be seen approaching. Chris and a com-rade shot at them – they fled – then fired a couple of cannon shots after them.

That set things off and the cannons bombarded heavily until dark – the nightwatchmen could hear firing through the night.

Chris also began the duties of taking part in disciplinary procedures. Two black African scouts of the enemy were caught and brought before the council, but no progress was made with their case, so they were sent to the 'main laager' of the generals. There was another case of petty theft over a sixpence, which was thrown out because the civil courts were closed, and a lawyer among them advised that it would only cause a needless fuss in the military court

On 19 January, Chris was requested to have his burgers pick up a dead person (possibly someone who had been shot while on sentry duty) – luckily 'only one'.

Later, when the post arrived, Chris received no letters and felt upset about this. 'I thought, how is this possible? I have such a big family and so many friends that surely I should get one in every post,' he wrote.

His short bout of self-pity was cured by the high jinks of the men the next day, which was pleasantly cool for a change. 'The young burgers had a war – they were shooting each other with jam tins full of sand that looked very much like bombs when they fell. More than one was wounded. I laughed myself silly.'

That night it rained 'into my ears' so he had to cover his head, which made conditions stuffy. Then the guards saw what they thought was the enemy creeping up on them. They shouted 'Danger!' and ran for the fort. One of them forgot about the wire fence and ran straight into it, and it flung him back.

The men jumped into the trenches, ready for battle. Then the sentries realised that what they had seen were young ostriches. 'This caused much hilarity,' Chris wrote.

On another occasion he wrote that 'a horse ran through our laager; a thornbranch was hooked into his tail. One could hear all the shouting – this was because he ran over pots, kettles, tents and so on . . . this happens almost every day.'

These little scares helped to release the tension, for time weighed heavy on the men as they waited for the next big fight.

By now, Chris had found a sheepskin, the best bed he had slept on since leaving home. Their mood remained mostly cheerful. He visited a friend further along the trenches, who told so many jokes that their stomach muscles ached.

On 23 January, the pump was broken but the men washed their clothes in 'very dirty water' and had fun – it was a jolly job. Late that afternoon the Ladybranders had a tug-of-war with the Bloemfonteiners. 'The rope broke and there they all lay in a heap amid much laughter.'

This gaiety was also a welcome counterpoint to the heavier side of Chris's new responsibilities. On 22 January he was involved in a court martial of a man who had behaved badly on patrol and who pleaded guilty, and was reprimanded.

The most riveting event for the men during this long period of dawdling at Magersfontein was also the most unexpected. On 27 January, after Chris had recorded the arrival of three wagons from Ladybrand bearing cake, fruit and other delectables, he added, 'I forgot that yesterday something great happened in our camp, and that was a woman. When she walked through the camp, everyone stood, amazed. Few greeted her as a result of their surprise. It was the prettiest thing that I had seen for some time.'

It is no coincidence, therefore, that his entry the next day, 28 January, recorded that their commander asked that their wives join them, a custom among senior Boer officers that baffled the British. Chris's friend, Kriel, voiced his strong opposition, along with the dominee, and won.

Chris visited friends in their tents to relay this and found them recently finished eating; they offered him a small piece of cold meat, 'which I ate without relish, and thought about my loving little wife, who always served me with food so affectionately'.

Until that point, the men had managed to keep each other entertained, but the sight of one pretty woman had undone them. Chris could not sleep, talked late with a friend, and visited the sentries to make sure all was in order, in this way passing his lonely night of longing.

Chris went to Jacobsdal on the first day of February to pick up clothing for his commando, and also visited the wounded in the hospital there. There were 21 patients, including one English soldier who lay between the burgers 'and was as well looked after as the others'.

When he returned to Magersfontein, the big cannon of the enemy was firing at the Boers' forts, making the earth shudder. The Boers gave this cannon the name Onrecht (Injustice), Chris recorded, also noting that its shrapnel blasted the bushes around them as they rode in.

The eagerly awaited post was given out and Chris received several letters, but it was too dark for him to read, except for the 'most important' one, which confirmed that all was well at home. Because they had also managed to bring in fresh milk, he had a big jugful with dumplings, pleasing him enormously, because it had been more than two months since he had had such a treat, and such a full stomach. That night he slept 'as comfortably as a minister'.

The men had managed to rig up a bathing tub outside their *laager*, and Oubaas and Chris used it: 'I sat in a tub and he threw a bucket of water over me. It was lovely.'

On 3 February Chris had to attend another court martial. The man was charged with leaving his post without permission, but claimed that he had, in fact, got leave to do so from Veldkornet Jan Diederichs. The result, Chris wrote, was that the man was let off, but was severely reprimanded because he had not told the other officers.

Incidents of burgers going off without permission needed to be curbed – their independent natures were unaccustomed to asking for it – and the officers instituted a new system of 'permission notes', sometimes scrawled quite hastily, offering explanations of the person carrying them (these were also used by the British army). Chris collected and saved some of these in a battered brown envelope, which he marked '*Ou oorlog korrespondensies ens. op die veld: Anglo-Boer oorlog*' (Old wartime messages etc in the veld: Anglo-Boer war). They provide an insight into the daily minutiae of veld warfare.

One, dated 9 May 1900, was from Chris's brother-in-law, SE 'Oubaas' Terblans (married to his eldest sister, Non), to a senior Ladybrander, presumably carried between the two by a youngster called Adam: 'I send you the bread that I mentioned to you, with the boy Adam, share it with Comdt. Cruiter [Crowther], your friend', it read, with the postscript, 'I send you a bottle of milk [for] coffee.' Other notes refer to orders and information passed from one officer to another; yet others are 'permission notes' for travel from one place to another after the Free State was occupied.

5

Fight and flight

UNEASE IN THE Boer camp was growing – they expected the enemy to retaliate soon, and Chris no longer slept well at night. Then orders came for them to move. On 5 February 1900 they were instructed to go to Koedoesberg, three hours away by horse; a report noted that the enemy had captured it and entrenched themselves.

Chris and his commando left under his general, whom he noticed seemed in a hurry, with burgers arriving from all sides despite the heat. He could not have known this, but the English army had been heavily reinforced and the Boer leadership had realised that they needed to abandon Kimberley and try to save Bloemfontein. The war was about to begin its long trek eastwards across the Free State.

At two o'clock Chris and his general reached the mountain occupied by the enemy; on the way there, they had killed three British scouts, who were replaced by about twenty others, firing at the Boers. Chris and his men chased them back up the mountain, and were showered with a hail of bullets, killing one of the horses.

> My horse did not know which way to go, left or right. The worst of the bullets were directed on my burgers who were nearest the ridge. We stormed [it] from the northern side, left our horses and climbed the mountain, the bullets whistling over us . . . our little group with our Commandant and the General fought until dark [but] we were very thirsty and could not remain there.

They went to a nearby farm to get water, then slept out, on a hill.

Their active war had commenced again, and now they were at far more of a disadvantage than at Magersfontein, where the Boers had controlled the high-rise koppie and had had trenches already prepared for them. This time, their fighting would be uphill, in the open, and more dangerous.

Their council of war the next day decided to request cannons for back-up, which arrived promptly that evening, after the Boers had lain 'all day in the blazing sun', now experiencing some of the misery felt by the High-landers as they had lain on the battlefield of Magersfontein.

On 7 February the fighting began in earnest, first with the cannons on both sides, then with the Boers advancing on the British-held elevation. Under heavy fire, Chris and his men were forced to drag their horses into a furrow, two of the animals wounded. A horse without a Boer is one thing; a Boer without a horse is quite another, so the wellbeing of their horses was always foremost. They were able to hide their horses in a safer place but could not leave them unattended, and asked for further reinforcements as they were chased out under a hail of bullets and took refuge in a river-bed, behind sandbanks.

As they lay there in a row, Chris realised that the English cannons were right above them, just as they began to fire at his troops – the second he rose to tell his commandant that he could no longer hold the position, the bombardment burst over them. He and his men crossed the river and took up position on the opposite bank as the gunfire intensified, the maxim also now aimed at them.

The fighting raged back and forth around a house, which was shot to pieces. Chris, trapped on the wrong side of it, tried to aid someone, who died.

The later it got, the more violent the fighting. He was now struggling to survive.

In the middle of this fierce battle, a pitiful herd of *boerbokke* (hardy goats) took refuge in the river, bunched up and scared, some of them already killed by the bullets. The enemy thought they were burgers and fired their cannons at them, killing a great number, observed Chris.

When darkness fell, he seized the opportunity to order the Boer horses to safety, despite the bullets still raining down on them, while he, his commandant and two others remained behind, shooting, to provide cover.

From his earlier position in the river, Chris had been able to see what his fellow burgers could not: that the Boer cannons had shot the enemy's entrenchments to smithereens and that they could, in fact, have occupied them.

Their exhausting day was not yet over. They received news that an officer had been left behind on the mountain with the cannon, and his commandant asked Chris to take a party up to fetch him. Chris called for volunteers, and with about fifteen men 'rushed through the bushes' to rescue the man, then helped him back to the farm for water.

They slept nearby. Chris lay down and quickly fell asleep, but woke at midnight from the cold because his shoes were wet (from the river) and were making him feel uncomfortable. He lit dry grass to warm himself 'and walked around like a wet dog, looking to see whether I couldn't creep under a blanket to share with someone, but there was no space'.

The next day was spent under heavy fire again, as British lancers arrive in huge numbers, but more burgers were coming to their aid, too.

On 9 February, although they expected an attack, none materialised. Then Chris's contingent of men were ordered back to a farm where there were reinforcements, and when they arrived, at four o'clock, their senior officer, Piet Ferreira, 'cried from joy, because he had heard that we had been encircled and could not escape'. Such were the close emotional links between the men.

Then there occurred a puzzling incident during a tense time of waiting for enemy patrols on 12 February.

> One of our horse guards arrived and told us that there was a body on the mountain, apparently a woman in man's clothing. The Commandant, the doctor and I went to see. We found it was a Chinaman; the long plait made him look like a woman.

Chris offered no further explanation, though they were not far from Kimberley's diamond fields, where there was a community of many foreigners, including those of Chinese origin. Why this poor man was lying dead in the open veld was anybody's guess.

The day dawned so brightly on 13 February 1900 that the Boers' heliograph, which signalled via flashes of sunlight reflected by a mirror, could not transmit (if it was too bright or hazy, the mirror might not be able to catch the rays to signal).

Chris stopped on the way back to his camp, to feast on grapes and water-melon sent by the wife of his commandant. He was in no hurry to return from this unexpected feast, then had a long conversation with Boer war historian Nico Hofmeyr, who was busy taking photographs for his records.

When Chris eventually arrived back at his tent, there was an urgent message that the enemy was moving past Jacobsdal, and that reinforcements were needed there at once. Senior officers and 55 Ladybranders left quickly, along with other commandos, while Chris was ordered to stay behind to take charge, named as the 'acting assistant combat general'. Suddenly, he had to make all the major decisions. He ordered the remaining horses and saddles to be readied and they left at 5 pm, riding late into the night to join Commandant HPJ Pretorius of the Jacobsdal commando.

Because of his new responsibilities, Chris noted, he rose early the next morning and climbed the hills, to look and listen.

Back at the tents, he discovered from newly arrived officers that the enemy had captured five Boer camps and fired at his own laager with their cannons. He was frustrated by the lack of accurate information and struggled to get details via their heliograph and from incoming messengers; he had only word of mouth about their situation.

The British balloon went up and down three times – something the Boers had learned was not a good sign, as it signalled an attack – and they could hear cannons and the big British maxims. Burgers arriving from Kimberley said the fighting was fierce there. The relief of Kimberley by the British, which the battle of Magersfontein had thwarted before Christmas, had finally begun.

Chris spent the day making tactical decisions, one of which was that if Pretorius had to fall back (he had few burgers left), Chris would send his own mounted men to intercept the enemy if they passed by; he worried all day long. In the evening he heard that the British had reached Alexander-fontein, a pretty resort just outside Kimberley.

The thundering of cannons next morning indicated that

> a dreadful battle was taking place, and people were continually com-ing from the battlefield and bringing disturbing reports ... [later] Commandant Froneman arrived and said that the enemy were through to Kimberley. We were still sitting and talking when a letter

arrived from General Cronje to the effect that we should evacuate
the forts and move to the east.

They had not even finished reading the letter when all the burgers arrived,
streaming down from the Boer forts, as word spread.

> Then everything was in confusion. Everyone saddled up quickly.
> As we only had one wagon, we couldn't take anything with us other
> than what we normally took on our horses. So all our goods, tents,
> boxes of clothes, kettles, pots . . . everything stayed behind – blan-
> kets, pillows, mattresses, ammunition and many other articles.
>
> I put on my best suit of clothes [the rest of his kit was aban-
> doned] . . . and went over to the forts. I retrieved my blanket and
> a canvas and a waterbag full of water, which the others had left
> behind.
>
> When we returned everyone had already left, [and] only G Del-
> port was waiting for me.
>
> Not far away we found our wagon, the only one we had, with the
> ammunition, food and so on. The wheel was broken. It was un-
> hooked and left in the road with everything on it. This all made a
> poor impression on me. Then I recalled the flight of the English
> from Dundee.

Dundee (also known as Talana Hill in Natal) in October 1899 was an early
fight for the Boers. The English at one stage had had to evacuate fast during
the night, and lost their entire kit – much welcomed by the Boers.

> We went in a long column. When we arrived at the farm from where
> we were all leaving, Gen Cronje had just left but we met up with his
> rear guard. The column was about three miles long, if not longer.
> Such a scene is difficult to describe. There were wagons, carts, spi-
> ders [carriages], cannons, horseriders, pedestrians, sheep. Everyone
> seemed to be in a hurry. It was very disorderly.
>
> I rode ahead to see the General, to tell him that it was dangerous
> to trek in this manner, should the enemy attack us. But I could not
> reach the front of the column. And so it continued.
>
> I could not get all my burgers together. The one did not know where
> the other was.
>
> We trekked right through the night without a rest or outspan.

The decision of Chris to ride forward to confront General Cronjé in allowing this disorderly, spread-out retreat was an unusually confident action by this younger, more junior officer. Had he been able to catch up with the general, one has to wonder what the senior man would have made of it. In the event, despite the urgency of his concern, Chris realised he could not do two things at once: reach the senior officers far ahead, and at the same time care for his own men, now far behind him. He turned back to those for whom he was directly responsible, though his misgivings would prove well founded.

His last day in the saddle for a while was 16 February 1900:

> When the sun rose, [we] went out to a spring where there was drinking water. At about seven o'clock one of the sentries came to tell us that the enemy was approaching from behind; we were thus past them.
>
> The horsemen returned to the hills as the wagons and pedestrians carried on. At the hills we found our burgers who had been there since the previous day – they were cut off when the enemy passed through to Kimberley. We occupied several hills.
>
> The enemy approached along the river, just like red ants. They shot, but I forbade the burgers to shoot . . .
>
> The position was dangerous. Some officers from the Transvaal insisted that we should leave this place, which we did. In the meantime, the wagons were outspanned near the river.
>
> We occupied another hill where we quickly started fighting. The fire from the enemy was tremendous. They were lucky in getting us under crossfire.
>
> At about one o'clock I was wounded in the leg, so I had to leave the hill and go to the camp to have the wound bandaged. There we had no doctor.

This last of Chris's diary entries for some time ended abruptly, leaving us puzzling over the exact nature of his leg wound (he recovered soon and rejoined his men). His first war wound had shocked him, though; for the rest of his life he kept the blood-flecked linen binding and bandana he had used to bind it up. In any case, this particular diary was now completely full and he posted it back home from the place where he was recuperating.

From this point until the day of his capture at Slaapkrans at the end of

July 1900, there was a gap in Chris's daily records. For a meticulous diarist, even under extreme war conditions, this was uncharacteristic. Given
that he routinely posted his diaries home, the next one either went missing
in the post or was confiscated by the enemy. It is all the more frustrating, for
he would have recorded the vital period of the long retreat across the Free
State, east to the Brandwater Basin, before the huge Prinsloo surrender.

But someone else had recorded what happened to him, and his fellow
Ladybranders, during this period.

Chris had a particularly loyal friend throughout the war, IA 'Andries'
Meyer. When Meyer was 85 years old, in 1952, he wrote an invaluable little
forty-page booklet of his war recollections based on his own war diaries.
It is in this, *Die ervarings van 'n veldkornet in die Engelse Oorlog 1899-
1902* (The Experiences of a Field Cornet in the English War 1899-1902),
that there are first-hand accounts of the Muller brothers during the time of
Chris's missing diary entries in 1900.

Meyer's own story before the war began is briefly but movingly recounted. In 1880 he married Alida de Villiers in Ladybrand, with whom he had
four children; by 1894 he had bought a farm, Damplaas. But five years after
their marriage his beloved wife died, and, as was the custom then (and at
Alida's own request), their little children, three boys and a girl, were farmed
out to relatives. Meyer managed – just – to survive the rinderpest cattle
plague of 1888-1897 (which killed over ninety per cent of African cattle and
countless wildlife) with a third of his herds intact, and after a considerable
struggle, saved his farm. In 1897 he remarried, to Judith Jacoba van Huys-
steen, and gathered his children back. He was settling in nicely to a new life
when the war broke out.

On 3 October 1899, even before the declaration of war – which was by
now no more than a formality – Meyer and 30 others responded to the
call-up and presented themselves, each with the required horse, saddle,
bridle and weapon, at Jan de Wet's farm Juistzoo near present-day Hobhouse.

Andries Meyer left the Hexrivier camp in the same commando as Chris
and Pieter Muller, on 26 November 1899, though he briefly returned home
again (his place on the front line taken by temporarily by his brother, a
Boer custom[12]), on 1 December, to harvest his corn, before returning to
his commando carrying a Free State flag as a gift from his wife. Just a week
or so later, on 12 December, he heard the dismaying news that Comman-

dant APJ Diederichs and Jan de Wet, plus another two Ladybranders, had been killed in what he described as 'the fight on Scholtznek' – the battle of Magersfontein. (Scholtznek is an elevated flat-topped ridge connecting two higher koppies which bend southwards at the extremities; one side slopes down to the veld north of Magersfontein.)

Meyer wryly recounted his first real test of war. On 4 February 1900, in the Modderrivier area close to General Cronjé's camp, he saw his first *kakie* and took his first shot of the war. Then he realised, to his consternation, that he was alone, because all the other burgers had retreated, and he made haste to follow them.

The commander-in-chief, General IS Ferreira, who had observed all this, called him over and asked him what his first lesson of warfare was. 'To look behind me,' answered Meyer, and Ferreira replied that it was sad but true.

Ferreira was killed within days, and it fell to Meyer to wrap his body in a blanket and later convey it to the churchyard in Petrusburg.

Meyer had just returned from this burial duty when the most famous feat of the legendary master scout, Danie Theron, took place, when General Christiaan de Wet sent the wiry former lawyer Theron through tight enemy lines to try to extract Cronjé from the mired-down Paardeberg disaster. Cronjé's large, slow-moving column had been intercepted at Paardeberg Drift, on the banks of the Modderrivier. Cronjé refused to leave with Theron as he felt he would be abandoning his followers. Had he acceded to the expert scout's mission, however, thousands of his loyal men would have been freed to search for escape routes, although slower units in the column, which included women, would undoubtedly still have been captured.

Theron's eel-like ability to infiltrate enemy territory led to the newly appointed Supreme Commander of the British forces in South Africa, Lord Roberts, calling him 'the hardest thorn in the flesh of the British advance' and putting a reward of £1 000 on his head, dead or alive. He was killed in action just months later, in September at Gatsrand, to De Wet's dismay; for him, Theron had the 'heart of a lion' while 'bearing consummate tact and energy'.

After a ten-day siege Cronjé surrendered, on 27 February 1900. He was a huge trophy for the British, along with the capture of thousands of his men – the first significant British victory of the war and a massive blow to the Boers – one that could have been partially avoided had De Wet's plan to rescue Cronjé been realised.

At this point, Chris was sufficiently recovered from his leg wound to join the Ladybranders who escaped, alongside the slippery General de Wet (for whom surrender was unthinkable), by fleeing ahead of the fast-pursuing enemy, as well as running the gauntlet of cannon fire on either side. The great wonder, he wrote, was that only one man died during this headlong flight.

At the beginning of March, the Ladybranders were able to regroup at Bleskop, where officers had to be chosen to fill their thinned ranks. Jonathan Crowther was elected commandant, Chris was chosen as his alternative, and Jan Diederichs was named veldkornet; Meyer was chosen as assistant veldkornet, personally responsible for 200 men divided into four corporalships.

They were plunged immediately into the Poplar Grove Skirmish on 7 March, as De Wet tried to halt the British advance, and again, three days later, at Abramskraal, where the Ladybranders took their stand between two cannons. But Bloemfontein fell to a vastly superior British force on 13 March, after which they began the long, successful push eastwards across the breadth of the Free State. This was the slow beginning of the end for the Free State republic, though fighting would continue for many months yet.

After the loss of Bloemfontein, a very low point in the war for the Boers, the Ladybranders were sent home to recuperate, commandeer more men, and find fresh horses. (Lool wrote of these few days in the middle of March, and the joy of returning home.) During this brief R&R, Chris's wife Dorie fell pregnant.

This furlough, in the middle of a hotly fought war, puzzled not only the British but also some of the Boers. The decision to send his men home for some rest and restocking by General de Wet was criticised by, among others, veteran general Piet Joubert. The edgy exchange between the two headstrong men is well documented: 'Do you mean to tell me,' Joubert asked De Wet, 'that you are going to give the *English* a free hand, while your men take their holidays?'

'I cannot catch a hare, General, with unwilling dogs,' De Wet replied in his usual colourful way (recorded in his war memoir), and added, for he could see that the old warrior was not satisfied, 'You know the Afrikanders [sic] as well as I do, General . . . Whatever I had said or done, the burgers would have gone home; but I'll give you my word that those who come back will fight with renewed courage.'

By 19 March these burgers were indeed back in the saddle, 300 men strong under their commandant, J Crowther.

Here, Meyer's memoirs replicate Lool Muller's almost exactly. All of their commando, including the four brothers, rode to Clocolan. Then they heard that the *English* were surrounding Ladybrand, and raced to return while their scouts were sent ahead to verify the news.

Soon word came that Danie Theron had been involved in a skirmish there, and that *een van sy spioene* (one of his 'spies') – Lool – had been captured. Lool's reconnaissance had indeed ended in capture, and he was now on his way to the Green Point POW camp, but he was not one of Theron's team. He had simply been chosen, on a single, fateful day, for a routine survey near Ladybrand after news of fighting there. He was not a trained scout: he was simply unlucky.

Under heavy fire, the Ladybranders were able to drive the enemy out of their town, but not for long. The town would change hands several times during the next few months, during which time toddler Pieter, Michael's son, saw his first 'man in a dress', the kilted soldier who made such a life-long impression on him.

Early in May, after a council of war in Senekal in which Chris and Jan Diederichs participated, the Ladybranders and the Thaba'Nchu commando left first for Wonderkop, a high, small farming area in the Senekal area; then, hearing that the *English* were behind them, they moved to Hammonia in the Ficksburg area, keeping ahead of the enemy yet still within fighting distance. At this point, the Ladybrand commandant Crowther was too ill to continue and Chris took his place. Until the end of the war, Chris held the senior rank of commandant of the Ladybranders.

As the enemy moved out from Senekal, one of Chris's veldkornets, Pieter Ferreira, engaged in a skirmish with them, and was in danger of being cut off from the rear by British reinforcements. Chris spotted this danger and galloped to warn him, and was shot through the hand. He bound up the bleeding wound with a large white handkerchief until he could receive treatment. He was taken to the hospital in Bethlehem to recuperate, which he quickly did.

Exact details of his hand wound survive: a small piece of almost transparent paper, with a tiny note written by Chris, '*2 koël gate*' [sic] (2 bullet holes). When the waxy paper is held up to the light, a faint outline can be seen of his left hand and wrist. A small hole just below the cuff of his wrist is marked '*In*' and a second small hole, below the third knuckle, is marked '*Uit*'.

The wound was typical of that caused by an almost-spent bullet. At close range, the hand would have been shattered; at a short distance, there would be an explosive effect if the missile struck a bone. At a thousand yards, however, it could pass neatly through a femur.

Chris had been lucky again.

6

Their last stand: the chaotic
Prinsloo surrender

WINTER WAS NIPPING at their heels, along with the enemy, and the nights were dark and brutally cold in the high eastern area of the Free State where snow is not uncommon.

In June 1900, at Doringberg, the Boers came across a sleeping commando without sentries and had to shake them awake to see if they were friend or foe. It was Commandant Haasbroek's commando, wrote Meyer, and it was a sight to see, when someone's eyes opened to the barrel of a gun!

Soon they were in the middle of the Brandwater Basin chaos, and this time there would be no way out for the Mullers and their comrades.

The British force that had pushed the Boers right across the Free State had done so in spite of some serious obstacles, the most surprising being that, in the early months of the war, there was an incredible lack of proper maps of military quality on their side. The post-war Royal Commission was shocked enough to ask Lord Kitchener to repeat one of his statements: 'There was no map before [the war] of the Orange Free State.'[13]

Still, despite this and other areas of ignorance – including that some senior British officers claimed not to know that Boers could ride horses and shoot – the British had regrouped and, due to their vastly greater numbers, had the Boers on the defensive.

In the middle of July 1900, the Ladybranders had harassed the hotly pursuing enemy with five cannons 'in all directions', but soon their commandos were on the back foot as the massed British troops drew nearer. These 8 400 Boers led by President Steyn and General de Wet, and including, of course, the Muller brothers, were increasingly alarmed about the approaching

16 000 British troops. Roberts had, by now, a shrewd idea of what it took to win against these elusive Boers: persistence and overwhelming odds.

The Ladybranders and the Ficksburg commandos were instructed to take control of Retiefsnek – by now all the commandos remaining were fighting together, and the Ladybranders and their neighbouring Ficksburg commando were chosen to shore up the area, as they were from the district and knew it best.

General JBM Hertzog, at the time an assistant chief commandant of the military forces (commando units) of the Free State, appeared there after a couple of days, to inspect their horses. Finding them 'too thin', not in good condition – the Free State is a summer-rainfall area and by now, in deep winter, the veld was dry and brown, with scant grazing – he ordered the men to go to Ficksburg to find fresh horses. Not even in the middle of a desperate fight for their survival would the Boers ignore the state of their mounts, which, though sturdy, had endured months of heavy riding.

They left their wagons behind, along with a group of men to dig trenches; the kloofs and valleys in this border region were now filled with soldiers from both sides, as well as civilians.

After their return with new horses, and following days of heavy fighting without a break, they were given permission to go to Fouriesburg, now the alternative capital of the Free State since the fall of Bloemfontein – in this early commando phase of the war, they provisioned wherever they could. But within half a mile of reaching the town, they realised it had just been occupied by the hugely swollen British forces.

Had they known that such a long commando-style war lay ahead, they might have slipped quietly on past Fouriesburg without the enemy even realising they were there, for the Boers knew the terrain intimately – Meyer regretted not doing this for the rest of his life, though it would have technically meant they had gone AWOL although able to continue fighting. Instead, under orders to retain contact with the main Boer force, they retreated into the bottleneck of the mountains at Slaapkrans in the Brandwater Basin, in the Golden Gate area, with the enemy closing in.

Realising their peril, the officers, including Chris, spent the whole night burying their excess ammunition to prevent its falling into enemy hands. The following day, 300 Ladybranders and Ficksburgers had to dig in and fight in the most chaotic and distressing circumstances: 'alles hier was in 'n warboel' (everything here was bedlam). Free State families who had been hiding in these mountains for months were trying at the same time to escape this horror with their children, cattle, sheep and the few goods essential for survival.

The Boers now felt the power of the lyddite 'bombs' of the enemy – the crags shuddered with explosions, followed by a horrible smell, then yellow dust showered down on them.

They buried their dead when they could.

When the shooting ceased, the *English* stormed at them with bayonets.

The view cherished by the Boers, of their democratic right to choose who they would fight and perhaps die under, sowed the seeds of their imminent though unsought painful surrender – they were defeated by the very process they held so dear.

There now unfolded an episode that made General de Wet still seethe with rage years later, despite his own responsibility in the unfolding events: the fight over who should be in command of these 'rearguard' Boers. This jealousy among the senior officers almost has elements of farce, though the consequences for the Boers, and the Muller family, were anything but funny.

De Wet decided to abandon the Brandwater Basin area as the large contingent of *English* edged ever nearer, and he split his considerable force of thousands of men into four parts. He then slipped away through Slabbertsnek on the night of 15 July 1900, taking President Steyn – he refused to leave so great a prize for the British. Steyn's serious illness was not yet manifest though as the war progressed it became increasingly difficult for him to ride or care for himself.[14]

De Wet also took with him a commando of 2 600 men and 460 wagons containing essentials such as arms, ammunition and food. 'Whatever I did, it seemed as if I could not get rid of the wagons!' he complained ruefully (these had partly been the downfall of Cronjé, too). Next, 1 500 men under Fourie and Froneman left.

Those who remained had been carefully chosen by De Wet to be left as trusted 'watchguards', picked because they were intimately acquainted with the 'rough and difficult territory'; they included the Ladybranders as well as the Ficksburgers. De Wet's plan was that these men would hold the fort until all the other commandos had got away, and then get away themselves. In this watchguard group were Commandant Chris Muller and his brother Pieter, as well as Meyer. Meanwhile, their eldest brother, Michael, was up at Witsieshoek (today's Phuthaditjhaba), a particularly high hamlet in the QwaQwa area, on the Free State side of the Drakensberg peaks, part of a reconnaissance sent ahead to try to find another way out through the mountains towards Natal.

At this critical and dangerous point, the wheels fell off. No sooner had the strong-willed De Wet left the scene, having bought time to save Steyn, than the row began. General Paul Roux had been placed in charge of a section of the remaindered men, but they, unhappy with Roux's leadership, rejected him. They demanded a council of war, which replaced him with General Marthinus Prinsloo. But a new election was supposed to include *all* officers entitled to vote, so a number, including Roux himself, left the war arena to canvass for ballots. The new general, Prinsloo, was not fully confirmed in his post and therefore was unable to count on the support he, or any other commander, should have had.

In a bigger surprise, the council also voted to surrender to the *English*, 17 votes to 13. This jolted everyone, including the council itself, which decided to review their decision with the idea that they ask the *English* (with whom they were in full battle mode) for an armistice of six days to consult. What a vain hope.

The more pragmatic of the Boers opted for a plan B: they resolved that if the enemy did not agree to their request (and they did not), then they should continue fighting in the direction of Witsieshoek, with the objective of breaking through and passing out of the mountains there.

This lack of clarity led to some Boers obeying the council's original decision to surrender by pouring back into the chaotic Brandwater Basin from Natal, while at the same time other Boers were trying to avoid surrender and get over the Drakensberg mountains and away from the English in the opposite direction – two tidal waves colliding.

By 28 July, General Archibald Hunter, the British leader of operations in the eastern Free State, and his force had advanced eastwards in a pincer movement towards Slaapkrans, which fell into British hands at midnight. Prinsloo's negotiators were ordered to surrender on 29 July: his Boers were surrounded.

Prinsloo's messenger, who had asked vainly for more time, returned with two *English* officers who 'arrogantly' demanded to see Prinsloo. The sturdy veldkornet Meyer bristled, after which they became noticeably more cordial. He attended the hopeless meeting at which Prinsloo asked for a short amnesty so that the Boers could figure out the problematic who's who of their remaining command.

General Hunter refused, of course; he would have been mad to accede when he had the upper hand, and he knew it. The only concession Prinsloo secured was that his men would not have to surrender on foot – the ultimate indignity for Boer soldiers. But their fitter horses were immediately swopped for 'thin ones', British mounts in poor condition.

Prinsloo had had to face both an inappropriately timed leadership battle, and a huge British force of about 20 000 men. At his headquarters, aptly named Verliesfontein (Fountain of Loss), his personal, dignified surrender took place.

The *English* respected Prinsloo for this painful decision taken in unenviable circumstances not of his making; but hardliner Boers never forgave him.

General de Wet's incredulity when he heard the bad news knew no bounds. Always the escapologist extraordinaire, he was temperamentally incapable of understanding how a fighting man could surrender (he never did, remaining uncaptured throughout the war), and was still fulminating against Prinsloo in his post-war memoir, describing the circumstances as 'nothing short of an act of murder, committed on the Government, the country, and the nations, to surrender three thousand men in such a way' (it was actually more than four thousand, in the final counting).

De Wet also managed to get a swipe in at the jilted Roux, whom he accused, with justification, of having behaved like a child, and who foolishly had gone to General Hunter's camp on the grounds that it was he, Roux, who was really in charge, and not Prinsloo, and that the Boers' surrender should therefore be nullified. Needless to say, he was immediately taken prisoner.

This surrender of a large number of Boers in the eastern Free State in late July 1900 is variously referred to, confusingly, as Brandwater Basin, Slaapkrans, Golden Gate, Surrender Hill and the Prinsloo surrender. They are all essentially the same event, over several days.

It had not all gone the way of the *English*, though: 275 of their soldiers died in this fierce ordeal.

The captive Boers were taken in groups to Surrender Hill near present-day Clarens. Disconsolate commandos trickled out of the kloofs: the war was over for them. The three Muller brothers, Michael, Pieter and Chris, along with their comrades, were about to become prisoners for far longer than they had been active in combat.

Meyer, despite believing they ought to have at least *tried* to escape to fight another day, defended Marthinus Prinsloo. He never doubted that the brave general had done everything within his ability with courage, and moreover, had 'stood his post' in dangerous conditions – a view shared by most of those, including the Mullers, who had been at his side.

But Prinsloo's reputation was ruined. He spent the rest of the war as a POW in Simon's Town at Bellevue camp: he lasted little longer than the war itself, dying isolated and scorned in January 1903.

PART II

LOOL'S WAR
1900

7

Cheerfully off to Colesberg

LODEWYK – 'LOOL' – began the war as a lively young fellow, keen to get at the enemy. The youngest of the four Muller brothers who fought, he was only 22, an age when war might seem more like an adventure than a deadly risk, for he was fit, active and cheerful, ready for whatever came his way – the keenness of young men who look forward to playing their part. His mother would have had a different view, as mothers do. So would Lool, but not yet.

Lool's neat, vivid and sometimes jolly descriptions of his experiences are well captured. They began, as did the diary of Chris, with him leaving home under 'a cloud of grief' from those left behind, although, with the slightly callous self-involvement of youth, he seemed cheerful enough in himself. They ended with his final, scrawled, faint words immediately before his death, just five months later. His actual time in direct combat lasted only two and a half months.

Lool left home along with his comrades on Sunday, 7 January 1900, from the muster at Hexrivier farm in the Ladybrand district, just as his brothers Chris and Pieter had done on 26 November the year before. They were fêted by women bearing coffee and cake; and speeches were made by the *landdrost* (magistrate), dominee and local dignitaries as a fitting send-off.

But in a single day, riding to Sannaspost and Springfield, and then Bloemfontein, a distance of about sixty miles, they turned saddle-sore and complaining, in spite of all of them being experienced horsemen. It also rained heavily, adding to their woes, and on the second night, at Bloemfontein, because of the deluge, they were forced to cram 200 men into one house, lying down

like sardines in a can. It was a difficult sleep. Here, you hear that
someone complains about being kicked, and there someone snores
so loudly that people around him can't sleep. But I slept very well.

It was still raining when they woke up on 9 January, the day they exchanged
their Martinis for the more efficient Lee-Metford rifles, and boarded a
train for Norvalspont, en route to southerly Colesberg, on the Cape side
of the Free State border. This was a more difficult exercise than it might
seem, because their horses had to entrain as well.

When they reached their destination the next morning, the men rushed
to the trucks to let the horses out. This was Lool's first, but not by a long
way his last, reference to the primacy of horses in the war. Like all Boers,
Lool could not conceive of being without his horse: this would reduce him,
he thought, to a 'pedestrian', useless in the enormous, rangy veld.

Care of their horses mattered to the Boers not only because of the close
personal relationship they had with them, especially their 'principal'
horse (along with their 'spare wheel', which was essentially a pack-horse
and potential remount), but also because their lives depended on mobility;
the reliability and condition of their sturdy mounts was paramount. Boer
horses were often able to carry their riders for the entire duration of the
war, the most famous example being Fleur, General de Wet's beloved grey.

President Steyn's war horse, Scot, was neither young nor fast but was
steady, and adored by his master: he was later buried with honour, in
retirement, to Steyn's deep grief. Bokkie, General de la Rey's 'Basuto pony'
(really a small horse), was so *op-en-wakker* (alert) that De la Rey called
her 'the best watchdog I ever had'. The general, no longer a young man,
made one of his miraculous escapes from the British (who never laid
hands on him) by hanging on to Bokkie's tail as she pulled him over the
Magaliesberg.

To the Boers, their mounts were not just 'sacks of meat' – an accusation
made by some of the British themselves about the way they used up their
war horses – but companions that received tenderness when there was so
little of that in warfare. For them, careless or deliberate cruelty to horses
was unthinkable, even though they were forced to ride them harder on
commando, or in battle, than was safe. They were incredulous at the way
so many of the *English* (most of whom had never touched a horse before

this war) treated their mounts as if they were disposable, to be ridden to death.

Though many of the English officers were accustomed to riding, those from the rank-and-file had had little or no former contact with horses, and had no idea, nor instruction, of how to handle them. Their big remount station at Stellenbosch was staffed mostly by incorrigible soldiers, British 'war rejects', or officers who had fallen out of favour with the high command; the pejorative term 'to be Stellenbosched' became a common insult. Few there had training in the care of horses and their incompetence deeply affected their horse casualty rate. There was little acceptance of how much punishment force-ridden horses, especially those not yet acclimatised, could take, nor what their needs were, including for fodder and clean drinking water.

So this particular war took a terrible toll not only of human life, but of horses, too. Indignant senior British officers unpacked their accusations and complaints about the disgraceful treatment of horses, too late, during the Royal Commission: the 'wastage' of British horses in the South African war was a 'revolting' 120 per cent.[15] Even the enormous horse carnage in Crimea – which, because of the long distances, tough terrain and weather, had up to that point held the record for being the worst of all Empire wars for horses – was lower, at 80 per cent.

On their journey, two large shells were fired at the Boers from the hills. Not being familiar with such bombardment, they fled into the nearby river without waiting for orders to do so. It was their first taste of battle, and alarming.

They camped at Thaba'Nchu that night, and Lool was, unsurprisingly, not at all sleepy after his first encounter with the enemy – his adrenalin was still running high. He was also worried that it was a very dry environment and he felt the horses would 'become thinner' (lose condition) because of it.

On 12 January he experienced his first commando ride under General Crowther, a Ladybrander of note. They were divided into three groups, each of only 18 men; this meant that they were 'few', though luckily it was a quiet night.

The following morning they spotted, from their hill, an enemy commando riding out, and their artillery fired three cannon shots, after which their opponents retreated speedily. Back they went to camp, hearing, from time to time, shells falling near their position.

Then, only a week into his war, something happened that had long-term consequences for Lool, on 15 January.

> Because of the carelessness of those looking after the horses, some have disappeared, and among them is mine. This day I have looked for them but found nothing.

That evening, ordered to go out on patrol, he had to borrow a horse from his corporal. Fed up, he wrote the following day that

> this morning, D le Roux, [Coenraad] Bekker and I are going to look for our horses again. While we searched, we came in the vicinity of the police camp [there were mounted police units on both sides], until the noise of the shells was so great that we could not proceed. We went to sit in a small *kloofie* and we listened to the noise and whistling of the shells.
>
> When we returned to our camp, we were given orders to go and dig trenches for protection. We slept there.

He wrote about this taste of war (the only complete letter found of Lool's) to his 'Dear Brother', Michael, on 16 January, but he was as much concerned about his missing horses as he was about the cannons.

> We arrived here last Thursday but still haven't yet engaged in fighting. On our arrival the enemy greeted us with bombs [explosions] but caused no damage.
>
> Yesterday we heard that they were moving out. We immediately saddled up and when we arrived at our positions, we heard that General De la Rey's barrage had forced them back. It seems as if the enemy is very afraid to engage us in the open veld. What they do is to shoot at us from the ridges with their cannon. While I am writing, I hear their cannon continuously shooting at our camps, but without success. At first, I found the roar of the cannon quite strange, but I am now so used to it, I no longer notice it.
>
> It is very dry here. You see nothing but scrub and *ysterklippen* [iron-stones]. Because the veld is so poor, the horses want to wander

at random. Through the neglect of the sentries, about ten of our horses are missing, including both of mine. I have been looking for them for two days, but found nothing, but I am still hopeful that I will find them.

We are about a half hour from Colesberg, under a ridge, and our position is on the other side of it. In the evenings we go there on foot and it is a strange sight to see so many men climbing the ridge with bundles on their backs . . . [Colesberg is surrounded by stony, hilly ridges which were used by one or the other side for observation and siting cannons.]

Further, dear brother, write quickly to me about how things are with you. I have had no news from home since I left, and I long for news from them. Also send me the latest news about other places, because here, I hear nothing.

8

Hunting for horses

THE FOLLOWING DAY a comrade returned one of Lool's horses that had been found in the police camp. Then, again, four of them went searching for the other lost horses, without success.

This was now the pattern of their lives: to go out looking for the missing horses, to get shelled at, and to stand sentry duty at night. They occasionally saw enemy searchlights.

A couple of days later, on Sunday 21 January, they attended devotions led by Daniel F du Toit of Bloemfontein – 'Oom Lokomotief', a journalist and an important figure in the first Afrikaans language movement founded in Paarl, in 1875.

The next day, Monday, five of them went to Colesberg to have their photographs taken, but as the photographer had been taken to jail in Bloemfontein, they returned empty-handed.

They took their horses to be shoed; they had to wait a long time, as there were so many mounts waiting to be seen to.

On their return to camp, they heard of an exploit by four fellow Ladybranders who had gone off to eat prickly pears – a great delicacy and delicious, but with fine, almost invisible spines on their thick outer skins, so they need to be handled carefully. The local burgers had thought the Ladybranders were the enemy and had shot at them; the Ladybranders had had to hide in a kraal and send a message for help. The commandant then had to ride out to intervene, and assure the angry farmers that these fruit-lovers were not their enemy. One can only imagine what he thought of this waste of his time.

After a church service, on 27 January, once everything was quiet, Lool determinedly went out yet again to look for his still-missing horse; again, this was without success, though he was pleased to find three letters waiting for him on his return.

There is a break in Lool's diary here, a missing page. Someone had later attempted to stick it back in, for the sticking-tape marks are visible.

Fragments of another letter, written to Michael on 2 February, and again marked from Colesberg, noted:

> This day I received your letter, which made me very happy. With me, and all of us . . .
>
> . . .
>
> . . . a few days with their cannons. They have been shooting a great deal during the last week, with a huge ship's cannon, but did not cause any damage. Here, also, is the protective hand of God clearly visible . . .
>
> . . .
>
> . . . Things are going very well with Oubaas. He is just the same as always, full of all kinds of jokes. His job is to cook food, something he understands so well. He is the best cook in the . . .

Their brother-in-law Oubaas ('Old Boss', a teasing nickname), married to the eldest Muller sister, Non, was clearly a character, and was always referred to, in letters and diaries, in a positive context as a cheerful comrade. He had five children when the war began. He was captured with the surviving Muller brothers in the Prinsloo surrender.

Boer cannons let go a 'violent bombardment' at the enemy fortifications on 7 February from the direction of Colesberg. This spurred Lool on to live it up a little, while he could. Off he went to buy fruit with his friends, Coenraad Bekker and Dawid Kriel, and found some at 'Joubert's farm', the first fruit they had eaten since leaving home. It was a rare, good moment in the dismal daily routine, with violent bombardments starting before sunrise and continuing until the afternoon; men were constantly wounded.

Lool was now in the middle of the battle of Colesberg. Australians were fighting on the side of the *English* on the central front, where the Boers had occupied Colesberg, and were pushing south into the eastern Cape. On 9 February the Australians prevented the Boers from outflanking the British position by defending what was known as West Australia Hill.

On that day, Lool recorded:

> Violent bombardment, starting before sunrise until the afternoon.
> On this day, five of our artillery were lightly wounded by the enemy's
> shells. This evening, about nine o'clock, Johannes Bezuidenhout
> arrived to tell us that General De la Rey is asking for support. Each
> corporal must supply three men. The two Dawids and I were nomi-
> nated by our corporal.

The following morning at 2 am, they formed part of 50 Ladybranders who
rode for more than two hours, first to the nearest camp, then on to a stream,
where they unsaddled and braaied meat and ate *stormjagers* (dumplings).
They then continued to a place where they found prickly pears for eating.

The men arrived at De la Rey's post at around four in the afternoon, teth-
ered their horses to bushes, and lay down to sleep, for it had been a very
long day. But they had barely closed their eyes when they heard the rousing
call '*Opsaal!*' (saddle up!) and they rode on wearily in the moonlight to a
more secure place, where they were finally able to sleep in a dry dam.

From this point on, there was a sustained period of fighting and finding
food and foraging. They relieved Jan FG Celliers (later General Celliers),
and then move on to the Rensburg siding, where there had been 'vigorous
fighting', and heard that many of the *English* had been chased from there.
They helped collect the dead and wounded – 10 and 12 February had seen
the battles of Bastersnek and McCracken's Hill, respectively, at Colesberg.

They managed to fortify themselves with green mealies, potatoes and
carrots from a nearby farm, and at Rensburg camp were grateful to find a
surplus of feed for their horses, including 'oats, bran, chaff and mealies'.
Lool was so pleased that he joined in singing Psalm 146 ('Praise thy Lord
the King of Heaven . . .'), managed to write some letters home, and had a
good night after the sleeplessness of the previous ones.

It was Lool's 23rd birthday on 15 February 1900, and he naturally spent
much of the day thinking about home. The men received orders that they
would soon outspan for Scholtznek, and spent the rest of the day packing
up and baking *stormjagers*. That evening, their tent was flooded and all
their things were soaked, making it difficult to sleep. It was not a jolly
birthday, and it was the last Lool would have.

They rode back to Norvalspont, and on 17 February left by train; despite the locomotive breaking down and having to wait for another, they arrived in Bloemfontein the next day. The first order of business was to feed the horses and rest them up, then at two o'clock in the afternoon they set off, sleeping on a hillock in the veld that looked 'very beautiful' after the rains – in this summer-rainfall area, the veld can experience great deluges.

The next day, while buying watermelons at a farm, Lool and his comrades met a number of men returning from battle who told them

> terrifying rumours of the fighting that almost discouraged us. From there, we carried on. The wind blows strongly. The red sand blows like clouds towards us, and prevents us from seeing much ahead.
>
> We unsaddled. I tried to sleep and I was just shutting my eyes when I heard the call, *Opsaal!* We left from there. Still nothing ahead but dust and sand. We slept on a plain.
>
> [The following morning] we wanted to leave early but we had to look for a long time first for our horses.
>
> We unsaddled on a hillock and waited for the Commandant, who was still behind us. From here we heard the thundering of the cannon. When the Commandant arrived, we proceeded.
>
> We unsaddled at Modderrivierspoort. Here we met various people from the battlefield. We also found out who of our people were dead and wounded. Here I also heard that my brother Chris was wounded [his first war wound, in his leg].
>
> This evening, we take our position on a red ridge.

The next morning, the enemy appeared on all sides. They were in the thick of it now, and ill prepared. They were ordered to flee, and charged 'over a barren place' while being fired at from all sides by cannon, maxims and rifles.

Lool was still dodging bullets when his borrowed horse weakened, so he could only proceed slowly. Coenraad Bekker remained with him, a brave act of comradeship.

By the time they were able to join up with their mates again, Lool's horse was so poorly that he could make little headway. Another man's horse had also weakened; he took both their horses on a lead, with Lool following behind, walking.

They eventually arrived at a dam where the men had unsaddled. It was dirty, 'but never has a drink tasted so good to me as this water'. An ox had been slaughtered for the men who were 'very hungry', so they were able to cut meat for themselves, and then take up positions on a ridge.

It is unsurprising that the next day Lool recorded feeling depressed. He had heard the news of his older, battle-hardened brother Chris (who had fought unscathed at Magersfontein) being wounded, and had himself come under heavy fire, his borrowed horse failing under him. The news from Bloemfontein was not encouraging, and he had seen enough dead and frightened burgers to know that war was not turning out to be either glamorous or thrilling. It was noisy, dusty, sleepless and dangerous.

All this could occur to young men going off to war, but, in the middle of rousing speeches and brass bands and bunting, and waving supporters, it rarely does, until reality kicks in. This had now happened to Lool.

It was with immense relief that, having thought all day about his 'other' brother, Pieter, he heard from the just-arrived Commandant P Ferreira of Ladybrand that he had seen Pieter two days before. This gladdening news certainly improved Lool's spirits, and again reflected the intimacy and kinship-relatedness of not only the Mullers, but indeed all the Boer commandos. The men who fell around them were brothers or cousins or close kin, or friends or neighbours since youth. Seldom were they strangers; for the Boers, it was a very close-knit war.

Lool spent the night of 23 February being shelled, and shooting back at 'waves of lancers'. Once the enemy began to retreat, so did the Boers, but Lool was left on the ridge. Only 13 men were with him by the time he was relieved by CC Froneman, still commandant though soon to be promoted to general.

Once again on a borrowed horse, Lool had to return the animal to its owner on the ridge. Another man lent Lool a horse but without a saddle.

They made their way to the dam to water their mounts, then spent the rest of the night on sentry duty back on the ridge, being heavily rained on, with nothing more to cover them than a coat and a blanket. They were soaking, Lool wrote, but because they were so tired, they slept. This happened again the following night, but this time the rain was so heavy that Lool and one of his comrades were compelled to spend the night sitting up, leaving their bodies sore the next morning.

A day of prayer had been declared by the Free State government for

25 February, wrote Lool; they were certainly in crisis mode. He and his companions were left with no officers, who were all away at a council of war regarding the seriousness of Roberts's march towards Bloemfontein, with the bogged-down General Cronjé being cornered at Paardeberg with his thousands of Boers. All elected Boer officers, including his brother Chris, were entitled, and expected, to attend: the mood was grim.

Two hundred men were told to move out, in case their help was needed for the 'main camp' (Cronjé's), but they were not called on, and returned. It was too late to do anything about the huge Boer force mired at Paardeberg, despite De Wet's seething rage at their quandary.

There was a hard day ahead on 26 February for Lool and his comrades. They had to make a road for a cannon, to pull it up to the ridge.

> About 100 men were roped in front of the cannon, and we towed it up to this high hill. When this was completed, a wagon arrived with goods from Ladybrand and to my great joy, I got tobacco, coffee, sugar and so on.

He then spent the night on patrol with about 200 mounted men, and the next morning visited the wagons to see if he could find his borrowed horse that had foundered, but was unable to do so.

On his return he heard, to his surprise, that President Steyn wanted to address the men.

> His Excellency made a lovely speech in which he encouraged us to trust in the Lord.
> [That evening], 200 men went out and because I was very sleepy and my borrowed horse was very tired, I was granted leave to stay behind.

The exhaustion of hard days of labour, nights of patrols, and the neverending search for the horses was beginning to tell.

Good and bad news arrived the next day, 28 February. At about 11 in the morning Lool's brother Pieter and others rode into camp; Lool's great joy was shared by all around him.

But that afternoon, they received the awful news that the main camp of

General Cronjé had surrendered, a disaster difficult for them to grasp.

Two days later, there was more bad news: on 2 March, post arrived from Chris, writing that his baby son, born before the war in January 1899 and nicknamed 'Mullertjie', had died – he would lose two tiny children during the war. Lool was again plunged into sadness: as the youthful godfather of Chris's eldest child, his daughter Joey, he keenly felt this loss within his tightly knit family.

The next day, a Saturday, he joined others on a swimming trip to the Modderrivier.

The following night, as they lay down to sleep after the church service, the rain came down in torrents.

> We jumped up. One hides here, the other there.
>
> When the rain cleared up we could not find a place to sleep; we saw nothing but water. All that was left was for us to stand and laugh at one another. Eventually, we lay down in spite of the fact that we had to sleep in the water, and we were just asleep when the rain started coming down again and the only solution was for us to sit up while sleeping until day arrived.
>
> [The next day] because for several days we had had no meat, to our great delight three oxen were slaughtered. Then you could see the Boere really braaiing meat.
>
> This afternoon we again went out to make a ford [across a stream]. While we were busy, the enemy loosed a few shells on us that gave us a fright. We worked at the ford until about nine o'clock in the evening.

Lool continued to fret over his missing horse, for he was aware of its intrinsic value. His familiar mount was his best means of survival, especially as the war was turning against them.

On 7 March, exactly two months since he had left home with such high hopes, he asked for leave to search for the animal again, but just as he had saddled up a borrowed mount, the enemy began to move and he was ordered to report to his position.

Now he began to see the real, unnerving effect of the huge Paardeberg surrender.

Not long after that, we saw the burgers who were on the 'red' [most dangerous advance] positions fleeing. Pieter [his brother], Jan Houmann and I tried to better our positions. While busy with this, we saw some of our men saddling up and riding away. The Commandant did his best to stop them.

There were still two cannon on the ridge that had to be secured. Some went to fetch the cannon, others loaded the wagons. Others retreated as fast as they could. During all the chaos, I marked the position of our burgers and watched how they were fleeing on all sides. A grave feeling of sadness overcame me and into my thoughts came, 'Look how the Afrikaner *Volk* lost their faith in their God.'

When everything was ready, the Commandant ordered us to ride. We left under furious bombardment from the enemy. In the throng of people we got separated from the Commandant. The three of us searched for a while but when we were unable to find our people, we went to the camp of General De Wet which at that stage was also in disarray. From here, we could see how the burgers were retreating on all sides.

We carried on a little way but the enemy advanced on us from all sides; we are being held back by our cannon, which retreats, then fires, then retreats. After we had covered some distance, the Commandant [who arrived later] ordered us back to take up positions.

During the afternoon I had great problems with my stomach. I could hardly sit on the horse and I was very glad when we unsaddled for a while. We rode until late in the evening and during this ride I thought continuously of my country, of which we have conceded so much to the enemy, and an uneasy feeling overpowered me.

At about nine o'clock we arrived at Abramskraal and slept there.

For the next couple of days they tried to regroup, moving to and fro in the area between Modderrivier and Abramskraal.

While on patrol on 10 March, Lool came across two Ladybranders drinking coffee at a 'native hut' [sic]; one of them was Jollyman (JDT) Prinsloo, a close Diederichs relative: Jollyman was the brother of Kotie, wife of Jan Diederichs who had fought alongside Chris Muller.

That night Lool and the men came under heavy bombardment, and on Sunday 11 March, after about three hours' sleep, they were ordered to *Opsaal!* In the dawning light Lool noticed with alarm that his borrowed horse was weakening. In a short time, it collapsed. Another man loaned him an old mare that was 'very lazy' and also difficult to ride.

At Bainsvlei, about five miles outside Bloemfontein, they stopped for food – a relief, for Lool was really hungry. After an hour they were back in the saddle again, riding towards Bloemfontein, now under heavy pressure from the *English*.

> We unsaddled next to our wagons on the ridge at Bloemfontein. Here, it was my turn to look after the horses. I was so sleepy that I feared I would lose them. When I was relieved, I went for a sleep and had a few hours of refreshing rest. In the evening just before sunset, we took up positions on a bushy ridge to the southwest of Bloemfontein.
>
> [The next day] shortly after sunrise, we held a service led by Mr Van Rensburg. Afterwards, we were ordered to dig ditches for ramparts. We were busy the whole day.
>
> In the afternoon, we noticed that the enemy was surrounding us. The burgers of Ficksburg were on a koppie. For a while they gave a good account of themselves but then they had to flee.
>
> When evening fell, there was great disorder. The burgers were retreating and there were no officers to command them. We also had to leave our ditch, seeing that we were alone.
>
> When it was dark, the Commandant arrived who by then was also at his wits' end. We rode this way, then that way.
>
> Eventually, [brother] Pieter with twelve of his men were sent out to do sentry duty. We were painfully cold and tired but seeing that the enemy was so close to us, we had to be very alert.

The next day was even worse. It became clear that many burgers who had read the situation accurately realised that Bloemfontein was lost. They began to leave while they still could – not for them the horror of capture, as had happened at Paardeberg. For the Boers, a strategic retreat was always preferable to surrender; one could live to fight another day.

Lool admitted to longing to leave, but his older brother Pieter refused, until their general granted them permission. They managed to escape without being shot, passing Bloemfontein to its west. 'With that, the enemy occupied Bloemfontein,' Lool wrote, although the capital city of the Free State was not formally occupied by Lord Roberts until 13 March.

To me it was terribly discouraging. We rode ahead in the direction of Brandfort and unsaddled in the afternoon at Renosterspruit, where we made coffee and ate a little, and we noticed that we were painfully few in numbers. From there we left for Modderrivier. Continuously, I dwell on the fact that our capital city was so easily taken.

Few could have felt as badly about the fall of Bloemfontein as President Steyn. Not only had he lost his capital city, but had also fallen out with his own brother, Matt (known to his family as Tewie). This was yet another version of the *broedertwis* (serious disruption, or 'twist', between brothers) within Afrikaner families, between those who deeply disagreed with one another's politics, as would the two generals De Wet.

Worse followed: at the fall of Bloemfontein on 13 March, Matt Steyn was recorded as stepping forward to 'entertain' Lord Roberts, describing his president-brother as a fugitive and a nonentity, according to numerous newspaper reports circulated in the British colonies. This perceived slur came as the president strove to rally the Free Staters, while himself struggling with the effects of his growing neurological illness.

On 14 March, Lool reported that their commandant had left for a council of war and returned with the news that more men should be rounded up to continue the fight. The hope by the British, that the fall of Bloemfontein would bring an end to the ever-lengthening war within a matter of weeks, would be dashed by the determined Boers.

Lool, at least, did not have to worry about the steadfastness of his own Muller brothers. He struggled on (*'sukkel, sukkel'*) with his 'weak horse', and arrived home on 15 March, for four wonderful days of R&R, finding his family 'in a good state'. 'They were happy to see us. We spent a few really enjoyable days there and we felt again how lovely it is to be at home,' he wrote.

This was the final time the whole family were together, the last time they would share company with their cheerful and youngest soldier, Lool.

9

Ladybrand: farewell to war

LOOL RECORDED HIS farewell to his family on 19 March: 'This morning, we had to part again, which is always a difficult task.' He would often think about that moment of leave-taking in the coming months.

At 10 am he and Pieter arrived in Ladybrand, where they had been ordered to muster under the leadership of Commandant Crowther, along with 300 men, rested and properly equipped.

The two brothers decided to make straight for Clocolan, where they were expected. It became dark along the way, and rained. Lool recorded that they had to travel a long distance through the veld and moved with difficulty, though they continued undaunted. 'At about nine o'clock we arrived at Mr Frans Ferreira [a family friend]. We had a very pleasant night.'

The following night, in Clocolan, they were redeployed to a nearby ridge, while the townsfolk were supposed to be guarding a prisoner. At eleven o'clock, they heard shouting and yelling in the dark and, jumping up, heard that the prisoner had escaped. Despite a search, he got clean away.

There was some relief in this, for the Boers were not equipped to deal with prisoners, and had no camps or facilities in which to hold them for any length of time – on top of which they could barely even keep themselves, as food was becoming so scarce as a result of the scorched-earth tactics of the British, who aimed to destroy anything that might be useful to the enemy.

After that excitement, there was more in store. The following day, 22 March, the Ladybranders gathered at Zandspruit to hold another election, for the Ladybrand commando had now been refreshed and reconstituted. The results were something of a foregone conclusion, and significant for the Mullers: Chris was chosen to permanently fill the prestigious position of commandant. It was a poignant moment, for he had seen and recorded the death of his admired predecessor, APJ Diederichs, at Magersfontein; his son Jan Diederichs, as well as Chris, had already been elected by the Ladybranders as veldkornets in late February 1900. Also elected were veldkornet Pieter Ferreira and assistant veldkornet Andries Meyer.

Lool's brother, Pieter, was chosen by the men as corporal, a rank in the Boer army that was a much more responsible role than the relatively junior rank in the British army. It was a busy, organising role directly responsible for marshalling and coordinating the men. Pieter had already shown strength of character in the skirmishes at Colesberg and Bloemfontein, earning the confidence of his comrades.

Now there was much to-ing and fro-ing. They were ordered back to Clocolan, and from there they spent the next few days riding out and returning to this small Free State town.

Lool's last day as a free man was Sunday 25 March. He noted that in the afternoon scouts were sent out.

Soon after sunrise on Monday 26 March, after arriving at Bytelsspruit (a small hamlet), they were ordered to unsaddle, but had not completed this when a corporal (likely his brother, Pieter) told him to go on survey duty with three others.

> Eight of us went out and at nine o'clock we arrived at Ladybrand where we found everything quiet. Here, we found feed for our horses and then, after that, we left.
>
> I, with three men from the town, was sent to the mountain above Newlands. [A comrade] and I were separated from the rest. We came upon a ridge, and saw about ten spies of the enemy. We thought it wise to go back to join the other two. When we arrived we could not find them – they had already fled. There was for us no other option but also to flee.
>
> We went in the direction of Lelieshoek [a Ladybrand beauty spot]. Here, my mate rode so fast that I lost him. I arrived at the side of the mountain and discovered that I was in the middle of the enemy.
>
> I left my horse and ran down the mountain and lost my weapon, and then noticed that they were also below me. And they already had theirs pointed at me. There was no other choice for me other than to stick my hands up.

The captain who caught me kicked up a big fuss because my weapon was missing, and when he took my bullets, he gave me a scolding because I was shooting dum-dums.

Hollow-point dum-dums are deliberately exploding (expanding) bullets.
Germany had successfully protested about their cruelty at the Hague Convention of 1899, forcing the British to replace the hollow-points with new
full-metal-jacket bullets. When the Boer War began that same year, the
two Boer republics had not had time to sign the Convention, and many of
these dum-dums were already legally in South Africa. Some were in the
hands of the Boers who had bought them, or had gathered whatever weap-
onry they could from their successes on the field. Lool's firearms, primarily
a Lee-Metford, and his ammunition, were British and had been legally
bought, so this scolding baffled him.

There were British troops who 'unofficially' used dum-dums in the early
part of the war in South Africa, though their war office made strenuous
attempts to keep that under wraps (as did some historians, later). This is
likely why Lool's 'infringement' was not taken any further.

> Then I saw that our burgers were already storming into town. The
> *English* who were with me shot off a few rounds and then they
> ordered me to get [back] on my horse and to retreat with them. It was
> a fast gallop until we were off the mountain and then it went slowly
> again. And just before sundown we arrived at Leeuwriviersdrift.
>
> I had just arrived when Landdrost [Magistrate] Van Gorkum and
> Tom Smith also arrived as prisoners. We were placed in a house
> and looked after well. I spent the night in a good bed and slept well
> despite the fact that I felt very bad because I did not know what
> was happening at home and with my commando, and also because
> I am a prisoner.

Here, in this house-prison, the shock of surrender kicked in for Lool. One
moment you are quite free and the next, a sudden, inexorable change of fate
holds you captive. It is always a traumatic moment, in any war. For these
Boers, these Free Staters in their own land, it was an additional terror, for
what had happened to them, their capture, could foretell what lay ahead
not only for their comrades but also their families, and their country.

The following morning, 29 March 1900, Lool, the *landdrost* and Smith were put on a small cart and taken to Thaba'Nchu, which had fallen on 19 March. They were held in an office along with four other men, two of whom were Transvalers.

By then they were all hungry and, because no food seemed to be forthcoming, the *landdrost* ordered food for them from the hotel; Lool reported they had a really nice meal.

They spent the night and the whole of the next day there; Lool admitted that he was deep in grief. The *landdrost* tried to cheer them up; he seems to have been something of a character and spent much of the time trying to enliven his fellow prisoners. He also made their evening shorter by telling them 'about other countries'.

Despite being told that he could go home immediately if he signed the oath of neutrality – a promise to the British by Boer farmers that they would take no further part in the war; those who took the oath were assured safe conduct to their homes and would not be made POWs or deprived of their property – this hardy Muller brother refused. Albert, a wavering fellow captive, asked Van Gorkum why he didn't just sign the oath, and Van Gorkum crossly replied, wrote Lool, that it was because he was not a filthy *smeerlap* (rag).

They were then taken on a wagon to Bloemfontein, to the prison there, which, for the time being, was fitted out to hold POWs. Arriving there on 30 March, Lool wrote that he was overpowered by an extreme feeling of misery.

> But at least I felt a little more free because I was allowed to walk around without a guard.
>
> I must note that since we were caught, we have only once been given food by the *English*, and apart from that, we had to buy food for ourselves if we were not to starve.
>
> Here are also three Transvalers and three Free Staters, a young Dutchman, and an Irishman, who were also caught. Here we are given food fairly often.
>
> This evening, we were allowed the privilege of holding a religious service.

On 31 March, the next day, Lool found out from soldiers who had been captured that 'the battle at Ladybrand is still being hard fought'.

> Then I felt even more sad because I am a prisoner and not there to fight alongside, and because I do not know anything about the battle, nor have heard news from home.

He knew that his brothers were out there, fighting on.

On Sunday 1 April, he attended a church service for the newly captured.

> And then I thought about how often, in church, I had not listened with much attention, and I yearn to have that privilege again.
>
> This afternoon I struggled with a sombre and dark mood, a feeling I can't describe. I pondered on what lofty ideals I had imagined for the future, and it seems, for me, as if those ideals have been crushed.
>
> Here I sit in prison as if I am a criminal, and I experience a feeling of regret that I was not rather shot dead in battle, rather than to have become a prisoner. Yet, I consider that so many people have been imprisoned and, of course, many who are better than I am. And I decide to earnestly ask the dear Lord to give me patience and humility, in order to look up to Him, and to carry my burden.

Two days later, Lool was among 19 POWs who were told they would be leaving for Cape Town by train. He reported having a 'good journey', and listed the names of some of the stations they passed, De Aar, 'Baufort Wes' (Beaufort West), Matjiesfontein (the large remount station for British troops), Worcester (which Michael some months later also found beautiful when he passed by as prisoner), Wellington and Paarl.

On the evening of 7 April 1900, Lool arrived in Cape Town, three months to the day after he had first left home to do battle, the most eventful three months of his life.

He spent a couple of quiet days in a 'three-storey house' where the prisoners were given good food and were well cared for, but this was the last contact with civilian life for him. On 9 April, the Free Staters were ordered to the Green Point camp.

Lool and 16 others had to endure tramping through the streets of Cape

Town, 'jeered at by the *Rooinekken* ['red necks', the English] and *Hotten-totten*' [sic].[16]

After this 'walk of shame', Lool was uncommonly pleased to see the POW transit camp on the open ground in Green Point, next to the sea.

On arrival at Green Point we were placed with others of our men. Oh, what a joy. I was delighted to meet them and they were glad to see me. Everyone had questions and I had my work cut out to answer them all. We were shown our tent and that night I slept very well. Here, I had the pleasure of seeing the sea.

He would not enjoy that pleasure for long.

PART III

CAPTIVES OF WAR
1900

10

The Great Vlei of Green Point:
Lool's last days

A winter yacht race on the Green Point Vlei, 1891. The central yacht,
Good Hope, was owned by one of the local Juritz brothers.

Green Point common had been used every winter as a marvellous place for
sailing yachts. Dry in summer, cattle comfortably grazed here during the
warmer months, but it turned into a natural wetland from May onwards.
At times, in a wet winter, the Great Vlei was up to two kilometres in length.

There was a cycling track there from the late 1800s, as well as a pretty
pavilion from which spectators could cheer yachts scudding across the
Great Vlei in the winter months, their sails snapping in the gusts, in popular, eagerly attended regattas.

The Juritz brothers, John, Charles and Walter, who lived on its doorstep
at Three Anchor Bay, were keen sailors and founded the Green Point Ama-
teur Boat and Canoe Club in 1887, with its own smart badge and festival
days; they built many boats used on the Great Vlei. They even persuaded
the city's municipality to widen and deepen the natural lake.

But wetlands were not yet understood or valued as a vital natural resource, and as homes began to spread along that part of Cape Town's coastline with its wonderful views, distanced from the crowded city centre,

residents started to complain both of the inconvenience of a marsh/lake on their doorstep every winter, and also of its potential (largely imaginary) 'health hazard'.

The two sides, yachties and residents, faced off, and in the end it was no contest. The local ratepayers won, although letters bemoaning the loss of the lake and its watersports dragged on in newspapers such as the *Cape Argus* for some years. In the last decade of the 1800s the common was gradually drained and filled in, and by 1900 the task was deemed complete. Despite this, in the rainy months, the commonage would have been difficult, if not impossible, to cross on foot. And the first winter of the war, in 1900, was very wet indeed.

It was here, to the convenient Green Point common, that Boer prisoners were first brought, after being entrained to Cape Town, during the last months of 1899. Because the overconfident British war office had given out that the war was meant to be over by Christmas, housing prisoners in large numbers had not been given much thought, along with so much else. Their administrators were left scrambling to find places all over for the growing numbers of captive Boers, including women and children, during the next two and a half years, as the resilient Boers refused to give up.

Green Point was designated as a transit camp, and thousands of Boers passed through it, including all four Muller brothers, at one time or another. Prisoners were supposed to be moved 'elsewhere' as quickly as possible. But 'elsewhere' still had to be determined, and constructed.

Veldkornet Charles von Maltitz of the Ficksburg commando was taken prisoner early in the war, and arrived at Green Point in November 1899. He complained about the powerful summer southeaster wind which 'almost lifted men off their feet' and annoyed them with its incessant pummelling, although without it, as any born Capetonian knows, the city would swelter with heat. And in winter the common turned into a great, soggy sponge that soaked up the rain runoff from Lion's Head and Signal Hill above it.

Long rows of hundreds of white pointed tents (in the old black and white photographs, they look rather like Klan hoods placed on the ground) were anchored with guy ropes, though that was not enough to secure them in the worst wintry weather, when the Cape of Storms decided to live up to its reputation.

As the war dragged on past 1900, the camp expanded enormously, with many huts, new clusters of tents in various areas, a large number of barracks, double-storeyed buildings, stables, sorting and cooking sheds, and other structures necessary for the war effort. Fort Wynyard, on the hillock overlooking what is now Granger Bay, was a commanding presence in the background.

Green Point POW transit camp. The lighthouse is the oldest in South Africa, first lit on 12 April 1824, and is still in use. Part of an old cycle track can be seen on the right.

After Lool's embarrassing walk through the streets of Cape Town, humiliated by Cape Town's mainly British-aligned population, he was thankful to see friendly faces surrounding him in Green Point Camp, even if they were all prisoners.

The camp was nonetheless a restless, unhappy and unhealthy place, and many of Lool's entries were about unrest among the prisoners, or death from sickness; he gave 'the fever' an early, ominous mention. The camp was rigidly run, and because of its transient nature there was no regular, comforting routine.

Men were no longer grouped in the close camaraderie of their commandos, where everyone knew everyone else. They were now cheek by jowl,

Transvalers with Free Staters (who regarded themselves as separate and not necessarily on an equal footing); and there were also the foreigners assisting the Boers, and the Cape Colony's Boer sympathisers.[17] There was visible hostility between the prisoners and their *English* captors, and even between each other. The POWs were miserable and angry and, as often happens, they took it out on those closest to them – their fellow sufferers.

The first major incident came soon after Lool's entry into the camp, on 16 April.

> There is a small Afrikaner in the service of the *English* as a bugler. He sided, however, with the Afrikaners and he spoke to us often about the war, and expressed his sympathy with us. Today he spoke again with us in favour of the Afrikaners.
>
> Jan Bender [a fellow POW] heard him and reported him to the officers, whereupon the young man was dismissed from his work and sent to prison. That caused great indignation among us.
>
> We were all fed up with Jan Bender and, added to that, the same Jan Bender signed a petition in support of signing the oath of allegiance to England, and many people who were weak characters signed it. This causes us to be even more angry with Jan Bender.

A couple of days later, on 19 April, the men heard the hard news that

> a young man, Du Plessis, died in the hospital. Later this afternoon, Ds Alheit held the funeral service. The coffin was brought in covered with the Transvaal flag, but only the father and brothers of the deceased were given the right to follow the body.

On top of the stress of the Jan Bender incident – the men were not finished with him yet – and the death of another comrade, several hundred Transvalers arrived in the camp within the next few days, overcrowding it. One did not know where to look, Lool wrote, crossly.

On Sunday 22 April, he was not even able to find a place to sit and listen to Ds Alheit's service; despondent, he returned to his tent. But he received two letters to cheer him up, one from Nellie Oosthuizen, a relative in Riversdale, and one from his brother Michael, who sent him £1. It was a very welcome gift from his eldest brother, who was by no means wealthy. This windfall enabled Lool to buy some longed-for 'extras' at the prison shop, little items such as tobacco, sweet goods and fresh produce that made such a difference for those who had some cash.

Then there was a fight. It had been brewing for a while, and Lool recorded it in some detail on 27 April.

> A certain two people came into our camp, and when they reached the Transvalers they were recognised as people who were previously with us, and who went over to the English. Quickly, a large crowd of people surrounded them, shoving them to the gate. One gave them a push, another threw coffee at them, and others threw tins at them, and yet others tied dirty rags on them, so that they were relieved when they were out of the gate and I am quite sure they will not visit the prison again.

This stirred the Boers' blood, and Lool recorded that they began to

> look for more traitors. I did not mix with them. I stand at a distance, observing them. There I see them coming closer with Jan Bender, calling out that they have found another traitor. [A senior officer] tried in vain to stop them. They would not listen; they said that all traitors should be thrown out of the camp.
>
> The English officers witnessed this and immediately a number of armed soldiers were sent to stop the men. Bender was left alone and everyone went off.
>
> This evening, Bender had to point out the men who had accosted him. He pointed out two from Bloemfontein, and Abram van Huissteen [a Free State burger soldier, and a friend of Lool's].

The following day the three men who had been pointed out by Bender were summoned, and they were given seven days' arrest, amplifying the bitterness towards him.

Yet another Boer died in the hospital, an increasingly frequent event.

On 30 April, a controversial and tragic event occurred in the camp. Lool, witness to the proceedings, wrote:

> This evening, some people were holding a service near the wire fence. The young man, Philip Cronje from Ficksburg, who was leading

the singing, was shot by the guard who was closest to him. When this rumour went around the camp, there was great outrage because we saw it as a cold-blooded murder. I went to see what his wounds were and saw immediately that he could not survive.

[The next] morning, the men were called [and told] that Cronje is dead. A feeling of grief overpowered all of us. We then adopted a motion that our officers make our indignation known to the government, and that we protest most strongly at this manner of behaviour.

In the afternoon, Ds Alheit announced that two more have died, one who had been wounded and one of the *koorts* [fever]. So we held a service and he spoke the words, 'Be faithful until death and I will give you the Crown of Life'. He was visibly grief-stricken, because he knew Cronje very well and he was very taken by Cronje's exemplary demeanour. During the service, there was a general feeling of grief among the people.

The worldwide controversy that broke around the fatal shooting of Boer prisoner Philip Cronje, who had surrendered at Paardeberg along with General Cronjé, was badly handled at the time, and no honest explanation was ever offered. The British authorities tried to brush it aside, laying the blame on Cronje for 'provoking' a sentry. The Boers who had been present saw it very differently, as a persecution, and what is more, right in the middle of one their devotional services. For them, he might as well have been shot in a church.

Cronje's death was in part due to the fraught conditions in the Green Point camp. Angry prisoners, twitchy and inexperienced sentries, a dark night, a state of war – anything could have happened, and on that evening it did. It would reverberate not only among the shocked Boers in the camp, but among all the Boer camps in South Africa, and in later exile, on their transport ships, and in news reports across the globe. It was bitterly felt, and had long legs.

Neither side disputed that Cronje had been taking part in a religious gathering (habitual at the end of the day for many Boers) and that a sentry on duty, from his post above the fence near to which they were standing, had shot him in the back. It was not an affair that could be hushed up. The British authorities issued a statement saying that he had been shot because he was standing 'too near the fence' and after having been warned repeatedly. Then a different statement claimed that he had been shot while making a break for freedom. Several more versions followed – always a sign of a weak story.

The Boers protested that their gathering near the fence was a normal, regular event. Because this was where lights had been erected to illuminate the perimeter of the camp, it was the only place where they could see clearly enough in the dark to read from their psalters, which most soldiers – British and Boer alike – carried in their packs. By May, heading for midwinter, it would have been getting dark soon after 6 pm.

There was no hope of an independent investigation, but the many Boer witnesses ensured that the legend of Cronje lived on in poems and songs. A well-known nine-verse version was written by Bostonian James Molloy, a Boer sympathiser. Molloy had known Cronje in Green Point camp, and witnessed his death; after the war he would describe the shooting as 'nothing short of wilful murder on the part of the sentry'.

This 'Ballad of Philip Cronje' was written with genuine emotion but also to evoke the greatest possible indignation, and it succeeded, becoming a rallying call, crystallising the many injustices and indignities the Boers felt they had suffered.

> Have you heard of the death of young Cronje
> who was killed on the Green Point track?
> He was holding a Bible in his hand
> when the bullet entered his back.
>
> They were holding a meeting for prayer,
> they had stood there, night after night . . .
> . . . When suddenly came the report of a gun
> which scattered the praying band
> and he, whom they loved, fell down by their side,
> his Bible still clasped in his hand.
>
> He died in the night. No mother was near
> to kiss him or hold his dear hand,
> but he told the doctor he did not hear
> the sentinel's rough command . . .

Aside from Cronje's controversial death, deaths caused by disease were now occurring in the camp almost every day.

On 5 May, frightening news arrived with a new batch of prisoners.

> As far as they had travelled, they saw the cattle being confiscated and many houses burned down. It was for me, and for all of us, a bitter tiding.

After Sunday devotions the following day, Lool recorded his most emotional entry yet.

> After the service I went to eat, and after the meal, I went back to the stand [pavilion] and for a time I sat reading. Then I put the Bible down and I looked over the blue mountains in the direction of the Free State and, oh, the longing for home that burned in my bosom, such that I cannot describe – a longing so strong as I have never felt in my whole life. When I thought about our country and my wonderful home, then tears just sprang out of my eyes.

Lool read in a newspaper on 7 May that the prisoners were going to be transported to Ceylon, and he recorded that he and his fellow Boers hoped profoundly that this exile would not happen – though it did, for two of his brothers.

On 11 May Lool received, with delight, a suit of clothing from the good-hearted Nellie Oosthuizen, his Riversdale relative. He would have little chance to wear it, however, for on Sunday 13 May, after a service in which the dominee preached that 'God's faithful will receive rest', he recorded that he was really sick the whole day, and had 'a terrible headache' that kept him awake most of the night.

The following day he felt slightly recovered, thinking continually of home, but gradually realised that he had 'the fever'. On 15 May he drank castor oil, almost the only remedy readily available (and useless for what ailed him).

That evening, he recorded that he had 'an unbearable headache'. A severe, crippling headache is a classic sign of the onset of 'enteric', typhoid fever.

All four Muller brothers contracted typhoid after being interred in POW camps: Michael in Simon's Town, Lool in Green Point, and Chris and Pieter in Ceylon – Chris very nearly died of it, too. It is linked to insanitary conditions, particularly regarding water. The combination of the location of the Green Point POW camp on land that had only just been reclaimed from the Great Vlei, and the winter of 1900 being especially wet, even for the Cape ('abominable weather' was recorded deep into September and October, when it was soaking and bitterly cold), meant that proper sanitation, difficult in an overcrowded camp, became impossible to manage.

On 16 May, Lool woke feeling again a little better, but later that day he became so ill that, he wrote, he simply did not know what to do. The seriously ill Lool, who had tasted so little of adult life, had to struggle on without the comfort and care of his family.

His last entry was on 17 May, in a faltering hand:

> This morning again a little better. During this unwellness, I think more and more of home. It is as if these heavy thoughts make me more ill.

At the end of his final entry, another hand writes the word *'voleindigt'*, finished.

Lool survived in hospital for another couple of weeks, but there were no further entries in his diary until a neat commentary, in black ink, on 2 June 1900:

> Our tenderly loved brother has departed this life. Brother in the Lord, LT Muller, after a sickbed of fifteen days. How heavy his loss may be, we want to remain silent, and say that what the Lord does, is well done. His will be done: Psalm 90:3.

11

The shock of surrender – Chris, Pieter and Michael

SURRENDER HILL: the place where hope went to die. Here, on the farm Boerland (not far from Clarens), with the beautiful Rooiberge as a backdrop, a thousand men sadly laid down their arms under orders on 30 July 1900.

The next day more surrendered nearby, as did nearly 1 500 Boers at Klerks Vlei, just beyond Golden Gate. In all, 4 314 men and three big guns were captured.

These thousands of Boer captives passed across this large incline over several days, amid crescendos of chaotic noise as their guns and other weapons clanked onto piles, the frightened horses jinking, the rumble of many feet. There were explosions as the munitions were destroyed; the earth there remains barren, blighted from the detonations, to this day. The sheer volume of sound could be heard for miles.

It was here that they discarded their freedom and their ambitions; all those who were now defeated and in despair, and most of whom are now unremembered.

Chris recorded his surrender in the first entry of his newest diary, on 30 July 1900.

> This morning at about 8 o'clock General Crowther gave the order to saddle up, also the carts and wagons were inspanned, and we head in the direction of the enemy.
> While we were riding we came across [British] General Clemens (General R.A.P. Clements) with about a hundred soldiers, who took charge of us. Then came two divisions of their troops, who accompanied us to Golden Gate and Nauwpoort.

> We went further to the camp of the enemy, and rode two by two, between two rows of their soldiers. At a certain place, our rifles and ammunition were handed over, and that evening we were kept under close guard.
>
> Early [the next] morning, the horses were examined, and all the good horses were taken except from the officers. Their horses, too weak to be ridden, are given to us.

The disconsolate Boer prisoners were taken over several days, in groups of 200, to Fouriesburg to be processed. This little eastern town had been a haven for the Free State government until 26 July 1900, when it was entered by British forces.

Chris was given his prisoner number, 9069. Each prisoner received a Red Cross card with his details, including his postal district – Chris, and Pieter, prisoner number 9915, listed their address as Palmyra, their parents' farm; Michael, prisoner number 10803, gave his as his own rented farm, Bankfontein. It is possible from these numbers to see in what order the brothers were processed – Chris, owing to his high rank, was first, then Pieter, a corporal.

In Fouriesburg, Chris 'found a number of courteous officers. They invited us officers for tea, which we accepted.' To be offered tea by enemy officers! This was the first taste, literally, of Chris's discovery that the British army took seriously the disparity in rank between officers and men, and extended that practice to the Boers.

Boer soldiers in the veld generally knew each other well, and slept, ate, bathed and joked together without undue regard for social distinctions, apart from the most senior generals (and then more in deference to their mature ages). Generals de Wet and Botha would think nothing of sleeping in the same tent as ordinary burgers, nor were there any official badges of office, or medals. They were leaders, not bosses, obeyed because of trust.

Yet Chris quickly realised that he and his fellow officers were now to be treated better and with more civility than the rank-and-file. If he had to be a prisoner, at least he would not lose every last shred of dignity – for the first time it was a clear advantage, rather than a burden, to command men. He later admitted, frankly, that he came to appreciate the privileges.

The surrendered Boers, including all three Muller brothers, were to be moved as quickly as possible to the nearest railway station, Winburg, not

especially close by. From there they would be transported via Bloemfontein to Cape Town.

On 4 August the POWs were marched to Senekal, though Chris was
lying on a wagon, for he was too sick to ride (his brother Michael rode his
healthy horse, which as an officer he had not lost). He described having a
'sore throat' though it must have been more serious – perhaps influenza.

The central road in the town was lined with locals, including the wives
of men who were now prisoners, though they were kept at a distance, permitted to do nothing more than acknowledge them.

When a wagon arrived to sell goods to the burgers the following morning, there was such a stampede that Chris and many others were simply
elbowed out of the way. Two wagons nearby were stripped down to their
iron frames, every last thing taken off them, including the wooden planks
pulled off to use for firewood during the now-freezing Free State winter
nights. This behaviour, wrote Chris, somewhat judgementally, was learned
by the burgers from the *English* troops.

He, his brothers Michael and Pieter, and the other Ladybranders were
taken to Winburg, the oldest town in the Free State, to board a train; the
Thaba'Nchu and Wepener commandos had been sent on by train the day
before. Fortuitously, Winburg's railway station had opened only a year
before the war broke out; the first train had arrived in September 1898 on
a branch line from Bloemfontein. (Winburg had a large Boer concentration camp of women and children later in the war.)

When the brothers returned two years later, it would not be to their independent Free State republic but to the Orange River Colony, governed
by their former foe. Mercifully, they had not yet realised the permanent
loss of their sovereign state.

At Winburg, Chris had two traumatic moments. First, he saw a woman
among many thronging the station, hoping to catch a glimpse of their
surrendered men; she looked so like his Dorie that it was a complete shock
to him and his ears 'burned'. He also had to say goodbye to his 'trusted
horse', a great wrench for any Boer, knowing that he would certainly never
see it again.

As an officer, he shared a train compartment with three others who held
rank, while the burgers, including Michael and Pieter, were crammed into
wherever they could be squeezed. His route was, of course, identical to the

one that would be described by Michael in his own diary, for they were on the same train, although Chris was in much more comfortable circumstances.

It took three days to reach Cape Town; the train was diverted at Salt River junction (close to their brother Lool's body, buried at nearby Fort Knokke, had they known it), then steamed on to Simon's Town station, where they disembarked and marched along the main road to Bellevue Boer POW camp.

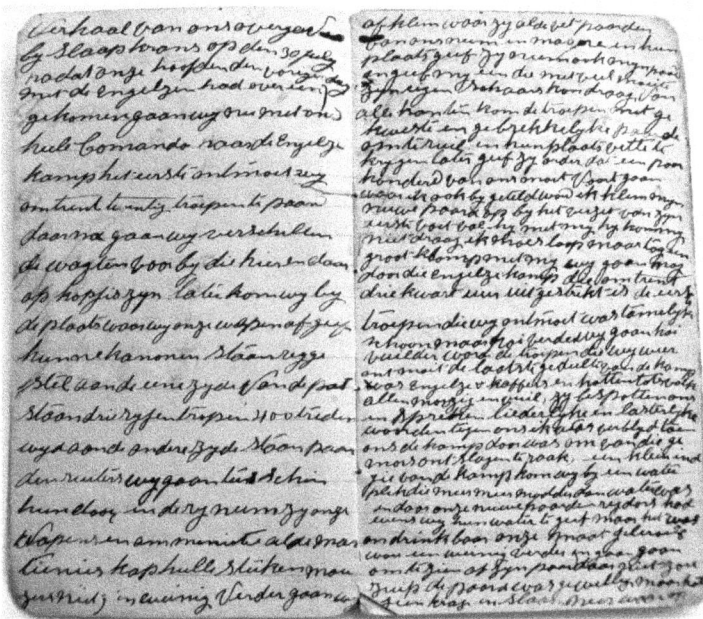

Early pages in Michael's diary, 1900.

At the time of the controversial Prinsloo surrender, Michael was up in the high mountains with his commando, not in danger of capture. A methodical diarist, he recorded exactly where he had been when news of the surrender broke: 'We were taken prisoners of war near Witsieshoek.'

He captured the beginning of his life as a prisoner in a long, stream-of-consciousness outpouring in his little diary. It was his first and longest entry, and his indignation still steams off the pages more than a century later – his personal Surrender Hill ordeal.

The story of our surrender at Slaapkrans on 30 July [1900].

After our leaders agreed with one another, we went with our whole commando to the English camp. First we met twenty troops on horseback. Thereafter we went past different guards . . . we came to the place where we had to hand in our rifles.

Their cannons are ready to fire. On the one side of the road stands three rows of troops 400 paces wide, and at the other side stand cavalry, and we pass between them. In the row, they take our weapons and ammunition. They smashed all the Martinis [rifles], not the Mausers [which were considered the very best weapons, and coveted by both sides].

After that we dismount where they take all the *vet* [literally 'fat', but also meaning fit] horses from us and in their place give us the thin ones. [His description to this point replicates Chris's.] They also take my horse and give me one that even with great difficulty can scarcely carry itself. From all sides the troops come with wounded and crippled horses to exchange for the fit ones, and later they give the order that a few hundred of us must go forward. I am also included. I climb on my new horse and with the first movement of his foot, he falls with me and he could not carry me, and I had to walk . . .

The first troops that we met on the way were reasonably clean, but the further we go, the dirtier the troops became that we met. The last part of the camp [which he estimated stretched over three-quarters of a mile] were *English* and *Kaffers* [sic] and *Hottentotsvolk* [sic], all of them messy and dirty. They make fun of us, and they say dirty and blasphemous words to us, and I was glad when we were through the camp.

Most prisoners struggle, in the first hours and days, with the sudden loss of their autonomy and dignity. This routine 'jeering' is always hard to handle by any soldier of character, and it was particularly hard for the devout, courteous Mullers, who, like others in their community, were not used to being treated as inferiors, especially by men of another colour.

This would be the first of many unpleasant surprises for Michael, one of which lay immediately ahead.

A small distance from the camp we come to a watering hole that was more mud than water, and because our new (unfit) horses were really thirsty, they could quench their thirst, but it was undrinkable for us.

Our friend wanted to go a little further to see whether his horse would drink. The horse was willing but it had no strength and it fell down, with his rider and all, into the mud. It was a terrible sight to view the horse and his rider. The rider's right eye and part of his cheek were visible; everything else was covered in mud.

This callous treatment was not what they had foreseen. When British POWs had been paraded in Pretoria during the early days of the war, President Paul Kruger had stood on his stoep and removed his hat, a mark of respect for their sacrifice. Now that it was their turn, the Boers felt treated like common criminals. (It is worth noting that Boer records of this surrender are markedly different from those kept by the British.)

Michael was taken to Fouriesburg for processing. On the evening of 31 July, he wrote that they were taken to Ficksburg, where they were 'well welcomed by the women'. But by 2 August, they had returned to Fouriesburg; he noted: 'My horse was weak and I had to walk on foot, and many others with me.' The incomprehensible back-and-forth of army life and capture had begun.

Early on the morning of 3 August they left with an English commando in the direction of Slabbertsnek. Michael had to drive his horse on before him for, unlike his own, confiscated mount, it was far too weak to ride (which had not stopped the English from allocating the poor beast to him).

My legs were really lame because I was not accustomed to walking so far and so fast, and I was overcome to see at Slabbertsnek how the houses there were burned and also the whole farm was destroyed.

Burning farms had begun early: the first homesteads were burned down as early as January 1900 in the western Free State.

Walking in the direction of Senekal the next day, the prisoners saw many charred houses, as well as two women with a cart, bringing bread for their men. At this point Michael confessed that he was really hungry and longing for home – that his mood was 'weakening'.

That evening, to stave off hunger, his brother Pieter and a comrade made porridge with grass in a bucket.

By the morning of Tuesday, 7 August, Chris was too ill to walk and had to travel on a wagon; Michael took over his horse.

> We still see many burned hourses and we go past a farm where a mother brings bread and coffee for her children [among the captured], also women for their men, which they were forbidden to do.

At this point he gave up on his horse, which 'doesn't want to walk any more', abandoning it in the middle of the road. He put his saddle on a wagon; he would not see it again.

They overnighted at Senekal in extreme cold; on top of that, all their kit was removed – waterbottles, jackets, saddlebags and the rest.

> Wherever we look next to the road we see dead cattle, horses and mules.
>
> Many women come here by cart to see their men. They all seem overcome about the departure of their men. At our halt, many women also arrive and wipe the dust from their men's faces and then kiss them on the cleaned place.
>
> Early in the morning [of 8 August] we depart from here. The whole road is full of women who have come to visit their men. My heart moves with sorrow for them.
>
> At every halt there is a line of troops set up around our laager, a line over which we dare not step.

Michael was experiencing a storm of emotions, but a more practical problem confronted him. Now that he no longer had a horse, he had to march, and Boer soldiers were unaccustomed to this, as well as having unsuitable shoes. It added to the greatest indignity for a Boer soldier – to be considered a 'pedestrian'. This tired him terribly, he noted, and his shoes fell apart. 'I cut off two cattle tails and bind them around each shoe.'

He struggled on.

By the end of his first week of captivity he was, by his own account, reduced from a mounted, self-sufficient soldier to a dirty, hungry, cold and practically barefooted vagabond. He had seen homes burned and destroyed, and weeping women, and feared for his family back home; his heart was 'sore' because he was unable to let his wife know where and how he was.

On 10 August, Michael described how he and Pieter were entrained at Winburg; Chris was on the same train, though in an officer's carriage. It was a relief for the footsore prisoners, as well as their guards, to clamber on board. Women were standing on the side of the tracks with eyes reddened from weeping.

Michael fell asleep at Brandfort that evening, and during the night their train passed Bloemfontein. During the three-day journey to Cape Town, he noted the stations they passed, including Colesberg, where his brothers Lool and Pieter had earlier fought.

On the morning of 12 August, he woke up in Victoria West and his observation was that 'this area has only shrubs and looks good only for *schildpatten* [tortoises]'. His practised farmer's eye saw this land as barren, compared to the rich Free State soil.

At Beaufort West they were given food, their first meal since leaving Winburg. Later, he slept until Matjiesfontein station, 'where they wake me up to drink tea. This was, for us, an extraordinary miracle.' Having been roughly treated since their capture, the coffee-drinking Boers were surprised by being offered tea, which they associated with polite company.

At Wellington, not far from Cape Town, the women tried in the early morning light to bring aid to the prisoners but they were 'forbidden to bring us anything'. It was here that Michael noted 'the first crop farm that we have encountered, and half an hour later we arrive at Paarl, a pretty place'.

At noon they arrived in the city of Cape Town, where they had

> a lovely view of the sea and also saw a large number of ships. From there in the afternoon to Simonsbay [Simon's Town]. From there, with our bundles on our backs, lined on both sides by troops, we walk to our allocated camp.

He had arrived at what would be his home over the next difficult months: Bellevue camp for Boer POWs.

Bellevue was not the first POW camp to be set up in the charming naval village, to the intense annoyance of its local citizenry. The authorities had scouted several possibilities, including the verdant suburb of Constantia, but those residents took fright at the thought of 'enemies' being housed in their well-heeled and well-connected midst, so it was Simon's Town that was landed with them. The oldest naval base in South Africa, it was situated about twenty miles from the city centre of Cape Town at the end of the railway track that runs, spectacularly, right next to the sea.

The first sizeable batch of Boer prisoners, about 200 men, were captured early, at the battle of Elandslaagte on 21 October 1899. No prison camps had been prepared, so these prisoners were brought to Simon's Town and held on board the three-masted armoured corvette HMS *Penelope* in Simon's Bay. The vessel, which had been built in the 1860s, was not at all appropriate for housing prisoners, and conditions rapidly became toxic.

The *Cape Times* reported on 6 November 1899 that these first prisoners included four 'Natives' [sic]; these were listed as servants. Yet both sides had insisted on, and then ignored, the 'rule' that black South Africans should not be combatants.

There has been too little recognition of the plight of black prisoners in this 'war between the two races', a term that included Boer and Brit but not black South Africans: irrespective of who won, black South Africans would discover that their own cause had been lost. Some were close to Boer families and served voluntarily, or at least without protest.

Once imprisoned, black captives resented the fact that they were expected to behave as servants inside the camp, and several refused to do so. Those who agreed under pressure to be camp cleaners were considered to be on parole (conditionally released while remaining under the control and in the legal custody of the British authorities); they were subject to lighter restrictions than the Boer POWs and were paid a nominal rate per day. The camp staff officer reported that by the end of the war, some had as much as £5-8 to their credit, however reluctantly earned.

Also at issue, especially during the first six months of the war, was the fear of escaping prisoners: two patrol boats guarded the *Penelope* at night, yet some POWs managed to escape, two of them leaving a cheeky note on a lifebuoy that read 'arrived safely – on our way'. The escape artists were captured the next morning by fishermen, although other Boers did manage to get clean away, one of them travelling, in minimal disguise, all the way to Pretoria on the same train as British military commander General John French.

If Boer POWs did manage to escape, there were allies in the Cape Colony to whom they could turn for help. The father of DC de Villiers (later mayor of Simon's Town, from 1957 to 1959) hid escapees under a pile of potatoes on the family's farm in the Glencairn Valley, for example; soldiers searched the homestead but they were not discovered, and got away. Others were not so lucky: a government contractor was arrested in his home for harbouring three Boers, who were dressed as clerics when discovered and taken back into custody.

While soldiers in the British army always considered it to be their first duty as a POW to try to escape, they did not extend that view to their own prisoners. Flurries of outrage were expressed long after such escapes had stopped. The *Cape Argus* huffed, on 9 April 1900, that 'it seems as if it would be neither peace nor safety for the civilian population of the Peninsula until all the prisoners have either been placed in transports or sent to [St Helena] island.'

Escaping from the *Penelope*, however, was not only a matter of enterprise but also an urgent matter of survival. The captain appears to have been something of a sadist, and there are records of the prisoners in his charge being dreadfully emaciated. Outrage erupted on shore over their treatment, with allegations that the prisoners were being deliberately starved.

Heavy pressure was put on local authorities by, among others, the active local dominee and another resident who, as an alternative, offered his land near Cape Point for a camp, although his offer was turned down as impractical, being too far away.

These two influential men insisted on meeting the Cape prime minister, William Schreiner, to inform him of the awful conditions on board. Their efforts were successful; prisoners were moved from the *Penelope* and two other prison ships, the *Manila* and the *Catalonia* (on which were crammed 400 men), to the first land-based camp in the Simon's Bay area. This was the temporary South Camp, with more than fifty bell tents, near the east dockyard.

In Simon's Town, local fears flourished: Boers plonked on their doorstep – who knew what would happen? And what about the strain on their resources?

(This fear proved not unfounded when their water began to run out.) Angry letters were written to newspapers.

As a result, or certainly inspired by this indignation, a town guard was raised by the mayor – two companies of about 130 men in total. They were dutifully drilled, sometimes twice a day, at the barracks close to the railway station. This added to the problems for this important naval town, as the men had to shut up their businesses and shops during drilling exercises.

However seriously they may have taken their duties, they were never needed. Nor does it seem to have occurred to them that the weaponless Boers had far more reason to fear an annoyed and armed local militia, than vice versa. Throughout the war there were no reported incidents of 'Boers behaving badly' in Simon's Town, despite the hysterics of local residents.

But a more palatable solution needed to be found for these prisoners, preferably as far away as practicably possible. Bellevue camp was laid out on land formerly known as Langebrune (today it is the golf course). It was usefully located just past the secluded beaches of Seaforth and Boulders, about two miles from the railway terminal, a decent distance from the small town but still close enough to be easily accessed by both the authorities responsible for the POWs, and the Boers themselves.

Had it not been for the fact that the Boers were prisoners, and for the lashing southeasterly winds that seemed to howl most days from October to February, Bellevue might have been considered to be a lovely spot. Also, there was the sea, that marvel most Boer prisoners had never seen.

Prisoners arrived mainly by train, for the station was the end of the new main line from Cape Town, while others travelled by ship from Cape Town harbour, or other ports, and disembarked at the adjacent quay in Simon's Town. Opposite the railway station was the Palace Barracks hospital, where explorer Mary Kingsley nursed sick Boers, and soon died from their fever, as a result.

The men were marched through the narrow Victorian streets, past the welcome sight of the small white Dutch Reformed church on the left, then following the curve in the road to the wide, flat field on which rows and rows of canvas bell tents had been erected.

The first Boer POWs filled Bellevue in mid-April 1900, and almost immediately there was a crisis at the new camp, for it could not manage the numbers required. Bellevue was meant to house 2 000 POWs but increasing pressure meant that it could not cope with the demand.

The authorities began to consider exiling those Boers whom they referred to as the 'troublemakers', a majority who would not sign either an oath of neutrality or allegiance to the Crown. From April 1900, these 'recalcitrants' were sent to St Helena; and later, much farther afield, to POW camps in Ceylon, Bermuda and parts of India.

All three surviving Muller brothers would meet this fate.

12

Simon's Town: a tent with a view

POWs in Bellevue camp in Simon's Town, 1900. Michael is seated left.

OF ALL UNLIKELY things, this POW camp had an astonishing view, 'Bellevue' meaning 'beautiful view'. (The name 'Bellevue' is never explicitly mentioned by Michael in his diary – he simply refers to their 'allocated camp'.)

It was on flattened ground, low on the side of the mountain and close to the sea. The prisoners were easily able to gaze far across the wide ocean, which the majority of them had never seen before, to the pale blue outline opposite, the Hottentots Holland mountains marching to Cape Hangklip, where the range drops down into the warm waters of False Bay. It is never a good thing to be a prisoner, but there were worse places to be held captive.

One of the first things the Bellevue prisoners saw as they were marched into camp was a bilingual noticeboard stating that 'no prisoners of war are allowed outside the limits of the Inner Camp. The sentries have strict orders to shoot any prisoners passing this inner fence. By Order.'

They were also instructed to follow a colossally long list of 'Regulations for the Discipline of the Boer Prisoners of War'. Most of the 23 regulations were to do with order and discipline, daily routine, hygiene and inspections, the cleaning of the tents and other facilities, and penalties for offences. Prisoners were not allowed to be in possession of money other than 'pocket money' for small items such as sweets, tobacco and stamps.

Regulation number 18 stated that all letters and packages would be subject to censorship; that is always hard to bear, and prisoners were painfully aware that the portions removed from letters held important news. Michael wrote, on 1 October 1900 from Bellevue, that when he received a letter from his wife Nelie,

> two sides were cut off, naturally as a result of something significant written. It causes me to smart, seeing that I wanted to hear how things are.

The final regulation prohibited the receiving of visitors apart from 'very exceptional circumstances', for which a special pass had to be obtained from the highest-ranking officer in charge. It was seldom allowed and was the subject of perhaps the greatest agony.

On arrival, POWs were given a couple of blankets and some cutlery and cooking utensils. All Boers carried their own hardy pocket knives, some made by themselves, considered to be as normal an item as a watch might be today. They were useful not only for cooking and minor repairs, but also for the whittling and carving of handicrafts, which increasingly began to occupy the prisoners' spare time. These included small boxes, walking sticks, pipes, rings made from coins, carved toys and model wagons. Some even took up knitting and produced socks, scarves and ties, which they sold for pocket money.[18]

On Michael's first morning, the camp was already filled with men captured in the great loss at Paardeberg, and from the Prinsloo surrender. Relief came immediately in the form of a 'good wash, which did me good. Added to that, we have a good view of the sea.'

But almost immediately there was a shock, another 'bitter separation'.

> A group of our people are told to leave and we don't know where to. It is a separation between fathers and children, between brothers and friends, among whom also a brother of mine [Chris] has to leave and I have to stay behind.

In the evening we had a beautiful church service which was also comforting.

The next day, 18 August, the men were all counted and 300 ordered to leave for the docks. Many of Michael's old friends, as well as his brothers, Chris and Pieter, were marched out of camp to the harbour. Within half an hour a large ship, the *Mongolian,* sailed out to sea.

Shortly after that, to Michael's astonishment, 12 men returned because the ship was too full, among them his brother Pieter. It was a joyful relief that would regrettably not last long. Two days later Pieter, with a hundred or so other men, were once more marched out of camp. They had no way of telling where they were being sent to, though rumours correctly guessed that it was '*Selon*' (Ceylon).

Discipline in the camp was naturally strict, as it would be in a prison camp, and the British tried to ensure as little contact between the ordinary guards and the Boers as possible. Boers with rank were put in charge of their men, and were expected to enforce discipline. There was little option. This was not a camp from which escape was possible. A few prisoners tried tunnelling out, but the spots were swiftly identified, and extra sentries posted.

What the POWs were *not* issued with was adequate clothing. Although most Boers had ridden off to war in decent clothes (usually their 'best', including smart suits and bow ties which would prove horribly inadequate), by the time they had been in the veld for months, their garments were shabby, dirty and often falling apart.

Some resorted to animal skins to cover their naked bodies, for the Boers had no grand army system to provision them.

The feisty Sarah Raal, who had ridden under fire on commando, recalled her shock at seeing her brothers after their first seven months in the veld: 'The poor boys, will I ever forget the sight of them that day? Tanned, emaciated, weather-beaten, neglected, their shoes almost worn to bits, their clothing all tattered and in shreds . . .' Months later their plight was worse: men no longer had hats, just bits of material tied around their heads, blankets instead of jackets, and were barefoot – a few had tied ox-hides to their feet with hand-cut thongs.

This lack of decent clothing was considered by many, even the most anti-Boer, to be the 'most valid' complaint of the prisoners, and clothing was collected for them. Many, including the Muller brothers, came from homes where 'proper' dress was considered the measure of a decent family, and even poorer Boers tried to wear clean, if patched, clothing. Photographs published in British newspapers, of Boer soldiers and prisoners looking like tramps, were not an accurate reflection of their usual way of being, although it was useful propaganda.

What different images the British public would have seen in the group and wedding photographs, the individual portraits of elegant and self-possessed Boers, prior to the war.

The bell tents were pitched close together, leaving as much open recreation room as possible in the camp's grounds. In theory, they were supposed to house eight men, with the officers sharing two-per-tent in the camp; in practice, overcrowding meant the tents usually held 12 men.

Each day, Michael wrote his diary entries sitting either inside the tent, squeezed in with 11 others, or outside if the weather was fine – always marking the date, the day of the week, and commenting on the weather, which had now turned to heavy rain; the tents leaked, and most of the men's scant belongings were sopping.

Michael remembered to send a telegram to Chris's wife, Dorie, with news of her husband's departure into exile, and included greetings to his own wife Nelie, who was still alone on his farm with their two small children.

Now the days became routine. The men cooked and ate. They washed clothes and sang. They swam, and smoked when they could scrounge tobacco. They yearned for letters and wrote some in reply.

Michael went to every post call. The post corporal would stand centrally, on a large rock, and call out the name on the envelope; then the letter was passed hand to hand, occasionally over the shoulders of three or four hundred men, until it reached the prisoner for whom it was destined. The post was sometimes in a sorry state by the time it got to them, crumpled and greasy with censoring and handling, but it was nevertheless received with joy.

The post has arrived and when they called the names we almost trampled on each other. The reason is hunger for news from home.

Michael carefully numbered each letter he wrote to his wife, and each he received from her. It was hard when there was nothing for him at the post call – '[when] the post arrived for the prisoners I also go with a happy heart thinking that I will get a letter but was cheated [of that pleasure]' – but when a brother or friend received a letter, the delight was shared by all around him. The news was read out loud, and messages passed on, and the contact with home was cherished. 'Wherever one looks, people are reading their letters that came from their families.' These were rare moments of happiness during the long prison months.

Regular Sunday services provided the only real break in the week, and were the greatest comfort for many. The services reminded these pious men of home and normality, and another world in which they had been the masters of their own fate under the watchful eye of their God. Once they had turned to their church for inspiration; now it was for solace and wisdom and the community they needed.

Though most prisoners in Bellevue belonged to the Nederduitse Gereformeerde Kerk (NGK, Dutch Reformed Church), there were also English-speaking prisoners, especially from the Free State. On Sundays, their English service was held at 8am by a reverend from St Francis' church, who, despite the simple surroundings, recorded that 'I must say I never celebrated with more emotion'. He was impressed with his flock, whom he saw as earnest and devout. A young man, 18 years old, wept after the service on his shoulder, and, the minister added, 'I confess, I felt inclined to weep also.'

The hardworking Dominee GFC van der Lingen, the second permanent NGK minister appointed to Simon's Town, attended the Boers. He was assisted by other dominees and elders in the camp. Michael's diary references about Ds van der Lingen are frequent, often with notations of the scriptures he used in worship.

A long-serving and able man, Van der Lingen ministered to the prisoners throughout the war, sometimes appearing two or three times on a Sunday (the camp was so large that services often had to be held in relay). He also served the all-important *nagmaal* (communion), and was still in harness at the end of the war when, in June 1902, he offered a special service to commemorate the peace. It was a heartfelt moment for him, for he had seen literally thousands of men, mainly young, pass through Bellevue over more than two years; fit and wounded, brave and sobbing, calm and anxious, healthy and some soon to be dead. He was often the only friendly link they had with the outside world, and his service and companionship could not have been more important to them.

Van der Lingen lived next to the NGK church on the corner of the main road and Church Street, in a handsome double-storey parsonage where, 20 years later, in 1921, Dominee ML de Villiers composed the music for the national anthem of South Africa, *Die Stem* (The Call).

Michael and Nelie on their wedding day, 4 June 1895.

At night the men dreamed of riding their horses on the open plains of the Free State, and they dreamed of home, and Michael saw his wife looking beautiful, 'like a lovely carved statue and all of the family being so beautiful and strong', and he thanked the Lord for such goodness.

But soon enough, and more disturbingly, the dreams changed and his sub-liminal fears rose up, of women and children crying, or missing, or every-thing back home going to pot. To sleep, perchance to dream, became a lottery: it would be either a longed-for escape into oblivion or an anxiety-filled sweatfest. There was no telling.

Who was this young woman, mother of his two small children, whom Michael yearned for in his dreams?

Nelie was born Cornelia Christina on 29 July 1878. Her parents had both been Van den Heevers, close cousins: her mother was Cornelia Petronella, born in 1849, her father Christiaan Mauritz, born in 1848, whose people came from Cradock.

Her mother died when she was 10 years old, and she and her sister San-nie went to live with a relative neighbouring the Muller farm, Palmyra, where she met Michael, whom she married in 1895.

Nelie was a pretty, open-faced young woman with a calm expression. She was athletic, well able 'to outrun the boys', recalled her second son, Chrisjan.

For a while after her husband rode to war, Nelie stayed on their farm in the Ladybrand district, with no security. All she had for protection was a basin of caustic soda kept next to the front door, to throw in the eyes of any intruder. She, and many of the eastern Free State women, moved around a great deal during the war to avoid the *kakies*. Before they did so, though, they buried whatever valuables they had, in Nelie's case including her cher-ished china dinner set, a wedding gift, packed in a large kettle.

But far worse than losing her possessions was the fear that she and her children would be captured and forcibly taken to the dreaded camps – the stuff of her nightmares, and with good reason. To be ordered out of your own home and to see it destroyed in front of your eyes is one thing; to be hauled off with your children to imprisonment under the heavy hand of a foreign enemy, without access to loved ones, proper food or sanitation, was entirely another.

Women went to great lengths to avoid being herded into the concen-tration camps, except for the families of joiners and *hensoppers* (hands-uppers, those Boers who took the easy route of surrendering at the first opportunity), and who therefore had good reason to seek the 'protection' of the camps (in fact, the first camps were called that – Protection Camps).

The detention of these unwilling women and their children in their own land was unlawful,[19] because they had never been tried or condemned. The vast majority of the fatalities in the camps were the very young – at least 20 000 Boer children perished in them. To be a captured Boer infant was in effect a death sentence – very few under the age of a year survived – and Nelie had two little ones to worry about.

The conditions in the camps were appalling, and especially so for the families of the Boers who continued to fight. No meat, and only half-rations, were given to families in concentration camps if their men were still on commando. As UK Member of Parliament (and later, during the First World War, Prime Minister) Lloyd George put it: 'The remnants of the Boer army who are sacrificing everything for their idea of independence are to be tortured by the spectacle of their starving children into betraying their cause.'

Black women and children held in camps were given even fewer rations than their white counterparts, and almost no medical care. They were not supposed to be regarded as foes, yet there were 66 recorded British concentration camps for black people in this war; at their highest capacity they are thought to have held about 115 000 people. By December 1901, their death rate had reached 380 per thousand (in the former Free State, 436 per thousand – almost one in two). It was a more severe rate of mortality than in any white camp in any single month of the war.

And it was not only in the camps that black people were more brutally treated by their British overseers; Sol Plaatje, working as a translator in Mafeking during the siege, recorded how blacks were starved, some dying, in order that white citizens might have sufficient food – those who escaped were so pitifully emaciated that the Boers waiting in the surrounds refused to shoot them, even under orders.

Starvation was a central fear of those civilians who suddenly found themselves in this unwanted war. Nelie's own neat hand lays out such concerns, and her frightening experiences, in a little *joernal* [sic], a small, school-style notebook, written in 1951. It is the only surviving record of a Muller woman writing of her personal ordeal.

> I was alone with two small children and my sister Sannie. We didn't want to hold our men back, and were determined to survive at any cost.

After the English took all our livestock, I had to work out how to manage, as long as we didn't end up in the camps. We were hounded from one place to another. There were always warmhearted 'good samaritans' willing to help transport our few possessions, so that we could set up home somewhere away from the frontline of fighting. But so often, just as we had set up home, the frontline changed again, and we were forced to look for a new place to survive.

Then we were on the run again and there were many days when we did not eat, and just cried. On other days, we realised that the Khakis were so stupid – these poor *voetgangers* [foot soldiers] were nearly dead with walking, trying to catch General De Wet.

One day a group arrived on the farm while the bread was still in the outside clay oven, which had a large pit to help keep the fire going. The Khaki opened the pit and put his hand in to take out the bread, and got so badly burned that he had to give up.

Then they killed our chickens and ducks and took the saddles, as there were always a few soldiers on horseback, along with the foot soldiers.

While hiding behind a dam wall with her small family, between crossfire, her son Pieter's little dog broke free and was shot – a grief the boy never forgot.

Nelie's birth family did not escape the camps. Two of her young half-siblings, a boy and a girl from her father's second marriage, died in the Bethulie camp, which was especially notorious and badly run, with ill-trained and drunken medical staff, and so poorly provisioned that the inmates often died of starvation or related illnesses. All three children from this second marriage were interned in this camp when it was first opened in April 1901. By the end of that year, Jacobus Ockert van den Heever, aged 5, had died of 'debility', as had his 10-year-old sister, Katie Naomi. The only survivor was the middle brother, CM van den Heever, aged 7.

Nelie's salvation lay, for at least part of the war, as a refugee across the border in Basutoland, along with many other women and children who took advantage of protection from the local chiefs. By staying on the run, often in hiding and/or protection, she saved her children.

On returning to their destroyed farm after hostilities had ended, Nelie found stolen or destroyed every single domestic implement, farm tool and anything at all that could be used to farm, including livestock and seed –

though she was able to dig up her precious wedding china plates. It was a blow the family never entirely managed to overcome. Nevertheless, she would remain all her life a warm, loving woman, her grandchildren fondly remembered, who baked the most delicious *hawermout* (oat) cookies. Her granddaugher Nella remembered her wonderful *boontjies* (beans), as well as 'meat and pumpkin', with a coffee pot eternally percolating on the cooker. These Mullers were kindly, quiet people who tried to help whomever was in need, though there could have been few in their community who had less.

Boer POWs swimming off Windmill Beach in Simon's Town, 1900.
(Photograph: courtesy of Simon's Town Museum)

The prisoners swam in the sea every day, both for hygiene and for exercise. They walked from the far end of the camp down the sandy path, secured within tall metal fencing, onto secluded Windmill Beach, named after the mill there to draw water. It was a small cove with fine white sand and many large flat rocks, and little shells washed up daily.

Though they had armed guards watching them, this was a time for the men to 'feel free' for a while, to horseplay in the waves, and wrestle and swim and chat. They had no swimming costumes so most of them swam naked, as soldiers often do.

The sea around Bellevue was relatively warm compared to the colder water on the opposite side of the Cape Peninsula, and was a hot spot for sharks. POWs were warned of their presence, and in any case most Boer bathers stayed in the shallow waters. Still, a gruesome strike happened the following year, on 30 July 1901, when 29-year-old John Henry Chandler (born English-speaking, but who fought with the Boer forces using the name Hendrik) was swimming fairly far out with friends in the direction of Boulders Beach – they would have been directly in front of Bellevue camp – and was attacked by a great white shark which bit off his leg. When he hit out at the shark, it bit his hand off, too. He was helped by his terrified friends onto a nearby flat rock, where he bled out and died. After that, the men swam in a small area protected by 70 yards of iron mesh fencing strung up between two big rocks over the water. Chandler was also a Ladybrander in the same commando as the Mullers had been; his was one of the most unexpected of deaths – to go to war on a horse and be killed by a shark.

The POWs saw wonderful, almost mythical creatures – jellyfish, and beautiful but stinging bluebottles and even fluttering seaweed – and occasionally less welcome intruders, such as the sharks. The octopus fascinated them; one Boer prisoner described it colourfully as looking like a frog with a bunch of snakes attached.

A ship's cat became a favourite with the men, often walking down to the beach with them. She was a good mouser, and something for them to pet.

September in Bellevue camp meant spring was in the air. The ferocious southeaster summer wind had not yet begun to blow, but the temperatures of both air and sea were rising, and the mountain fynbos that tumbled down to the camp was in colourful bloom.

On the first day of this month Michael received his first letter from home, an event he noted in his diary with 'great joy'. At least he now knew that his dear wife and children were alive and safe, and that they knew where he was.

While swimming on Monday 3 September, Michael's brother-in-law Oubaas mentioned to him that it had been exactly eleven months since they were at war, and how quickly the days had flown by. They, as well as the prisoners in Green Point, decided to make this a week of prayer for peace.

Michael wrote on 9 September:

> A nice, quiet Sunday morning, also really warm. We also saw this day three whales at the same time. It was beautiful to see such monsters wallowing.
>
> [The next day] A nice morning, a bit misty. Again, at about twelve there was a great number of things on the sea. They looked like pigs. The people say their name is *vark-met-die-Boer* (pig-with-the-Boer). It is a kind of fish, a wonderful thing to see.

He was referring to dolphins, which congregate here in huge numbers in spring – it is not unusual to see hundreds of them swiftly crossing the ocean in their familiar, rocking-horse motion. Never having seen such fascinating creatures before, the Boers simply named them after one of their most familiar domestic animals.

Michael was intrigued, too, to see seals for the first time, which he described as 'a type of fish about 6 ft long. Its torso looks like that of a dog'.

More tents were pitched in the camp, a sign that new prisoners would be arriving, and sure enough, the following day seventy men from the Transvaal appeared, all of them caught at home, hiding from the war.

Sanitation, often rudimentary, remained a major issue in all the camps, and when illness swept through the overcrowded quarters, the situation could quickly become deeply nasty and potentially lethal. Men who suffered from illnesses such as typhoid fever, with its attendant vomiting and diarrhoea, had to struggle with the indignity of their disease and the unpleasantness for their tent-mates in close proximity. The severely ill were removed to hospital, though by then it was often too late. In an age without antibiotics, and without recourse to the home remedies and diets used by the Boers for generations, many died who might have otherwise been saved.

This was also true – even more so – in the concentration camps for Boer women and children, and also for British troops who fell ill.[20]

So sickness in camp was a cause for deep concern. On 15 September, Michael reported feeling 'really sick' and drank a whole packet of *Engelse sout* (epsom salts), which 'achieved its goal'. But by the 19th, both he and others in his tent were suffering.

The following month he became more seriously ill, and on 11 October he noted that he had been forced to ask the camp doctor for *medicinen* on repeated occasions. He coughed a great deal, needing to wash out his fouled handkerchiefs; this continued for several days, but after a week or so, he recovered. His luck was not to have been so seriously ill that he needed the hospital, where many POWs met their end.

Bellevue, on the main road leading out of Simon's Town towards Cape Point, at first had an ordinary four-string barbed wire fence along the main thoroughfare, and along the shoreline. Tall (ten-foot) corrugated-iron fencing ran on either side, seawards down the slopes, and there was a guarded gateway on the north side, halfway down Bellevue Road.[21] The tents were in long, straight rows on the mountain side. A number of zinc huts were added lower down following the line of the shore, for cooking, washhouses and latrines, and work huts.

On the other side of the wire fences was a veritable zigzag of barbed wire, known as a zareba. A tall sentry box stood on each corner, with an armed guard, and on these and other areas of fencing were tall, bulbous lights. The centre of the camp was therefore dim at night, with only the perimeters well lit.

The POWs discovered, with dismay, one morning, that ten-foot corrugated-iron fences were being constructed along the main road and also the lower open-wire fences, effectively cutting off *all* visual contact with the immediate outside world (Michael complained about it in his diary). Hemmed in on all four sides, they now felt they were in a fortress, rather than a large, open laager; they were no longer able to see passing traffic or sense the expansiveness of 'life outside'.

The authorities claimed that one of the reasons for their high addition to the perimeter fence was to give shelter from the howling summer wind, but there was little logic in this. These new fences were constructed along the mountain and sea sides, not along the south side, where a high fence already existed, and from where the summer wind roared in – anyone could tell exactly which direction it blew from by the steeply bent angle of the trees. The ferocious summer wind covered everything with sand on its worst days, and these new fences did nothing to stop that.

Their height now prevented the Boer POWs from having any contact at all with the outside, including their loved ones, even from a distance. Their families – wives, parents, children – who had made the long, expensive and difficult journey to Cape Town to see their loved ones in the camp were now driven to desperate measures.

In a moving entry describing the effect of being so near and yet so impossibly far, Michael wrote on 11 September 1900:

> I see something that really grieved my heart. A woman came from the Transvaal who had last seen her man eleven months ago. She is not allowed to see or speak to him, and because around us there is a wall of ten foot high corrugated iron, she cannot see him.
>
> She climbs up onto the wall of a house about two hundred paces from our camp and from there she waves her handkerchief to greet him. From there she gestures above her, and stretches her hands out to her husband as if she wishes for a blessing from Above to him.
>
> She also holds a small child high in the air to show it to her husband, and then she disappears.
>
> How the feelings of her heart were, that I do not know, but to me, a stranger, tears come to my eyes.

On Sunday 16 September 1900, his birthday, Michael wrote that although he had received many good wishes, 'never was my longing for home stronger than today, because I am certain that today my wife also thinks

The Boers playing a form of jukskei in Bellevue camp. The large and resented iron fence effectively cut off the prisoners' contact with the outside world. (Photograph: courtesy of Simon's Town Museum)

of me'. He was comforted by the sermon 'revealing that all things happen for good purposes'.

What to do, what to do, with these endless wasted days? The POWs had to find things to keep themselves occupied, for the inactivity badly affected the spirits of these formerly active men. Perhaps writing a diary helped.

Gradually, those POWs who were kept in Bellevue for months on end began to organise pastimes. There were sports days, with handmade certificates and trophies handed out; these events were held in the overseas POW camps as well, and were keenly contested.

Michael recorded that on 2 October, President Steyn's birthday, the children held a sports day. One has to pause at that word, 'children', captives in a camp full of grown soldiers; boys were in all the prison camps, including those overseas. They had accompanied fathers, brothers or uncles when no one else was left at home, as a method of keeping them out of the deadly concentration camps – anything, even exile, was better than that fate. (A school was belatedly put together in Bellevue, permission for which was granted in April 1901; it taught more than eighty boys.)

In October, Michael was given a pair of shoes, the first proper footwear he had had since his shoes had fallen apart in early August, after being captured and losing his horse.

On the 10th it was President Kruger's birthday, and the young men held a sports meeting in excellent weather, and sang both the Transvaal and Free State anthems. That evening they carried a large, transparent lantern of different colours around the camp, on which was a portrait of Kruger and his familiar sayings. Throughout the evening, they sang familiar folk songs. For once, it was a good day.

There were frequent games, including a Boer favourite, jukskei. There were concerts and plays and song days, along with the formation of a *Boere-orkes* (Boer orchestra) with handmade instruments, and swimming and cooking and cleaning, and writing home or to friends in other camps, and washing laundry and reading. Some of the tents were lucky to have several books, ranging from devotionals to the classics. Michael borrowed one and noted in his diary on 7 December:

> When I reached [the part] where the husband and wife reveal them-
> selves to one another, I could not control my tears, especially because
> it is comparable to a part of my own experience, about the long
> separation from one another, and the rejoining.

Many single POWs would later remark that the married men suffered
more than they did, pining for their wives as well as their families. Few
younger men and youths had known intimacy, and, in resorting to relieving
themselves in the usual way, were not worse off than they had been before,
even though they may have longed for the sight and touch of potential
sweethearts. But for those men happily married, the loss of sex, of accustomed physical comfort, was agony.

It is a subject not often dealt with in war documents or diaries, though
both Michael and Chris did so, in carefully worded terms: Michael, in writing about Nelie in his dreams, and Chris, while in Ceylon. There was little
point in keeping a diary if it was not honest – though discreet. They burned
for their beloveds. Of course they did.

13

Food fears: tinned cat and a
ruined Christmas feast – Michael

MICHAEL'S LONGING FOR his wife and two small children festered like an open wound: he was now 34 years old, and frustrated.

By December 1900 there were frequent outbursts in the camp, based on petty or genuine grievances – one of the sicknesses of war is the pent-up frustration of active men, and the emotional and psychological strain of being forced into close quarters. And, as always in prison camps, one of the major grievances was food.

Michael's father, a prosperous blacksmith and farmer, had quite easily supported ten children, and his young wife Nelie had filled his stomach daily. After a day's labour, he had not gone hungry. Now, he yearned not only for familiar food, but also for the sight and smell of his household, the sympathetic qualities of his own home. He sometimes could not tell which was worse, the uneven quality and restricted rations of the camp, or his need to hold his wife and children.

Ever since his capture, Michael had been hungry, as were his fellow prisoners. On commando, the Boers had largely fended for themselves; they were familiar with carrying their own rations from home, including the hardy *boerebeskuit* (a durable rusk), and accustomed to living off the land. But as POWs they were at the mercy of the enemy's ability, or will, to feed them. This amplified their sense of vulnerability, for their daily survival depended on their captors, including those with a nasty whim.

The main meal at midday soon became the central focus of the men's daily routine, tapping into the most basic of survival instincts – will I be nourished? The rations of meat and potatoes were given out between 9am and 11am for cooking on the same day; everyone in the tent witnessed the daily issuing, and division, of rations. It was so important that, after the war, Michael was able to record, in detail, exactly how the food distribution operated. In the back of his dead brother Lool's diary, he recorded, in pencil, a precise account of how the system worked, overseen by the men for the sake of fairness.

> We stay in tents. Each tent elects a corporal and every row of tents chooses a captain.
>
> The work of the captain is to oversee the rationing of food, wood and everything [else] that is provided, and is done regularly. The corporal must see to it that the tent is kept clean on a regular basis.
>
> In the morning early, the bread (coarse) is dished out. Each corporal sends a man to get bread for his tent. After that, potatoes are provided in the same way.
>
> Then the bugle is blown and the inmates of every tent must stand on parade, two by two behind each other, to be counted.
>
> After that, the meat is issued.
>
> We have to make our food ourselves in cook houses without chimneys, and the poor cooks have a hard time with the smoke.
>
> At eleven o'clock the bugle blows again and then everyone except the corporal has to vacate the tents. Then the officers come to inspect the tents to see whether they are clean and in order. [The wooden floors, efficiently divided into four quarter-circles, to be taken out and scrubbed.] If a tent is not acceptably clean, then the pole is yanked out and the tent collapses.
>
> In the evening, shortly before sunset, we must be counted again.
>
> After that, coffee and sugar are distributed and then wood is distributed for the next day.

The meat ration was officially seven pounds a week, not unreasonable when the meat was actually distributed, or fresh, or even edible. They were given tinned meat every Monday, which they rather liked. It was something of a treat.

Michael had never been responsible for cooking for others, until now. At home, men were often in charge of the open fires, turning the meat over, tending the *braai*. Though the women were fully capable of doing it, it was also a chance for the men to talk among themselves about the things they thought women did not share. But the preparation for the ordinary, daily meal for his eleven companions in his tent – this he had not done before; it was novice work for all of them.

It seemed strange to him at first, and he worried about getting it right. Yet the daily ritual of sharing food within this formal structure became paramount, essential to their wellbeing, and eventually, a routine of fellowship, a centrestone in their transient existence.

The cookhouse was down at the lowest part of the camp, an open piece of ground nearest the sea. The smoke troubled him continuously.

> This day, I am cook again, and on the dot of twelve my dinner was finished for twelve men. The place where we cook holds a hundred and twenty big pots, so everyone can understand why my eyes are so red in the evening from the smoke.

When in charge of preparing food, first he had to safeguard the firewood. On 19 August he noted that the people in his tent were concerned about preparing food for the next day because their wood had been stolen; this was the only time he mentioned such an occurrence, as discipline was tightened after this unhappy surprise.

Prisoners should not steal from one another, but they do. The Free Staters blamed the Transvalers, whom they saw as rowdy and less God-fearing, a charge difficult to prove. 'A couple of our people were really badly behaved. They bellowed like madmen and fought. They were Transvalers,' Michael noted in his diary.

Michael was himself the victim of a small but painful theft. On 6 September he wrote of being 'busy packing small shells in a little tin to take home for my little sons'. He recorded despondently, a month later, 'My tin of shells has disappeared. I cannot find it.'

His babies had not seen shells. The collecting of them, small, coral-coloured 'ladies' fans', gleaming little perlemoen ears, tiny white double-sided mussel shells, these trinkets of nature kept alive the thought of seeing his children again. He hoped that one day, perhaps soon, he would be able to give these shells from Windmill Beach to them, as the only tokens he could glean from these wasted months. The loss of them was a silly theft, but it stung enough for him to write the melancholy words: 'Nine men around me in our tent lie in sleep while I am writing. I cannot sleep.'

Soon Michael became more comfortable with his role as cook, which came up every twelve days, though his eyes were always sore afterwards from the smoke. By 29 September he was able to write, 'A clear and sunny day. I was cook. The food was cabbage, potatoes and meat and a sort of onion, and from that I make nice soup.' He began to be a little more creative over the coals. On 15 October he noted, 'Today I cook *zouskluitjies* [sweet dumplings] and the smoke troubles my eyes.'

Once the food was ready, that day's cook took it back to the tent. On wet days they ate inside, but mostly they ate outside their own tents, forming a circle.

The chosen foreman of the tent, not the cook, supervised the sharing of the food, making sure that each man got an equal share. He did this by sticking his fork into the pots, first the meat, then the potatoes, and finally the vegetables and gravy, at the end using bread to dip deeper into the pot. They used what they had been given – large, unenamelled tin mugs with big handles, tin plates, kettles, pans, potjies and larger pots.

There was usually a battered tin, flattened, for smoke ash, along with bags of tobacco and boxes of matches. The ritual of pipes, cigarettes and snuff after the meal was soothing. For many prisoners, tobacco was as comforting as their food.

During this time spent over the communal meal, it felt not too different from a commando camp. Michael was surrounded by men who knew each other, sharing simple food, then coffee and a pipe.

The food was often very far removed from the Boers' usual fare. On 8 October, Michael wrote:

> As the twelve o'clock bell had already been heard, we came together to have our lunch. We opened the first tin. Some say it is horse meat but it tasted fine. When we opened the second tin, it was clear that it contained cat, whereupon many of our friends left the tent. Nevertheless, the cat was well prepared.

He was not a man who was used to luxuries and, as a prisoner, was not about to look a gift cat in the mouth. He ate it philosophically, though some of the others could not.

The following day an unexpected possibility of nourishment arrived in the form of a young whale 'which they caught and they hauled it out close to our camp. It was 40 ft long.'

Talking politics became more urgent as the war continued. At the time of Michael's captivity in Bellevue in 1900, the majority of the men were determined to stick it out with the strong faith that somehow their suffering, as well as that of those back home, would be worthwhile once their war was won. They did not allow themselves to think otherwise.

A huge argument took place in Michael's tent on 20 September, the day he also received news from his brother Pieter, posted from Durban on the way to Ceylon. One of them accused the Boers still fighting in the veld of being a band of robbers, nothing less. Michael was so horrified at this slur that he scratched out the man's name so it is unreadable.

Such differing and deeply felt views would flare into conflict, sometimes seriously. On 25 October he reported disapprovingly that

> two brothers fought until they were covered red with blood and had to go to the doctor urgently. They are both Transvalers, to the detriment of our nation.

The outbursts spurted like pressure valves, especially over matters they could no longer affect, such as the progress of the war.

On 28 November, after reporting a number of arguments over politics, he wrote:

> In the evening they have tarred and feathered a spy. The men were given a prison sentence of eight days.

By December, they had grown accustomed to the daily grind, the predictable scheduling of food. But on the 3rd, a rainy day,

> they bring us tins of meat that are spoiled. We refuse to receive it. They stack them in a heap in our camp and say that they were following orders. We then had a very lean dinner.

The situation festered. On 19 December, with a typically strong summer wind blowing up a rough sea,

> a man is taken from our camp to jail because he wrote home that the *English* had given us rotten meat to eat. Three others were also taken because they threw stones at the guards.

Feelings about the food situation had begun to run high, and the guards decided to assert themselves in a cold-hearted act.

Christmas Day, a Tuesday, dawned after a show of fireworks in Simon's Town the evening before, a day marked by 'beautiful rain' (appreciated by the farmer in Michael). The lighthouse, which they could see from their camp, was festooned with flags. By now, Michael had received fourteen letters from his wife Nelie, and was more confident that she was safe, as were his children. He had also had news from his brother Chris, in a couple of letters from Ceylon.

Days later, on the 29th, came the blow that drove the men to fury.

> Here comes many cases of goods sent by the colonial women before Christmas. Roast chicken, suckling pigs, apricots, vegetables, all sorts of cooked meals and fruit. It was all rotten. We received it four days after Christmas. It was all this time stacked in front of the camp gate.

This superb and generous feast had been sabotaged. While the usual officers and guards were diverted from their duties by Christmas festivities, other sentries, disgruntled by recent skirmishes with the prisoners, had taken this opportunity to teach the Boers a lesson. The food, collected, prepared and transported to the camp through the offices of good-hearted women in the Cape Colony for the POWs, had been deliberately left to rot at the camp gate.

It was crushing for the Boers, for they had seen nothing like this abundance, nor such delectables, since their capture. For it to be paraded before them like this, magnificent but inedible, was not merely a prank, but cruel.

The following day their nerves were slightly soothed by pastor Van der Lingen, who read to them from Genesis and pointed out to them that it is the 'end of the month, of the year and of the century, and that this day must not pass without the Lord blessing us, so that we go into the new century renewed'.

Matters were smoothed over the next day, the last of the year, 31 December. Word of the Christmas Day food calamity had reached the *English* headquarters, and the Cape colonial women, discovering that their efforts to provide a generous meal to the POWs on a holy day they all shared, were outraged. They were not women to be trifled with, and steps were hastily taken to mollify all sides.

> The English officer visits us in the camp. It is something out of the ordinary for us. He passes his tobacco pouch around for the Boers to partake and is really friendly. He hopes that the Boers and the English will not hate one another, but that they will live together with love and affection after the war.

At the end of December Michael wrote of 'the *English* promise to give every burger an extra suit of clothes, to the surprise of all. This puzzle remains unsolved.' The Boers never did receive the promised clothing.

Another, more upsetting surprise came the following day: the false news in the *Cape Times* (being pro-English, this newspaper was permitted in the camp) that President Steyn and De Wet had surrendered, and that there was 'no chance that the Boers would achieve any justice' – this last prophesy proved dismally true.

Michael's diary the next day was marked in bold letters: '1 JANUARY 1901.' The 'new month, new year and new century' had begun: it was an early, pleasant morning with some fine rain, and the tents resounded with songs of praise. He wrote that there was a beautiful church service, and, an extra joy, he received a letter from his brother Pieter in Ceylon: things were still fine with them, he commented, 'them' including Chris.

But this interlude was brief. Water was now scarce – the dry summer months and the overcrowded camp had put such pressure on the water supply that a breaking point had been reached. At last the local towns-people were able to trumpet 'I told you so' to the authorities.

The large camp of Bellevue needed around 10 000 gallons (almost 38 000 litres) of water every day. As far back as March 1900, when the camp was still being erected, the water superintendent had warned that Simon's Town's water was running 'dangerously low' because of the drain on it by POWs already in Simon's Town harbour.

The day after the New Year celebrations, 2 January, Michael noted that 'ten men from our camp go outside the camp to make a well because of scarce water'. But it was too little, too late, and urgent steps had to be taken at once.

A decision was made, in a rush, to ship as many prisoners as possible back to the Cape Town area, where there was plenty of fresh water from the many rivers and waterfalls that flowed into the Camissa network of underground water canals.

The authorities tried to cover up this glaring lack of forward planning by planting a rumour that these Boers were being moved because of intended commando raids on the Peninsula, during which they would try to escape. Yet no Boer commando ever came within a hundred miles of Cape Town, and anyway, the POWs in nearby Green Point would have been far easier for 'commandos' to reach first, rather than far-flung Bellevue, right down the long Cape Peninsula. The rumour bore no logic, but that has never stopped a rumour-mill in war.

PART IV

INTO EXILE
1900-1901

14

'The land weeps':
Chris and Pieter to Ceylon

AS THE LAST sight of shore slipped away from Boers sailing into prison exile from the ports of Cape Town or Simon's Bay or Durban, it felt to
them like a physical amputation. Boers were profoundly attached to their
land. They were not part-time Africans. Irrespective of how the land had
been bought or conquered (the way land has always been manhandled,
here and everywhere else), it, and not Europe, was their home – their
families had been rooted here for centuries.

Several Muller ancestors had arrived in the Cape in exile or slavery (as
had those of very many Afrikaner families). The Mullers, like many Boer
families over the centuries, had married brown partners in the seventeenth
and eighteenth centuries when such intermarriages in the sparsely popu-
lated Dutch colony were neither illegal nor uncommon. In the less-forgiving
nineteenth century, and especially in the legally racialised years of the
twentieth century, such knowledge was ignored or suppressed, though the
truth would out. The fifth and youngest Muller brother, Daan, was markedly darker than his four soldier-brothers. Their father, Michael, had mainly
European ancestry, but their mother, Martha (nee de Jager), had at least
six slave or free black ancestors.

Michael's wife, Nelie, and her sister Sannie, who struggled through the war
together with the two small Muller boys, also had brown ancestry, including
Krotoa's daughter, Pieternella van de Kaap (real surname Van Meerhof), and
also slave ancestors.[22] Nelie looked 'European', but Sannie, her full sister,
unquestionably did not. This may partially explain why she was publicly described as the *verpleegster* (nurse) of Nelie's children, in order to deflect gos-
sip, though Sannie was fully integrated in the Muller family, and much loved.

Now some of the descendants of these Muller forebears were to become *bannelinge* (prisoners in exile) too.

At eight o'clock in the morning of 17 August 1900, all the officers in Bellevue, including Chris Muller, and about sixty burgers from Ladybrand, were marched back along Simon's Town main road to the docks. The British had learned quickly to separate the rank-and-file from their leaders, to whom they were so loyal and would remain so, even in captivity, and saw to it that Boer officers were the first to be sent overseas. There, they boarded the *Mongolian*, rumoured bound for 'Ceilon' [sic]. Already on the ship were burgers from Ficksburg, Senekal and Winburg: the manifest recorded 719 Free Staters and four 'foreigner combatants'.

On 23 August 1900, the whistle of the *Mongolian* gave a great blast and made its way out to sea. On that day Chris recorded in his diary:

> I look back with a sore heart at the land of my birth, that for a long time, perhaps forever, I will not see again.
>
> Many thoughts and memories fly through my head. I think about the idea that, when I return, I may not be a free burger again, nor the land, for which I have fought for ten months and for which I twice gave of my own blood; and I sat mulling this when our servant came to call us for tea.
>
> After the meal, I sat again on deck, and I looked back where the land is disappearing in the mists, as if the land is weeping with us. A small ship passed us [and] we saw a whale close to us.
>
> It becomes dark, the land dwindles out of our sight, and from my heart rises a sigh of farewell, expressed from the depths, with the knowledge that I am in God's hands and He decides what my future will be.

Chris would not set foot back on his homeland for two endless years.

It was Chris's first time at sea, and though many men around him were seasick despite the calm water, he was only slightly 'dizzy' and enjoyed watching the large vessel cleave through the waves, leaving a foamy wake behind it, while birds such as seagulls and cormorants swarmed behind them.

His voyage as an officer was totally different to the dreadful one his brother Michael would, the following year, experience to Bermuda. He was not stuck below decks with hundreds of POWs in their hammocks, sweating their way through the tropics. He shared a *cabin* (he had resolved to learn English and began to practise these words in his diary) with two others known to him, including Andries Meyer, who would remain at his side throughout all of their exile.

He had free access to the deck, saloon and dining room, and officers were able to buy clothes, shoes, sweets, lemonade and other treats. He was brought coffee in bed in the mornings, then had a *bath*. 'At half past eight we were given *braakfast*, twelve o'clock, dinner, and at five, *lunsch*.' (It was during his return trip to South Africa at the end of the war, in 1902, that he would finally realise just how comfortable his outward-bound trip had been.)

Now, faced with the inevitability of exile, the officers settled down despite their seasickness, and were grateful for the 'refreshing air. We sat smoking, or we walked up and down on the deck.' Though many spent their time playing cards, Chris disapproved, and passed his time smoking a pipe and chatting with his cabin mates.

The views from the ship were beautiful, he recorded, as it hugged the coastline past Cape St Francis, Port Elizabeth and beyond, to Durban. They could see the landscape changing all the time – mountains, lighthouses, grassveld, and then lusher lands. Along the way they also saw sharks, dolphins and whales alongside their ship, new and wonderful creatures that fascinated them.

Within a few days they saw sugarcane plantations, and on 21 August they docked in the big port of Durban, Natal.

> In the evening, it was very beautiful to see the many lights in the town and on the beach, and on the ships. I go inside again, and then we heard the English officers on deck playing music and singing.

They chatted and smoked; some played cards, and drank 'ginger beer' poured for them by a servant. Not too shabby.

The sea was now calm, which was a relief, and while some POWs fished, others hung over the side to watch two whales cavort nearby. They could see the beautiful ridge of the Berea, 'where the rich people live', and at night, Chris wrote, the lights were like many large stars.

The *English* gave them two pairs of boxing gloves and the men enjoyed the sparring, while many steamboats plied back and forth to their vessel with supplies for the long voyage ahead. The Boers knew that they were about to depart South Africa's shores, and wrote letters home for the last time on this side of the ocean.

They were ordered to go below during the changing of the guard, and Chris took this opportunity to grab a quick, secretive chat with some of his burgers, who told him their complaints. First among them was their revulsion at the inhumane way in which livestock was butchered on board. They told him that the *English* sailors were too *kleinzerig* (squeamish), and unable to do the job efficiently.

Indeed, on 24 August, Chris saw, from his deck, a sailor trying to slaughter a large animal with an axe, 'torturing' it in the process, until a burger came up with his pocketknife and put the beast out of its misery. Two days later a similar incident occurred:

> The Tommies [a nickname for the British troops] slaughter a beast, just about murdered, as before. They ought to learn from the Boers how to slaughter.

This lack of skill and the wretched consequence for the creature upset the Boers. As farmers, they respected their food sources and considered it a failing not to be able to slaughter a beast quickly and humanely. After having seen so many men and horses killed in the veld, it was notable that they could not cope with this beastly suffering. But war casualties could not be helped – this could.

Chris was, he thought, the first of the three surviving brothers to cross the ocean as a *banneling*, a POW in exile, because he held the most senior rank. As far as he knew, Pieter was due to follow him soon.

In fact, Pieter had initially been with Chris's group, but was turned back at Simon's Bay harbour because the ship was too full. He had not escaped the inevitable for long, however, as a few days later he had had to board the single-funnelled, twin-masted *Bavarian*, filled with 1 300 men – mostly Free Staters – also heading for Ceylon and, as a matter of fact, arriving at the main port city of Colombo (today Sinhala), on the west coast, two days earlier than the *Mongolian*, having made good way.

As for the other brothers: Michael was still in Bellevue camp in Simon's Town, and Lool was dead – Chris would have known that by then. He had plenty to mourn.

Chris joined the other officers daily on the deck, where they played games for exercise and chatted about home and their families – anything to break the long monotony of their voyage.

As it got hotter, they began to feel the humidity, something most Boers were not used to. They developed the habit of going above in the early morning when the sailors were washing down the decks, and both sides had fun as they were sprayed with water. This soon became a relief as well as a game, as the heat intensified.

On 29 August, after their morning bath 'under the spray', they saw an island – Madagascar. It rained in the afternoon, very welcome to the men who now suffered from both heat and seasickness.

Chris's cabin was close to the kitchen and all night they could hear the noise of cooking, which disturbed his sleep, though he and the other officers had things far easier than the majority of the Boers below deck. Sweat seemed to drip off them all the time now. Soon they were sleeping on the deck, and welcomed the nightly showers of rain, which cooled them off.

A week later, the English colonel came to tell Chris that a burger was seriously ill, and the following day, 4 September, he died. A short funeral was held on the 5th. The body was stitched up in canvas and pieces of iron were inserted; it was placed on a plank and slid into the water. Chris wrote that his heart was filled with sympathy for the family, which would never have a grave at which to grieve.

The next day was more cheerful: it was his birthday. Emotions ruled his mind as it flew

> over the ocean to the silent house [Dorie and daughter Joey had by this stage fled as refugees] where I last spent some time with my wife and little child . . . many of these happy days come up in my mind and I could not bear these thoughts without tears coming to my eyes.

So began Chris's ever-intensifying longing for his wife, who would become an obsession for him during the months of exile.

Then he began to receive good wishes, and once the colonel heard it was

Chris's birthday, he allowed a few bottles of strong drink (usually banned) so that the officers could toast Chris's health; a lifelong teetotaller, he did not join in.

Chris's wife Dorie and their two children born before the war: baby 'Mullertjie' (Pieter), who died in February 1900, and their daughter, 'Joey' (Johanna), born in 1897.

Suddenly the voyage was over. After breakfast on 9 September 1900, Chris went on deck and could see land and also hear the gangplanks being prepared.

Soon they saw the harbour of Colombo on the west coast of Ceylon, with its beautiful breakwater against which huge waves were crashing. Chris was intrigued with this attractive place, as he would be with much of Ceylon, and described it as a

> lovely harbour. Behind the breakwater lay about 50 or 60 ships, that is, apart from smaller boats. The docks and the storage sheds are built right into the water, so that the small boats could be rowed right into one of these buildings. Continuously, ships arrive and leave . . . deeper in the sea there is a small young shark.

The next morning they were still on board, watching the many little vessels plying between the ships, laden with fruit that made his mouth water. The large ships surrounded by these little vessels made him think of an enormous sow with little piglets around her. He could see, further away, a beach with orchards, plantations, and many date and banana palms. Alarmingly, they heard that there was cholera on the island, and that there had been an earthquake on the day they arrived.

They finally set foot on Ceylon on 12 September: woken at 2am, given breakfast at 4am, and then rowed in boats to the quay and put on board a train that swiftly left the port city. For the first time, they saw the country they would live in for two years, and it made a favourable impression, despite their circumstances. Chris wrote a long entry describing this feast for their eyes after the monotony of the ocean voyage: the train passed bushes and waterfalls, and

> we see many beautiful palms: *koko* [coconuts] and dates. And after a while we see mountains and hills, with trees and bushes, climbers, flowers and many types of shrubs. Between the trees, we see everywhere the houses of the *Sengalies* [Sinhalese], mostly decked with palm-leaf mats. They are built with stones or wooden planks.
>
> It is a delicate nation, but industrious. It is difficult to distinguish between men and women. Many men have no beard, and they have long hair. The women have small busts and their clothes are similar. They do not seem to be fussy about their clothes, for with a *doek* [cloth] around their body the *Sengalies* is properly clothed.
>
> They marry when they are very young, and they are blessed with children.
>
> We saw very few cattle; even the chickens are few. They plough

with a wooden plough, using two buffaloes that resemble two donkeys with horns and [are] dull in colour. They sow a great deal of rice in the water, and on the slopes and mountains they plant tea, even between the rocks.

The beauty of nature, you cannot describe with any pen.

The railway here is a marvellous piece of work. The rail goes along the tops of the mountains . . . and then passes through 37 tunnels, some long, others short.

We see no birds sitting in the trees; we also see no veld. A few tame elephants are by the huts of the people and in a few places we see animals like our *boerbokke.*

In the first part of our journey, the trees consisted mostly of dates and coco palms – the cocos have ripe fruits; the dates are full of small ones – and also a lot of bananas, and when we reach the big mountains the rice fields become less, and the tea [plantations] more.

Since we left Colombo it has been raining, first softly and later very hard. And the streams from the tops of the mountains are lovely, with beautiful waterfalls and rivers. We can already see the camp in the distance, from the top of the mountains along which the train is passing.

At four o'clock we arrived at the camp, consisting of many large zinc houses. We, the officers, are brought to the houses set aside for officers. They are well appointed.

It was a joy to again experience such freedom, and mostly, to meet the burgers again.

He had arrived at the large hilly prison camp of Diyatalawa where, apart from when he was recuperating from a serious illness, he and most of his fellow POWs would spend the rest of their war.

The camp of Diyatalawa was in a natural amphitheatre in the high, central region of the island of Ceylon, about eighty miles from Colombo, at an altitude of just over 4 900 feet. The camp spread out as more POWs arrived: by the end of the war it covered over two miles.

Before the POW camp was erected there in 1900, under the supervisory eye of the governor, Sir West Ridgeway, it had been attractive open land but for an orphanage and parsonage, known locally as Happy Valley, and overlooked by high mountains.

Rows of zinc huts glittered in the sunlight, visible for miles. Each hut was built to house 56 men, with a camp bed each, and tables and benches for meals, which the men took turns to cook. Officers had their own communal huts holding fewer men. They had servants, *koelies* [sic], to help with cooking, cleaning and other chores. Each hut, whether of officers or burgers, chose a hut captain.

The huts were neatly ordered on either side of long 'roads' – it looked not unlike the mining camps of the Transvaal. A double fence of barbed wire, as well as trenches, formed the perimeter, which was dotted with '23 big lights on high poles and many oil lamps on wire poles'; the camp buildings inside were lit by electricity, which impressed Chris enough to record it.

Goods were ferried from the railhead to the camp by an aerial tramway raised on Eiffel Tower-like structures for a mile or so; there was also a wire chute for firewood running parallel to it.

Ceylon was thought by the POWs to have a good climate, similar to that of the Cape in South Africa, with plenty of water that was funnelled into four holding tanks in the camp. If there was an ideal place to house thousands of Boer prisoners, at its fullest tally about 6 000, it was here.

As in all the POW camps, there were black POWs who had been captured with Boer troops; those sent to Diyatalawa had been captured at Paardeberg. They were paid small sums for labour such as building and shovelling, even though there was plenty of local labour available. They also, of course, suffered from POW ailments such as homesickness; very little has been recorded of their experiences and trials as POWs, nor were they subsequently included in memorials.

The first POWs had arrived in Ceylon on the *Mohawk* on 9 August 1900, with many more shiploads following. There had been, as usual, anxiety among the local population about the invasion of 'wild and hairy Boers', but Sir West proved to be a capable negotiator and administrator, and allayed fears by poking fun at the locals – were they afraid that the price of pumpkins would go up, he teased them.

After initial misgivings – Ceylon's residents had been told *ad nauseam* that the Boers were rough, dirty in their habits, crafty and treacherous – the islanders began to accept that these POWs were, on the whole, decent human beings and no threat to their existence. Indeed, Ceylon benefitted from their presence.

Many of the POWs had been shabby on arrival, for they had been wearing their clothes for weeks, if not months, in the veld and then on the prison ships. But once they stripped to swim, the locals were impressed with their strong bodies. The local opinion of the Boers rose further, including the realisation that 'clothes do not make a man in war'.

For their part, the Boers agreed this country made a beautiful prison, one that many came to appreciate in its own right, despite their captivity.

The imperial powers believed it would be very difficult, if not impossible, to escape from this very large island, yet five Boers successfully did so.

These five men had just arrived on the SS *Catalonia* in the port of Colombo when they realised this would be their best opportunity for making a dash for it. On the night of 13 January 1901, girded with lifebelts and led by their ringleader, Willie Steyn, they lowered themselves into the sea with plans to find 'sympathetic ships'. After a nasty few hours in the water, all five made it to the Russian vessel *Gerson,* where they were hauled on board and given permission to stay by the chief officer.

Few ships could have been more sympathetic, for Russia was passionately pro-Boer, regarding them as freedom fighters. Tsar Nicholas II scoured the English-language papers daily, admitting he hoped for news of Boer successes, as did public figures such as Leo Tolstoy; some 225 Russian officers had taken leave to fight alongside the Boers.

When the *Gerson* docked at Aden, officials boarded it to search the ship for the five escaped prisoners. The captain swore he had never set eyes on them; meanwhile, they were hidden, squashed, in the ship's funnel. By this time their story had made world headlines. The men disembarked at St Petersburg and travelled through Russia to a heroes' welcome.

These Boer escapees eventually made their way to Utrecht in the Netherlands where President Paul Kruger was staying. When they were ushered into the room where their respected president was seated at a table with a huge bible on it, smoking, he greeted them with, '*Goeiemôre, is julle die vyf swemmers?*' (Good morning, are you the five swimmers?)

On his first day in camp, Chris was tired from the long trip that had started so early the previous morning. He did little more than stretch his legs, while greeting those he knew. Many now began to feel exhaustion and/or depression.

The next day, 14 September, he and the other officers were taken to a house outside the main camp. Each was given a cork hat with a red band (non-officers wore blue bands on theirs). This was a signal to the sentries that they had officer status, and could walk unhindered outside the camp 'up to the white flags', which stood at quite a distance.

The camp's shop was opened in the morning for officers, from 8.30 am to 10 am, with a sentry posted at the door to ensure that only those wearing red bands entered. It was then opened to the other ranks. Officers were also allowed liquor, unlike the burgers. Chris disliked the amount of drinking that went on, as well as the card-playing that happened straight after the devotions held mornings and evenings inside their hut.

Very soon after they arrived, they were handed a form from the British authorities on which was printed the oath of neutrality. They handed it back, unsigned. This battle of wits went on throughout their imprisonment and would eventually cause deep rifts among the men.

The food took some getting used to: almost everything was foreign to their taste, from drinking tea (instead of coffee) to the highly spiced local dishes.

Each day Chris bathed, often late in the morning; there was a bath area outside the camp that he enjoyed using.

Everyone tried to make money, for they wanted to supplement their diet with local fruits and foodstuffs, and buy tobacco. They turned to pancake-making and baking goods, carving walking sticks, making cigar or cigarette holders and clothing, and holding lotteries. If someone had money, he could live well here, wrote Chris. He had a little, enough to buy small items including (he kept a record) coffee and cakes, stationery and stamps, socks, collars and toothbrushes and, touchingly, brooches and bracelets for his womenfolk at home.

Education classes were started – they cost one rupee a month – and Chris took lessons in English every Wednesday and Friday afternoon. He was a good student and advanced so efficiently that his very last diary of the war in 1902 was written in fluent English. (Learning English was a smart move by Chris: it reduced the area of misunderstanding with the authorities, and gave him an advantage in dealings outside the camp, where he would frequently roam.) Later, he expanded his lessons to Dutch, history, geography and arithmetic. He was determined to use his time well.

Hard-earned wisdom decreed that the burgers be separated by nation, into barracks named Krugersdorp (Transvalers) and Steynsburg (Free Staters), after the presidents of the two Boer republics. There was also Wilhelmina-stad for 'Hollanders' and other foreigners who had fought on the Boer side and been captured.

There were thousands of men living cheek by jowl, and they needed to get on with each other, but sometimes they did not. There was an imme-diate, rather shocking event in which two Transvalers fought each other and one of them died as a result.

The dead man – the only one during the Boers' incarceration to be killed by a fellow prisoner – was given a military burial the next day. His was the first grave in the cemetery, situated not far from the camp, on a grassy mound, a quiet place with fragrant lemongrasses scenting the air. Eventu-ally it would hold some 140 graves, most of them Boers, though there were also some British graves, mainly sentries: all now lying together. The young-est Boers buried here were two Free State boys of 16; the eldest was a 90-year-old, captured at Paardeberg and who survived in Diyatalawa camp until May 1901. They had succumbed to typhoid.

Some of Chris's friends also ended up in the graves; he visited the cem-etery often, both as a homage to them, and as a solace from the noisy, bustling camp.

Chris and his father-in-law Willem Nel helped tend the graves; for Chris, it was a comfort to have 'Father Willem' there, and they often spent time together. Chris grew saplings in tins until they were strong enough to be transplanted into the cemetery.

General Paul Roux was a POW, and Chris mentioned him often, visiting his *laager* and being visited in turn. Roux, despite having been a conten-tious central figure leading to the Prinsloo surrender, was the most popular Boer prisoner in Ceylon during their stay, not least because he was fluent in English, tall and lean, and with the easy manners of a gentleman and a good sense of humour. He had obvious leadership qualities, though he could be temperamental if thwarted.

He lived in a little cottage outside the camp's perimeter with his wife, who had been with him on commando, and they were in demand by local hostesses as dining guests. *Vrouw* Roux would regale (or perhaps stun) her audiences with accounts of her claimed successes with her rifle against the British troops.

They were fed the local 'Dutch' delicacies, which included very hot curries. After one such meal, Roux teased his hostess by saying, 'I have gone through many months of war without shedding a tear, but I very much feared I would do so tonight!' It was a *bon mot* much enjoyed by the local gentry.

The majority of the Boer POWs were from the Free State, and mostly farmers – there were 3 679 of them. But there were a further 152 occupations listed: accountant, wine merchant, a professor of mathematics, 32 engineers, three lawyers, several doctors (including four belonging to the Dutch Ambulance Corps), a conjurer and an undertaker.

Some of their skills were exceedingly useful for Ceylon. A prisoner who had worked at the state bindery in Pretoria before the war was employed to help improve the standards in the Government Printing Department in Ceylon.

Commandant Krantz, believed to be one of the finest shots in South Africa, had been a founder of the state museum in Pretoria six years before the war. He offered to mount specimens of local fauna for the Colombo Museum, which possessed none, and was allowed to do so on parole (on the honour system, allowed outside the camp on his own recognisance), shooting all the specimens himself before preparing them for display with the help of a Boer taxidermist. It is noteworthy that Krantz, despite being a POW, was given the guns and ammunition for this job. His wife, who joined him during his parole in Ceylon, was also an excellent shot and not slow in claiming to bemused hosts how she caught her own 'bag' of *rooinekke* while on commando with him. How the local gentry marvelled at these feisty Boer women.

Chris had fallen ill for a few days after his arrival. Once he recovered, he sat on the hill at General's Roux's *laager*, watching the burgers play cricket and the Tommies playing football (a game the Boers soon adopted). He found it fun to watch the liveliness, including the burgers busily laying out a tennis court.

On that same day, 25 September, General Jan Hendrik Olivier and some prisoners from Green Point arrived, and there was much chatter that evening about news from South Africa, though the post did not bring a letter from his wife, Dorie, his 'dearest'. He began to refer to her, in his diaries, in increasingly sentimental terms as the distance between them stretched out.

On 16 September, he recorded the birthday of his elder brother Michael, now separated from him by the width of a great ocean.

Chris took advantage of one of the best perks of being an officer: parole. On 27 September, he and Andries Meyer were given permission to leave the camp; he was ecstatic with the feeling of freedom for the first time since his capture at the end of July.

> Oh, it was wonderful to be in nature again. I leapt around like a deer, my joyfulness in the beauty of nature. We gathered flowers, and we also ended up in a tea plantation. It is beautiful. We also went up high, from where we had a beautiful view of our camp and its environment. We came back, me with a great bunch of flowers.

But on their return to the hut they discovered politicking on the go.

> There was meeting under way of hut captains about how to celebrate the forthcoming birthday of the President; also to sign the petition, asking that the enemy send us back to South Africa. When I heard that, I was very dissatisfied.

Chris and Meyer were opposed to any collaboration with the enemy, or anything that smacked of being a *hensopper*. This issue would lead to continual rows.

But being on parole was a joy, and every couple of days Chris's diary was filled with descriptions of the splendour of their environment, as they swam in rivers and under waterfalls, and wandered between trees and among flowers they had never seen before. They chatted to local *Singalies,* and he asked them to teach him words, from *rice* to *pineapples.* A local property owner came to know them, and confided to Chris that he enjoyed and was 'honoured' by their conversations, gratified that Boer officers were so approachable.

In quick succession there were some celebrations, including President Steyn's birthday (2 October), which also sparked a fight. It began when, after a religious service, some of the men began to cheer and celebrate, even as many were being carried off to the hospital with measles, a grave illness for grown men (it seems, however, that none died). Then men arrived with musical instruments and began to play, dance and sing 'worldly songs'. Chris was among those who objected (which seems rather a pity), and it was stopped; yet he had appreciated the day's meaning.

That night, though, his heart 'burned with longing' for his dearest wife, and home, where he could pray alongside her 'in quietude'.

Sir West Ridgeway visited and was introduced to all the commandants, including Chris, who was much taken with the governor's neat dress style: even his bodyguards had impressive garments, Chris noted. This impression would encourage him to pay attention to his own appearance, for he liked to be well turned out.

Chris's last entry in this diary was on 4 October 1900. At their midday meal, beer had been placed on their tables for the birthday of veldkornet Piet Kruger, son of the president (one of his 16 offspring), who kept up a correspondence with his father while he was in exile in Diyatalawa camp. And that evening Chris and Andries Meyer received another bottle as a present from a friend.

> Now it is late and my book is full. I wish I could put it into the hands of my beloved.
> Now I'm going to bed. May the Lord have mercy on us.

15

Deadly disease in Ceylon's camp

IN HIS FIRST entry in his new diary, on 5 October, Chris recorded that he and his friend Meyer took a walk outside the camp. They were able to buy fresh fruit and 'old coins' as souvenirs.

On their return there were letters waiting for Chris, though not the longed-for one from his wife, from whom he had not heard since he had left South Africa.

After another walk that afternoon, one of the sentries took fright and challenged them on their return with the traditional shout of, 'Halt, who goes there?' Chris explained they had been out on parole (his growing command of English coming into good use), at which the sentry said peevishly they should answer that they were 'friend'. Chris showed him his pass, at which the sentry restated the required formula: 'Pass, friends!' The poor sentry seemed 'as startled as a hare' to the two, and they folded with laughter once through the gate.

Two days later, with their friend Fred van Blerk, they climbed high above the camp and sat there, drinking in the beautiful scene and the revivifying fresh wind. While they were chatting, wrote Chris on 7 October, their hearts burned for their loved ones. 'More than ever we spoke about the love a woman has for a man, and how little we had appreciated it.' It was not surprising they felt this way: Chris recorded on the 12th that it had been five months since he had last seen his wife Dorie (who was pregnant).

As they walked back past the cemetery, with its wall of earth sods and a furrow around it, Van Blerk remarked that he hoped he would not end up being buried there. Chris responded that he would not choose that either, but if it were to happen, it would not matter much where he was buried.

He would remember those offhand words, when he and Pieter fell so ill that it seemed possible they may suffer this fate.

On 8 October Chris asked permission to visit the camp hospital, which was, alarmingly, filling up with POWs ill with measles, and also agreed to help start a debating society. Then he heard someone crying and he knew at once that Daniel Robinson had died (aged 23, of appendicitis), for he had just seen him on his deathbed. Another day, another funeral.

All the dead were buried with full military honours. After Robinson's coffin had been placed in the grave, the *dominee* held a short service, then 12 soldiers fired three volleys over the grave, and others blew trumpets. The dominee thanked the doctor and the colonel in charge of the camp for their medical help, and for the privilege of allowing them to bury their dead according to their customs. They scattered earth on the coffin and said the blessing. Once they returned to the camp, the camp servants closed the grave. The fifth, so far.

Three days later Chris could hardly get out of bed. He heard that his brother, Pieter, was also very ill. They were told that there was an serious outbreak of 'cholera' (in reality, it was typhoid), and it made them feel despondent. But the brothers rallied, even as the hospital and the cemetery continued to fill up.

In the following days Chris was unable to attend the funerals, for, aside from still feeling ill, 'my trousers are broken. I am getting another pair made but they have not arrived yet.'

A letter from his much-missed wife Dorie, the first, finally arrived on 25 October. He was thrilled: he was glad to know that she was alive but he also noticed that things were not going well at home, and that she was struggling with many discomforts. He left the camp and sat quietly under a tree to process her letter, and prayed for strength. Somehow he found it, and struggled on.

There were some diversions – a 'boxing concert', and books arrived, some of them very beautiful, which were displayed on a shelf in a makeshift library, Chris noted. On one of his walks he saw a 'wonderful ape with a tail two feet long. His face was black and he had a bushy white beard.'

Four of them strolled down to the station just as the governor arrived in his own grand carriage, and they walked around the village shops and houses. Among their group was Johnny Brink, one of the eight Ladybranders in that long-ago pre-battle photograph. Johnny had been eyeing the local women, and they teased him about it, though in truth they were all fascinated. Chris noticed that small girls wore rings in their noses and had pierced ears with heavy rings dangling from them.

On the way back they popped in to the workshop of A Strauss and E Meyer, who were building an organ.

As always, the first matter at hand for the POWs was to keep themselves busy. A workshop had been set up, and though they had no tools, they turned barrel hoops into saws, and table knives into planes, resourcefully using whatever came to hand. Their craftware was plentiful and of considerable quality, and an exhibition of their wares was held in Colombo to raise money for the 'poor women and children' in the concentration camps back home; it was well attended, with many sales. One of the items that they carved specifically for Ceylon's market was the tea caddy. Though the Boers were not used to drinking tea, they quickly realised this was a prime crop in Ceylon, and so they made some beautiful specimens.

Apart from useful enterprises such as handiwork, tailoring, education and music classes (one of the POWs was considered to be the best pianist in Ceylon, and was much in demand all over the island for concerts), there was also a pressing need to exercise those magnificent physiques that attracted such local attention. The prisoners worked enthusiastically to build playing fields and tennis courts, and even a swimming pool that could hold thirty at a time. They took to any sport they were introduced to.

Among them was a boxer of note, Irishman Jim Holloway, the lightweight champion of Pretoria before the war. He set up a boxing academy at Diyatalawa and trained his young charges so well that some were considered good enough to be sent on a world tour with him, though sponsorship could not be found before the war ended. He was probably the best-known POW in Ceylon, and on his departure in 1902, half the island turned out to see this celebrity, surprised by his slight build and quiet face. They had been expecting a giant of a man, like some of his fellow POWs.

The size and strength of the Boers was an ongoing fascination, particularly in contrast to the much smaller, smooth-skinned *Sengalies*. Among the most impressive was General Jan Hendrik Olivier, who had headed the Bethulie commando, one of two generals in Diyatalawa. All on the island were struck by his physical presence: he was tall, 'a magnificent physical specimen', with broad shoulders and a keen eye, though his long beard was streaked with grey in a V-shape. He was referred to with admiration by the *English* as 'Big John', for his stature and also his courage.

Olivier had won a great victory at Stormberg during 'Black Week' in December 1899, and he enjoyed regaling anyone who was prepared to listen to his story of that battle, which he won with 'only one big gun by adroitly moving it from one side to the other'. He seemed approachable, and was more of a diplomat than Roux. Having survived combat, he would have to suffer the loss of his son in November 1900 during the enteric epidemic in Diyatalawa: a monument was raised on his son's grave after the war.

Cricket history was made in Ceylon when Boer prisoners, who quickly mastered the game, took on the Colombo Colts in an invitation match on the posh Cinnamon Gardens pitch, a cricket ground set out in the most affluent area of the capital. Usually thin crowds turned out for local cricket, but when the Boer XI travelled from the camp to Colombo for the match, the place was crammed with eager spectators, including the vice-regent's party, and the impressive-looking Boer General Olivier. There were a notable number of women present, recorded the press – perhaps to gauge the Boer physiques for themselves.

The Colts won by 141 runs. When the Boer captain presented the legendary Tommy Kelaart, 'the wizard with the leather', with a memento of the match – a carved bone paper knife inscribed 'A Souvenir of the Boer-Colt Cricket Match' – the crowd was ecstatic. Reports of this sportsmanship were carried far and wide, including in leading London newspapers.

Athletics days were keenly anticipated and trained for, and the Boers ran barefoot like the wind. Not letting the facts stand in the way of a good story, a Ceylon newswriter conjured the myth that their speed was because they were 'ostrich herders' and that every day they had to chase young ostriches 20 miles into the veld for 'pasturage' and then back again in the evening.

Once again, enteric fever – typhoid – arrived to take its pickings. It was believed to have entered the island on the *Bavarian,* the overcrowded ship that Pieter Muller had travelled on, although it hardly matters which ship brought it in, for it would certainly have made its way there at some point. It had begun its grip at Paardeberg, and scored more deaths in the war than all the bullets and explosives put together.

Chris, a regular hospital visitor as part of caring for the men under his command, was one of the first to contract it, in November 1900, the worst month. On the 3rd, he started to feel rather ill, and began to lose his appetite, though he recorded trying to eat the next day, fiddling with a piece of raw meat and choking it down 'for my health'.

It got worse. His head and neck were sore, and he had pain in his legs. Every now and then he felt better after eating porridge. This fits: a simple nourishing diet is an essential part of recovery from typhoid, and by avoiding the meaty diet so beloved of the Boers, he was inadvertently doing the right thing.

As the days passed, more burgers died. Chris managed, one more time, to walk over to some new arrivals in camp, and talk to them. They told him that his father had been taken prisoner in the Free State; he had been released after two days, but his cart, horses and all his belongings had been confiscated.

This seems to have been the last straw for Chris, who now succumbed to the illness that had been waiting in the shadows. He was admitted to hospital on 14 November, six months to the day since his younger brother Lool, aged 23, had fatally contracted the same disease in Green Point, a fact not lost on Chris.

He later recorded that his first night in hospital was devastating. There were five officers lying in a row, all of them seriously sick, and on the first night two of them died, one on either side of him.

Over the next couple of weeks, the number of hospitalised rose to 300. Now the authorities had to scramble to contain the epidemic. The governor sent his best government physician to take charge. The first thing Dr RF Garvin did was strengthen the medical personnel, including the nursing staff under the firm-handed and experienced Sister Lucy, a senior nurse of the old school.

She took umbrage at some of the 'blunter Britishers' in Ceylon society who criticised her role in looking after the Boers. She retorted that she much preferred to nurse the polite Boers, from whom she never heard bad language, nor had to field offensive remarks or looks. This differed from her experience in hospitals among her own countrymen, she snapped, when young nurses were forced to appeal to her for protection, which she was more than capable of dishing out.

During the worst months of the epidemic, ice was brought in twice a day, a real feat as the nearest supplies were about a hundred miles away.

Chris's great friend Andries Meyer visited him regularly and asked to be allowed to stay at the hospital to nurse him, a request that was denied. Meyer noted the names of the men who died next to or close to Chris. Soon there were multiple deaths every night, and in a single terrible week, from 21 to 28 November 1900, 15 men died of the fever, all from the Free State, all captured with General Prinsloo.

The sickness in this same week claimed the tallest Boer in the camp. Francois Johannes Loubscher, who stood six foot five inches, had been captured in February 1900 in Natal (his POW number was the very low 49) and, with his brother, was sent to Diyatalawa. He died in hospital, aged 38, on 24 November, in part because he was allergic to milk. Both he and his sick brother were too ill to speak, and were unable to warn the staff not to feed them the standard milky diet. Thus his cause of death is recorded as 'dysentery' (the only such one), though it was in fact a fatal combination of the fever and the milk he ingested.

Around one in six POWs in Diyatalawa contracted typhoid, and had it not been for the emphatic and quick action of the governor in sending Dr Garvin, the results would have been far worse, especially during the critical early phase.

The epidemic reached its height in November 1900, with 370 cases, but by December 1900 that number had dropped to 196, then it decreased rapidly. In all, 756 men were infected and 68 died, most of them during the earliest period, though the illness lingered on with sporadic outbreaks throughout the war.

Inevitably, Andries Meyer had joined Chris as a patient during the dangerous November month. As the epidemic began to abate, they were among the fortunate who survived, though at times it was touch and go.

Three weeks went by until, on 7 December, Chris was judged well enough to be moved.

> I was so weak that I could not walk or stand. After two days, I could walk if I hung round the neck of someone else with a walking stick in one hand.

After a few days he was able to keep food down and couldn't resist a treat of blancmange with jam. It proved too much for his stomach, he wrote, and he had to return to bed for a week and live on milk.

His next stop was down to the coast, where a special convalescent house had been set up for recuperating Boers, who were initially unhappy with this relocation so far from their comrades in Diyatalawa; Chris even tried at first to insist on being sent back to the camp, though he was far too weak for a return journey.

It took all day to get there, the transport leaving at 7am and arriving at its destination at 8 pm, by which time he was exhausted. This resort area was called Mount Lavinia after the residency here of an early governor of Ceylon who had named it after his local mistress, a dancer (whom he smuggled in, scandalising the public). By now, it had become a smart hotel (Meyer called it 'beautiful') about 200 paces from the water's edge.

The Boer invalids were staying a little further back from the shoreline, in a roomy building on a ridge, surrounded on three sides by palm trees, with palm leaves for a roof, and a verandah right around from which they had a lovely view of the sea. There were also separate huts for a pharmacy, a wash house and a kitchen.

Marvellously, the recovering Boers had a mile of free access to the beach, set aside solely for their purposes in the early mornings, and again in the late afternoons and evenings. It was an utter boon for the sickly men.

Staffed with a medical doctor and a permanent chemist, the convalescent area was devised to hold 25 healing prisoners but was expanded out of necessity to hold as many as 150. There was also a cook, an 'inside servant', and a few more hands to carry water, fill baths, remove chamberpots and do other cleaning work. The only chore for the recovering prisoners was to make their own beds.

The doctor appointed Chris, the most senior officer present, as captain of their hut.

For breakfast at 8.30 am and supper at 6 pm, they were given tea and bread; for dinner at 1 pm there was meat, rice, potatoes and vegetables. They felt continually hungry, that they were not getting enough food, though the regime for recovery from typhoid insists on a light diet.

Chris was not yet allowed to swim in the sea, as his doctor felt it was too early, but on 29 December 1900 he, along with friends, went for a walk on the beach and were soon encircled by a curious crowd. And it was a hard moment for Chris when they saw some women walking from the hotel to the beach.

> This is an agonising memory – what I have left behind in South Africa and how long it has been since my beloved and I were separated.

On the last day of this tumultuous year he wandered the beach, reflecting back on it. It had begun with him still a soldier at Magersfontein, quickly elevated to veldkornet and soon after, commandant; surviving several main battles, and wounds; being captured and sent to Ceylon, where he, somewhat ironically, came closest to losing his life in the war because of severe illness. During this time he had also lost his younger brother Lool, and his baby son Mullertjie. He had a great deal to contemplate, while paddling in the waves and watching the local villagers fishing with hooks and nets, as well as from boats.

On the first day of 1901, he used almost the identical words in his diary to those written on that same day by his brother Michael, who was at this stage still in Bellevue camp in Simon's Town:

> Many thoughts flew through my mind, about a new day, a new year and a new century. Now the 19th century is passed and the question must be asked, what will the 20th century be in world history?

16

Ships, storms and fire in the Cape – Michael

STILL IN SIMON'S TOWN, Michael Muller continued to witness the anxious spectacle of men being transported to overseas POW camps; yet while he remained on South African soil, he remained strongly connected to his land and people, as did those around him.

But the spectre of deportation hung in the air, reminding the Boers of the perilousness of their position. On 15 November 1900, about sixty men had been sent to Ceylon, 'and we are frightened a number of times with the threat of Ceylon, like small children with a ghost,' Michael wrote.

On 3 January 1901, several of his friends were told to be at the gate at 10 am, and a large group of Transvalers left in the afternoon, he thought for St Helena (the first British colony to which Boer POWs were sent). Then he and his tentmates were told to be ready to leave the next day.

On 4 January 1901, they were marched out of camp, bundles on their backs, between two rows of troops along the main street of Simon's Town. This was the first time Michael had left the camp in five months, and he was in dread. Their life in Bellevue camp had come to an abrupt end. Whatever its demerits – the fact that they were prisoners, that it was a spectacularly windy site in summer, and sand turned their food gritty – it would soon be remembered with nostalgia.

The men were crammed onto a steamship which travelled across the water to a larger transport ship, and by 11.30 am they were fully embarked. They were given a rudimentary lunch, a piece of meat and a potato cooked without salt, and only a spoon to eat with.

The ship was the *Kildonan,* and from this point on everything would be different. Gone were the days of swimming on the beach, and of games in the space, generous by comparison, inside Bellevue camp. The POWs were now trapped on board, crushed into cabins, cheek by jowl, with further trials to come.

Michael's first diary entry on board, on 4 January 1901, described the *Kildonan* as 600 feet long and 70 feet wide, at anchor in Simon's Bay. He wrote of 'other miracles' he had seen, 'too many to name'. He noted that there were three warships anchored nearby, as well as another ship with prisoners on board. From the deck, on which they were permitted to roam freely, they could see three or four trains a day on the nearby shore, and a high lighthouse that marked the way for ships, during the day with flags, at night with lamps.

But there was much negative feedback. Michael heard complaints about the *benoude* (stifling) nights the men had to endure: 'such a tiny home for so many people. In the camp we were in well-aired tents,' he wrote, forgetting the grumbling about overcrowding in those same tents on their arrival in Bellevue.

On Sunday 6 January they were given knives and forks, although the cutlery did not help much because the meat was 'really raw'. No longer able to do their own cooking, they had not realised what a loss that would prove. The awful meat was somewhat compensated for by a 'delicious pudding'.

Now they were confronted with the fragility of life at sea: the possibility of sinking and fire, poor food, disease, seasickness, cramped quarters, no exercise . . . it was so much worse than Bellevue, a place they had never believed they would come to appreciate.

There were, however, two pieces of good fortune for the Boers on board. First, the ship was large, new and efficiently run. The *Kildonan* was the last mail steamer to be completed by the notable Union-Castle Line before the war. The 9 600-ton ship, with its many levels, was immediately converted for war purposes, and sailed for the Cape in November 1899 with 3 000 British troops on board – possibly a record number at the time.

Second, and perhaps more importantly, the captain of the *Kildonan*, JC Robinson, was a sympathetic man in whom the Boers felt they had found a friend. In war, this is no small thing.

Captain Robinson immediately made a good impression on his captives. He told his crew to treat the Boers as honourable foes, which seemed to have the required effect, because Michael recorded that

> the ship's captain and officers are friendly and good to us. In the evening, the captain held a church service, whereupon he invites the Boers who understand English [this included Michael] to attend his services. His service was serious. He also prayed for our wives and children, and for peace.

Captain Robinson's evening service was attended by great numbers, the space completely filled up. It must have been gratifying for prisoners to hear him say that 'the war was caused by the jealousy of the capitalists', a view many of them shared, though probably not his own Admiralty.

The relief at encountering a friendly 'enemy' was huge, and would make a great impact on the men, then and later. They trusted him as they did no other 'foe', and they needed to, because their lives were literally in his hands.

The first tremor of anxiety came in the form of sickness a week later, when on 13 January Michael recorded 'a serious outbreak of [enteric] fever; twenty have sickened'.

The next day, sick numbers had risen to fifty and were 'increasing fast'. This led to a shattering task for Michael: on 15 January he was ordered to clean out the ship's heads, which, he wrote, was 'a very unpleasant job'. It would have been nasty under any circumstances, but with so many men with typhoid fever on board, his initiation into this foul task was especially ill timed. Further, many of the Boers were seasick, as the ship 'rocks from side to side'. A sensitive man, Michael was so scarred by this filthy work that he repeated both the date and event on the inside back page of his diary, the only time he ever did this.

And there was now another urgent concern. The day following his confrontation with the gruesome lavatories, he mentioned that

> it looks like the coalroom is under threat of burning, but speedily they haul the coal out with *mazinerys* [machinery].

> We vacate our place under threat of fire. We go to another cabin about 200ft away, where it is absolutely crammed.
>
> [The next day they are] still busy trying to save the ship. Enormous effort [is] involved.

The struggle to put out the fire continued for several days, and during this whole frightening time, prisoners were transferred to and from other ships, as many as 150 at a time – men were separated according to nationhood (Transvalers and Free Staters), among other reasons, to discourage fights.

On the significant date of 23 January 1901, they received the news that the 'old Queen' [Victoria] had died the day before, and a salvo of 82 shots with the big cannon marked the official mourning. During this, men were still hard at work unloading the coal into another ship, presumably as a precaution, for the fire was at last conquered.

It had been a dramatic week, enhanced by some prisoners taking advantage of the chaos. Two men had escaped by swimming from another ship, which then put out to sea to discourage any further attempts.

All the plates, knives, forks and pots of Michael and his fellow prisoners were gone, and he worried – he was a perpetual worrier – what they would put their food in.

Then the men were forced out of their rooms for an inspection, during which 'something' was found. Though this issue was resolved, it was all unnerving, and it was during this time that he found out in a letter he received that Chris's wife, Dorie, had lost her baby on 29 November 1900 – the second child she had lost during the war. A devoted family man, he was grief-stricken by this news.

Perhaps this led to his next dream, of meeting his wife 'and one child' in a church in a strange place. He dreamed again, the same night, of once more meeting his wife and 'only one child' (Pieter, the eldest), and that her sister Sannie was with her. In his dream, he took the boy in his arms, and then he woke up to the chaos on board.

Pieter, Michael's first-born son, aged 3; he carried this photograph with him while a POW.

There was now a firm attempt to get things back to normal on the *Kil-donan*. On 28 January, the whole ship was washed down by the sailors, while Michael and his mates scrubbed the tables. That afternoon, they all received canvas shoes.

On the last day of January, the *Kildonan* set sail from Simon's Town at sunrise. On the way out, they passed another ship and they could see that men were lying about it, seasick. It was not an encouraging sight.

Here, Michael ran out of space in his slender diary, and resorted to using an 'appendix' of extremely small pages. There are only sixteen of these tiny, thin sheets, which are, in fact, doubled-up single pages he must have gleaned from somewhere, folded and written on. He then inserted them into the envelope of the diary's cover where they remained, cocooned.

His tiny writing on these pages – it is amazing how much could he cram into such a small space – described the sights of Cape Town.

Around ten o'clock we arrive in Cape Town's harbour, where we docked and we [were] also given orders to prepare our bundles, and return the mats that belonged to the ship. A little later, the ship left and when we were further out to sea, we were given our mats back.

The wonders of everything that my eyes see are impossible to describe. Here are around one hundred or more ships anchored. A section of them are busy loading and unloading. The manner in which they do this is wonderful. They have large built areas and walls on which there are buildings and railway lines where the trains bring goods to and from the ships – steamboats and small ships, too many to count.

The Cape is next to the sea, closely built up. Also, there are big houses. Further away are scattered blockhouses and as far as my eyes can see are more single houses. Plantations are against the highest part of the mountains, and for this reason it must be very fertile. I also see high towers rising above the houses.

And deeper into the sea we see a small island that just appears above the water, and the island's centre is a little higher. I can also see a little town there. Now I hear its name; it is Robben Island. Further, a wonderful animal [a Cape seal] swims next to the ship; the head looks like a lion, his length about six feet, his width about three feet.[23]

Six decades later, Robben Island will become synonymous with another, infinitely more famous prisoner who fought for his freedom: Nelson Mandela. This unwanted war, involving the Boers and their attendant suffering, sowed the seeds of that long, second freedom struggle.

'They say it is the funeral of the Queen,' was Michael's next entry, on Saturday 2 February 1901; he recorded the frequent firing of cannons to mark Victoria's funeral at Windsor Castle, so far away.

They were now anchored off Cape Town, and he noted that the next day, the stormy sea tossed the ship from side to side so that they were all thrown around 'like sea water'.

The next several days were distressing, not only because of the continuously howling wind (not unusual in summer), but also because there was yet another unnerving disturbance on board. On 5 February he wrote that about 150 Boers were told to pack up and leave their cabins.

When they were at the door of the cabin, they were all searched by
the *English*. Their bundles were shaken out. They allege that £25
and a gold watch was taken and yet they were unable to find anything but a pocket knife that one of our burgers had bought from a
trooper. Fortunately he could prove that with reliable evidence, and
the burgers were sent back to their cabins again.

This unhappy contestation took place while their ship, and those near them,
heaved around on the wild waves; so bad was it that the Boers commented
they could not believe that the small service steamboats did not sink, for
their decks were continually swamped.

On the morning of 9 February, all the prisoners' goods were returned
to the quartermaster, including everything made of canvas, such as their
shoes. The *Kildonan* docked in Cape Town harbour at 8.30 am, and at noon
the men disembarked, and boarded another vessel, the *Armenian*. This
8 825-ton cargo ship, built in 1895, had set sail for Cape Town from England
on 23 October 1899, carrying 658 horses and more than 700 British soldiers
for war duty.

Now that Michael was on a berthed ship, he had a bird's-eye view of the
world around him and it was of great fascination to him.

> Everything I see here, the dock, is built like an enormous *kraal* [live-
> stock enclosure] where fifty or sixty ships can go in at the same time.
> In the kraal there are also platforms [quays] pointing to the middle.
> At every platform, two ships can unload at the same time ... [He
> is so fascinated by this sight that he draws a rough diagram of the
> docks.]
>   There is a great buzz of people. Scotch carts [two-wheelers pulled
> by an ox] and trolly-wagons bring goods to and from the ships.
>   At 12.30 pm the ship pulls away from the docks and anchors about
> 2 000 paces from there.
>   In the afternoon we receive no food, and in the evening each man
> gets two potatoes the size of chicken eggs and a piece of meat about
> the same size and a little meat broth.

Despite his indignation about the insufficient food rations, Michael tried
to make the best of his situation. At dusk, he and his brother-in-law Ou-

baas Terblans stood on the deck and looked at the thousands of lights of Cape Town. Michael wrote:

> It made me think that it is actually nine months this evening since I last saw the light in my own house, when I had to tear myself away from all that is dear to me. And today is also my little son's [fourth] birthday. Oh, how I long for home.

Nostalgia began to hit hard, for they knew that soon they would be transported far away. He had just read the *Genevan Psalter*, a Calvinist songbook of psalms translated into Dutch in 1565, a devotional work much used by the Boers, which he admitted he could not read without tears, but said also that he had found much comfort in it. He remarked to a friend in the evening, as they stood on deck: 'How wonderful it is to watch the sun go down on the sea.'

In the afternoon of 13 February

> the ship *Kildonan* goes forth with a large contingent of troops. The ship's captain, who has become a friend of ours, sailed close to us to give us a farewell greeting with his handkerchief. He keeps on until there is a great distance between us. When he left us, he said that he recognises us as his brothers, and there is a strong bond of affection that has developed between him and us.

Thus they said farewell to the one true friend they had had since their capture, Captain Robinson of the *Kildonan*. The Boers cheered him as the ship disappeared.

The bubonic plague holds a particular grip on history, most markedly the Black Death which swept through Europe in the mid-1300s when a least a third of the population died (even the record-keepers died, so accurate data has never been established). Though there have been other bubonic plague epidemics, it was that particular one that set the yardstick for sheer dread.

The date of Michael's note about *de pest* (the plague) was Friday 15 February 1901, just a week after the first public admission of its presence, in the *Cape Times*, with predictable results. Panic gripped the city, and large posters with huge black lettering warned of the disease, with instructions on what to do if the pestilence appeared; in truth, there was not much practical help. There was no known cure, though an early vaccine – subject to much suspicion – was beginning to be used. Few, including some medical doctors, understood what caused it, although 'filth' was earmarked as a culprit (raising the obvious question as to why some perfectly clean, prosperous homes were infected). What actually causes it is the bacillus *Yersinia pestis,* and it arrived as a direct result of the war.

Britain's war effort needed huge amounts of fodder for its equally huge numbers of doomed horses, and also mules. Fodder supply ships, ploughing their way across the oceans to Cape Town from the Americas, also carried rats, which carried fleas, which in turn carried the plague bacillus. From port, the rats hopped on trains, and so began to spread inland.

A few isolated cases of plague had been contained in 1900, but early February 1901 a large number of dying rats in the Cape Town docks were reported to the officer of health for the Cape Colony. Of the 45 patients diagnosed with the plague that month, 20 had worked in the docks or nearby.

By the middle of March, over 130 cases of plague were reported in the Peninsula, 56 of them fatal. Port Elizabeth followed soon, then other key ports. A plague hospital was set up on the Cape Flats, with heroic work done by medical doctors and nurses, some of whom lost their lives.

Within a relatively short time, in early May, it was clear that the worst was over, with around a thousand fatalities. The plague was never totally eradicated, though; for the first time it became endemic, and it remains so among rodents far inland. Now and then, an unlucky human case is still reported, a long left-over of this war.

It did, however, have a peculiarly South African side-effect: the beginnings of enforced racialisation of living areas. Because rats prefer human congestion, and because dock labourers, usually non-white Capetonians, lived in crowded conditions, fingers were pointed at them. This led to the exclusion of Africans from the 'white' areas of British-occupied Cape Town; some 6 000 were forced to leave their homes in the city centre 'for their own good' and were taken under armed supervision to a tented area several miles away. There they remained until the end of the war when, by passing special legislation, their habitat, known as Ndabeni, was declared permanent.

The *Cape Argus* coolly noted on 20 February 1901 that the plague might therefore be a 'blessing in disguise'.

Johannesburg quickly used the Cape's example as a precedent to burn down the 'Coolie [sic] locations'. Watching this desperate spectacle in disgust was a young Indian lawyer, MK Gandhi, who served as a stretcher-bearer during the war.

As it had so often before, the plague again altered the course of history, this time in South Africa.

Meanwhile, on the *Armenian* things were not going smoothly. Something else had broken out on board, and this time it was a political storm. On 19 February, the ship's captain asked his Boer prisoners if they would allow General Piet de Wet to come on board to speak to them. He and a fellow contingent of 'peacemakers' – joiners – had arrived in Cape Town to speak to Boer groups, including those in the Green Point POW camp, which had caused explosive reactions.

Of the three De Wet brothers (from a family of 14 siblings) from the Free State who fought in the Boer War, the first two, Christiaan and Piet, became generals, while the third, veldkornet Jan de Wet, died at Magersfontein. (The especially awful war carnage in Jan de Wet's family[24] has been sidelined in the persistent controversy around his two more famous brothers.)

It seems there was an element of 'the war in the nursery' between the two competing brother-generals. Christiaan was known for his fierce determination, and agility in thought and in the saddle. He was the ultimate *bittereinder* ('bitter-ender' or 'irreconcilable', those who refused to surrender) whose fable grew as he eluded capture time and again.

Piet was more conventional, though no less brave, and perhaps more acutely sensitive to the destruction of 'family and farm' he had witnessed during the autumn of 1900, as British forces pressed towards the eastern part of the Free State.

Piet had frequent arguments with his brother and other senior Boers about the sense of continuing what he felt was an unwinnable war resulting in a conquered and bankrupt Free State. Christiaan was furious with this attitude, and refused to even entertain the idea of surrender. Piet differed, strongly, and offered his surrender on 26 July 1900 at Kroonstad. When Christiaan de Wet heard what had happened, he was reported as saying he preferred rather that his brother been shot dead.

Piet de Wet was considered even worse than a *hensopper*: not only had he surrendered, but he then played an active role in persuading other Boers to do so, and therefore crossed over into that cesspool of collaborators, the joiners.

It was this last act that blackened his reputation, not only during the remainder of the war but permanently, considered forever a traitor to his people still struggling for their freedom. He was undoubtedly right in his prediction that the Boers could not, despite their determined efforts, win the war; but he was wrong to assume a role that resulted in placing in jeopardy not only the morale, and therefore the lives, of his former comrades still in the field, but also their negotiating strength at the end of the war. That there were still more than 19 000 active and determined combatants at the time of the Treaty of Vereeniging in May 1902, by which time Britain was heartily sick of what 'should' have been a short war of invasion, was one of the few important cards the Boers held (no joiners or *hensoppers* were allowed to participate in this peace process).

General Christiaan de Wet never acknowledged Piet as his brother again; when they met by chance at a Kroonstad hotel at the end of the war, he had to be restrained from assaulting Piet.

So asking that Piet de Wet be allowed on board the *Armenian* to 'talk' to the Boer POWs was an incendiary move, and there were immediate repercussions, including a 'big commotion' among the Boers. The request was emphatically denied.

On the evening of 19 February 1901 Michael remarked with annoyance that a list had been going around the ship by those who were pro-English, suggesting that 'simple Boers' were being misled by their leaders. This was an interesting comment from Michael, the first directly political one he had made.

A couple of weeks later, on 7 March, he again remarked on these goings-on:

> Someone goes around with a petition and he claims that he represents those who would go home [take the oath of neutrality and therefore be allowed to return to their farms]. I think something is suspicious.

This thorny issue, of meeting De Wet's joiners, was not resolved.

On 12 March Michael recorded, with simmering alarm, that a meeting was held to send a representative to the *English*, though he did not know for what purpose.

This proposed meeting was put on hold for a while, as the *Armenian* set sail on 13 March for Simon's Town, having first taken on another hundred POWs.

On their arrival the following day, a great number of them were taken to Bellevue camp. Rumours flew. Another large group was marched to the camp the next day, while Michael and others remained on board.

The meaning of all this activity became clear when he heard, shocked, that General Piet de Wet was at Bellevue, trying to convert POWs

> to work against our government. And seventeen men spoke against him, and for that reason they were sent back to the ship.

It began to dawn on those remaining on the *Armenian* that there was method in this seeming madness of trekking them all the way by ship back to Simon's Town – it was precisely to entice them to listen to Piet de Wet's call to end the war. The men marched to Bellevue camp were seen as potential converts. The Boers left on board hastily chose new captains and corporals, according to Michael, to ensure that those ranks were kept in the hands of loyalists.

Their suspicions would later prove well founded; records show that when the *Armenian* eventually set sail for Bermuda, it was filled with men – including Michael – who refused to entertain the notion of 'giving up'. These POWs were *bittereinders*, those who refused to turn their backs on their leaders. How they rejoiced at snippets of news about the exploits of fellow Boers who remained active in their commandos, the De Wets and De la Reys and those alongside them, no matter the hardships – which were considerable.

For the rest of the war, Bellevue became a camp for *hensoppers*, Boers who agreed to sign the oaths of neutrality and allegiance to the Crown. They were given the label 'political prisoners', with some special privileges. By the end of the war, there were about a thousand of them left in the camp; they were finally released on 5 July 1902, after which Bellevue was turned into a transit camp for Boers being repatriated from the overseas camps – though many flatly refused to enter it, once back on South African soil, pointing out that they were now free men.

Bellevue finally closed for war business in 1903.

Michael had been trapped on board the *Armenian* for two months, and now it was March 1901, the hottest time of the South African summer. The men were terribly cramped, without the relative space of the camp and those sea swims every day, and the busy life of cooking, cleaning, singing and games that had kept them active.

He and many fellow prisoners felt their hardship keenly. They were not told where or when they were to be transported, though they daily dreaded the inevitable break with their parental subcontinent. Their fate lay as *banneling*, so deep a hardship that only those who have experienced it can understand its particular agony.

Michael was in many ways an innocent man, and would continue to be so, throughout his life. He believed in God, duty, country and loyalty. His notion was that those entrusted with authority were honourable men who could be counted on. He could not believe that his Lord would let His devout people down, and it was a shock for him to discover that so many men, more worldly, saw things differently. His world had begun to rock, imitating the ship's movement, seemingly firm underfoot, yet ready at any moment to fling him around, like the flotsam and jetsam bobbing in the busy harbours. Michael's dismay at his fellow Boers who had given up the war, and the stress of his months as a POW, became a crisis.

He had never before faltered, but now he did – not in his devotion to his God and his country and his family, which for him were indivisible; but to the tendrils of self-doubt, suspicion and dread that began to trickle through his dreams, both waking and asleep. His daily entries from now on became ragged, brief, even nonexistent.

> I feel this day the weight of a whole mountain resting on me. I told of my condition to three of my brethren, whereupon we knelt together and asked the Lord to help me. It slightly lifted my spirits but I was still heavily laden.

He reported the following afternoon that he felt a slight respite from the gloom, but later it returned, and so on 20 March he asked the leaders of the church to pray for him. They did, and during that evening prayer he felt released of his weight, as if the Lord had listened.

But the relief did not last long, for the next day his depression returned and he was in crisis.

> A thousand fires burn in my heart. I turned from the Lord through
> a lack of faith. My God, once more give me grace.

The next day he felt no better, with 'the fires' still burning inside him. But the nadir of his crisis had been reached, and, with the support of his comrades, he seemed to sink no further. A Sunday service on the 24th encouraged him, and a couple of days later he wrote, 'My head is clear and at last I come to rest.'

Although he no longer complained, it was evident from his diary that his crisis had taken its toll. No longer was he routinely recording every date and day of the week, the weather, and whatever slight information there was at hand. Now he began just to jot down the date, and/or day of the week (sometimes altered, indicating his stressed state of mind), and on Sunday, the last day in March, he simply recorded: 'I forgot to write.'

Then followed a long delay in his entries, the next on 13 April 1901, when he noted he had posted a letter to his wife, and again on 18 April, writing that a crowd of people were told to leave the ship.

His last entry in April is poignant. On the 21st he recorded an anxiety dream 'that Pieter has passed away and that me and my wife hold hands when he dies'. Pieter, his first-born and the only child he had had the time to know before the war, was the symbol of his future, his still-possible destiny. The child's death would, in his troubled mind, destroy that potential.

17

Michael's unspeakable voyage to Bermuda

IT WAS THE middle of May, a deceptive month in the Cape, for though it is autumn and many of the days are mild and lovely, it is also when the first great cold fronts stream in from the Antarctic; the most destructive Cape storms are almost invariably recorded in this month, as Michael found out the hard way. After a long gap, his 12 May entry read:

> We leave Simon's Town and encounter a storm at sea that almost leaves us dead. Fortunately, the captain found a mountain for protection, where we anchored.
>
> Around 2 pm we leave for Cape Town. We were in great distress. The sea was so rough that the ship lay first on one side, then on the other. No one could stand without holding onto something.

After this shocking voyage he was grateful to be on dry land for a while, in Green Point camp.

Yet again there are no entries, until the crisp, fateful day he had been dreading for almost a year: '29 May: We leave Cape Town.'

And this time it was not back to Simon's Town, that familiar ping-pong maritime game that had been going on for months. It was now the wide and turbulent Atlantic that confronted him and the other Boers, most of whom were unaccustomed to the ocean, many of whom could not swim, and who had already endured the unfamiliar terrors of ship life, from fire on board to wild storms. What lay before them seemed to contain awe and dread, in the full, biblical sense.

This, and the emotional crisis that Michael had just gone through, would persuade him that the present was unreliable, and embolden him to make a radical change of religious belief during his POW future.

The *Armenian* carried its human cargo to Bermuda, where camps had been especially, and reluctantly, built to accommodate them. Michael was jammed in with nearly a thousand other men, crammed into compartments that were originally designed for horses. There was heat and seasickness and homesickness, and just plain sickness. The single blessing was that none of the 963 on board died during the voyage. (The *Montrose,* which later carried two shipments of POWs to Bermuda, lost 28 men during its trips; the survivors nicknamed it the *Morte Rose.*)

James Molloy, who had been a POW in Green Point camp with Michael's brother Lool, was on the ship, and during the voyage, his 'Ballad of Philip Cronje' was heard by the POWs. It seems probable that this was how Michael found out about the shooting of the hymn-singing soldier, and also firmer details of what had happened to his own brother.

Michael offered almost no details of his voyage, though records by others reveal how terrible it was. Their plight was recorded vividly in the war diary of one GJ van Riet. There were 580 men in hammocks in his compartment alone; the only way that men could reach their own hammock was by crawling on their hands and knees underneath them.

Crossing the equator was pure hell in those confined quarters, even more so for the 'maniac' who was kept in a cell in the sweaty bowels of the ship, whom Van Riet volunteered to watch over (and who died). It reminded Van Riet, he recorded on that horrible night, of Milton's description of Hades. After midnight, drunken British troops rushed down among the POWs, cursing and beating tin plates. There were 3 000 miles of water between him and his native land, he wrote bleakly: it must have felt like three million.

The food was dire: breakfast consisted of almost-raw oats and a cup of dirty water called tea; dinner was oats boiled up as soup. One day they got animal protein – in the unwelcome form of a dead rat in the soup.

Dysentery broke out on board, and three corpses were carried out.

On Christmas Day 1901, the men, to their surprise, actually received pudding with their dinner – their other 'Christmas present' being the discovery of lice.

The POWs, including Michael, were extremely anxious about Bermuda, of which they knew nothing. During this voyage, a group of prisoners tried to hijack the vessel and sail it to Holland. The coup was foiled and the mutineers were locked up on arrival.

Nothing, including warfare, had prepared Michael for the frightful trip to Bermuda, added to which was the fear that he would never see home and his loved ones again. Perhaps because it was so unspeakable, he simply could not bring himself to write it down.

On 16 June he recorded briefly that they had arrived, en route, at the island of St Vincent, one of the Cape Verde cluster of islands in the shallow waters of the eastern Atlantic. This stopover was mainly to pick up more coal, but it was also a very welcome sight of land with its lovely mountains and active volcano, and boys diving for pennies.

And his last entry in his only known diary, on 1 July 1901, was simply: 'We climb off at Bermuda.'

18

Touchy days in Ceylon – Chris

STILL CONVALESCING AT Mount Lavinia, in early January 1901, Chris had woken early and felt very unwell, and dwelled on the pain and suffering of the year past. The men had ordered a special pudding but he could not eat it.

Then he had a skirmish with a British lieutenant who arrived to confiscate all their money; they reluctantly relinquished some, but not all. Chris remonstrated with him that this was insulting, but the officer replied with the old adage that he was just following orders. Stung by this, the men lay on the grass and sang folksongs of the Free State and Transvaal and fulminated until late.

Chris was prickly at this stage, complaining about the food, tea without milk, bread without butter or jam, and the Tommies who searched for them if they went walking after dark. He was annoyed they were treated with such mistrust; he felt that as an officer, his word was his bond – a nice thought, though not always true in wartime.

The bickering continued about the food. The governor arrived for a visit and ordered that fish be given to them twice a week. Then there was a pleasing arrival of tablecloths, saucers, mustard pots and teapots, the tables now set for dining 'with everything shining and a bunch of flowers on each table'. Their complaining had paid off. Gradually they settled in as the conditions and the food improved.

They were getting used to the stir they caused when they went out in public: a 'beautiful young lady' followed them to the beach and they were happy to pose for her. While chatting, she told them of her surprise that they all spoke and understood English.

Chris remembered on 5 January 1901 that it was his brother Pieter's birthday, and two days later that 'today is Mullertjie's birthday. I think a lot about him, and this takes me back a long way.' He was referring to his little son, Pieter, who had died early the previous year, just a year old.

They managed to get their hands on a copy of the *Ceylon Standard* and devoured it for news, noting that the Boers had advanced deep into the Cape Colony under the leadership of Smuts, and that prisoners were still being loaded onto troopships for exile.

General Roux appeared with news that a ship filled with burgers had docked, but that he had not yet been allowed to speak to them. He was accompanied by two local youths bearing a box of delicious bananas from one of their mothers, with a card, 'To my Boer friends', and an invitation to visit when Chris was able.

Another milestone: on 12 January 1901 it was his 'dear Johanna's birthday', his only surviving child.

The Dutch consul visited, promised them fatty meat, as they felt theirs was too lean – Boers were used to fatty cuts – as well as coffee and books. He kept his word and a few days later the promised rations arrived, addressed to Chris, who also received letters from his sister Johanna, and his brother Pieter in Diyatalawa.

The doctor agreed with Chris that they were not getting enough food and visited the kitchen, after which portions increased.

To his delight, Andries Meyer and other friends arrived at Mount Lavinia to recuperate.

On 18 January there was a sudden fright. They were sitting at table when they spotted a long snake at the door, which they killed. Then they spent the afternoon playing *kennetjie*, a children's game of flipping sticks, until the perspiration poured off them.

A man and a woman, obviously newlyweds on their honeymoon, were seen strolling down the beach from the hotel. They were walking with their arms around each other's waists. The man casually slapped his wife's bottom a couple of times, Chris wrote, and the men made 'many remarks'. His thwarted desire oozed off the page.

This available beach was a democratic space, the only one they had. It was open to the public, as to them (within certain hours), and as they strolled along it, swimming and chatting to passersby, they had a feeling of freedom and normalcy that they had felt at no other place in the war. Once they became used to it, this relaxed, quieter atmosphere was a tonic, a convalescence from not only their severe illness but also from daily discord in their POW camp, and from the dragging war.

They heard 'in secret' that General de Wet was fighting a brave battle against the *English* – no newspapers arrived for them on that day, and they thought this was why. Then, on 23 January 1901, they read that the Old Queen had died.

The next evening there were high jinks in the hut; after lights-out the men begin pulling each other off their beds.

> One of them took the leaf of an arum lily and stuck it between his legs. He was in the nude and the sap from the leaf burnt him like fire on his dangerous places.

This was considered a good joke, though not for the sufferer.

On another occasion, the young burgers dressed up as Scottish troops with paper hats, no pants, and towels for 'dresses' – kilts – which made them all laugh.

Sometimes it got out of hand – a lamp was broken – and Chris, as the most senior Boer, tried to stop it but their high spirits returned once he went to sleep. It was clear that they were getting better.

Mrs Mack, a local of Dutch descent, was extraordinarily generous to them, frequently sending food and other treats. On one particular day she sent a banquet of foods, including bread, salads and two suckling pigs. Though Chris should not yet have eaten meat, he tucked into one of the heads, a delicacy.

The Macks continued to do what they could, not only for the convalescents but also for those who returned to Diyatalawa after their stay at Mount Lavinia; Chris recorded with appreciation the parcels they sent to him there.

But worry still lurked below the surface. On Sunday 10 February 1901 he received an alarming letter from a friend at home, who advised him that his family had been told to be ready to be sent away at a moment's notice to 'headquarters', meaning the camps. He was overwhelmed with anxiety and grief, and just six days later he noted that it was exactly a year since his first war wounding, his leg.

More pranks and pitfalls at Mount Lavinia: one night a man somehow managed to fall into a wild prickly pear tree, an awful mistake. His legs were so full of the fine sharp spines that he had to seek medical help, and he was so crippled he could scarcely walk.

Abruptly, their time there came to an end; they had several last swims until they were quite worn out.

On 23 February 1901 Chris arrived back in Diyatalawa camp, having been gone for three full months, in hospital and then at the coast. He immediately visited Father Willem and several cousins who had arrived during his absence.

But it would be months before Chris felt fully well. He veered from recovery to relapse, and frequently referred to his recurring headaches.

Chris (seated right, with a cane and hat on knee) in Diyatalawa camp with other POWs in Ceylon, 1901. Chris's father-in-law, Willem Nel, 'Father Willem', is seated next to him, his hand also resting on a cane.

Back in Diyatalawa, Chris remembered Cronjé's surrender on its anniversary, 27 February. A slew of rumours and lies were now flying around the camp about the war's progress.

A lie can be a big one, but as long as it is in our favour and against the enemy, they believe it and cheer it.

Despite his steadfastness, Chris hoped for eventual victory, but was not convinced of it. He had seen too much of the giant imperial machine to imagine that the Boers had the resources to conquer it, though many around him could not recognise this.

On 8 March 1901, after attending a debating society meeting, Chris and others rolled out to watch the Tommies have a mock battle.

The band played beautifully as they marched . . . it was a beautiful sight, everyone in red jackets and white hats and the band playing so well. In such moments, no one can know what goes on in the minds of prisoners who are far from home . . .

Meyer and Strauss had, rather astonishingly, completed their organ, and on the afternoon of 13 March, Chris and Father Willem went to hear it played.

Then Chris heard that his brother Pieter was in hospital, and the earlier shock of young Lool's death rose like a spectre. He visited Pieter during the following days, including on 17 March, when he noted, compounding his misery, that it was his five-year wedding anniversary; he wrote a letter to his wife Dorie and little Joey with a 'sorrowful heart'.

An emotional event occurred on 21 March, when 3 000 POWs attended the farewell sermon of *Dominee* Murray, on his way home. Chris later sent his wife a clipping from one of their several news sheets that included the *Diyatalawa Dum-Dum* and the *Prikkeldraad* (Barbed Wire); it carried two newsprint photographs of an enormous group of men on the side of a small hill, on top of which are perched a few zinc huts. It was a deeply moving ceremony, especially when the choir sang, beautifully, 'God be with thee till we meet again', and Chris was among many who 'cried a lot'. How hard it was to say farewell to their minister when they, too, longed to leave; it would have been even harder had they realised that it would be another 18 months, at least, before that happened.

On Sunday 24 March 1901 Chris attended a service for young people by General Roux (who was also a *dominee*). Late that afternoon, he walked out of the camp alone and sat above it, watching all the bustle. 'Oh! Then the thoughts surged through my mind and an involuntary tear comes into my eye, and a thousand tears in my heart.' A year before, he had been a toughened commandant leading his soldiers into pitched battle; now, he was a sickly and helpless prisoner. No wonder he was nervy.

He took refuge in small tasks.

> On 4 April I took the whole day to mend, darn and wash. I also hemmed a handkerchief which I made from flannelette. By 12 o'clock I was finished and all my sheets, etc, were pure white. I folded them and let someone sit on them. This is my ironing. At 3 o'clock, debating society. It rained hard.

Despite the mundane, there remained an exotic quality to their lives in Ceylon that never quite vanished. He tried a 'Ceylon peach', a sweet, new fruit; and on 15 April he recorded that an elephant procession had arrived. The villagers were celebrating their New Year wearing flamboyant costumes.

> Some . . . had bells on their legs, and still others were beating on drums and so on. It made a deafening noise – in the evening there were fireworks . . .with rockets bursting in the air.

Cheerful, girl-mad Johnny Brink had left Chris's hut to join General Roux in his cottage. Chris was sorry to see him go, but luckily he was replaced the next day, 21 April, with the return of his friends, including Andries Meyer, from Mount Lavinia. This was a 'great joy' for Chris.

The next day, however, he had to take leave of his brother Pieter, who was only now being sent to Mount Lavinia for recovery. The brothers wrote to one another while apart, but those letters have not survived.

One of the men returning to Diyatalawa was grief-stricken. He told Chris he had received a letter informing him that his wife and three children had died in the concentration camps. 'Oh!' wrote Chris, 'this was a heavy burden for a man to bear' – and one that he himself dreaded, as they all did.

Almost every post contained news of the deaths of loved ones, mainly children, sometimes wives and occasionally entire multi-generational families. The fearful fatalities in the British concentration camps would end in a frightful tally of more than 30 000 Boers, mainly the young (not including the even worse conditions in the black concentration camps, where accurate records were not kept).

This ongoing domestic death tally was shattering for the POWs. They had willingly committed themselves to war, never imagining that the small bodies of their children would be the price. There would be consequences.

Chris was hypersensitive at this stage, and to a large extent remained so for most of 1901. He complained of the rowdiness of officers letting off steam in his hut at night, keeping him awake; he was fearful that some real injury would be caused. These high jinks were important for keeping up morale, but he couldn't see it. What did the Tommies think of us as officers, he wondered. And what about the poor wives and children in misery, praying for their menfolk and pitying them?

> And who knows but that some of us are widowers and our children orphans. And, above all, our position and the state of our country. Such carryings-on should be forbidden.

He was not strong enough to insist they stop, but his glumness showed.

May arrived, and Chris noted that it was exactly a year since he had last spent a whole day with his 'darling'. The following day, 12 May 1901, was even harder for him, a year since he had said goodbye to his wife and child

> whom I long for. The farewell would have been even worse had I known that the separation would be so long . . .
>
> At 2 o'clock I went to the service for young people, as I still consider myself a youth.

This was an interesting comment. On the battlefield he had seen himself as a man among men, a 'commander'; just a year back, he would not have offered such a comment about himself.

On 15 May his close friend Andries received the horrible news that his wife had been captured. Chris anxiously scanned his own letters now, from his wife, his sister Johanna and other family members, though none of them were imprisoned in camps and all would remain free, some as refugees in the nearby protectorate of Basutoland.

Continued news of the plight of their women and children had two diverse effects on the imprisoned Boers. On the constructive side, they set up another exhibition of their handiwork, which was sent to Holland to raise funds for those in the concentration camps at home; on the other hand, some of the men began increasingly to act out their anger.

A few tried to escape and were recaptured after six days (there was a bounty on the heads of escaping Boers). Camp regulations were tightened and the Boers were ordered to sit at their tables to be counted. Though this was not an unreasonable request, it provided a crack through which the pressure-cooker of rage and resentment boiled. Some of the Tommies and burgers got into a scrap, the face of one of the Tommies was badly injured, and the camp turned raucous.

A Boer officer out on parole returned so drunk that he was taken to the cells, though later that night he was returned to the hut without his blankets, which had been left behind. Out of pity, Chris lent him one of his own, for the high altitude meant that nights were now cold – the camp was so high that frost sometimes occurred in winter. Chris was upset by this episode.

Agonising news was received almost daily of the fatalities back home; it consumed them. Chris, thankfully, received letters from his 'darling Dorothea', confirming she was still fine.

On 18 June, the head of Chris's school told the men that some women had died of starvation in parts of the Transvaal. Each burger was asked to give six cents to send to South Africa for the women and children; those who had no money (and there were many) could save their sugar and send it. A few days later, most of the officers added a rupee.

Despite their suffering, the women in the camps continued to support their soldiers; their resolution never failed to astonish, given what peril they faced. One defiant woman announced: 'I can get another husband, but not another Free State!'

On 26 June 1901 Chris and other officers were photographed, and in the evening they listened to the band playing beautifully.

Dorie's birthday was on 28 June.

> Oh! how I thought of her today. First of all I thought of the kiss I would have given her this morning.
>
> On my return [after a walk] I receive a letter and portrait of my wife. Oh, what joy, and a feeling of heartsore and longing. That night I dreamed of my Dorie.

The next day, on returning from the hospital where a relative was recovering, he saw 'three ladies' walking in the camp and thought of his darling wife again. Here, he closed his latest diary in Ceylon. 'If only I could place it in her hand,' he wrote.

The first six months of 1901 sapped more from Chris than had his whole active war, and his woundings, the previous year. Those days of saddle and veld seemed as distant and elusive as the mountain mists.

For the remaining six months of that year, Chris's thoughts turned more and more to his wife, Dorie, whom he progressively idolised. He placed her portrait in a frame and it stood on his bedside table, and he sometimes picked flowers to decorate it. He created a shrine to his love, and enjoyed other men complimenting him on her attractiveness. He was also thrilled when a letter from 'Mrs Kriel' (of the Kriels who fought with the Muller brothers) told him that Dorie was 'just as beautiful as when I left her'.

As time stretched their forced separation, he increasingly sentimentalised their relationship, harking back to it as the perfect, still centre of his world during a happier time. His diaries, so bold when he was on commando, were now filled with effusive terms: 'my dear', 'my darling little wife'.

In a brassy, all-male prison world, it is not unusual to retreat into a kindlier memory for comfort, for consolation. The three Muller diary-writers engaged in the emotionally soothing rituals of memory in differing ways: Chris turned to his wife, Michael to a new relationship with his God, and Lool to the memory of his mother as he lay ill and dying.

Chris had been carefully observing what he considered the civil and refined behaviour of the officers who were his captors. His diligence in his lessons were part of a conscious programme of self-improvement, and though he was never other than an Afrikaner, he internalised some of the enemy's genteel habits and mannerisms. It was one way of surviving captivity with an intact ego.

His handwriting was no longer a hasty scrawl, but regular, well formed and precise. For the rest of his life he would be a neat, erect and well-groomed man who would strive for 'the better things of life'. And he would become the most successful of the three surviving Muller brothers after the war.

Keeping busy, he and Father Willem found time to walk and talk, and visit the cows in the dairy. He placed a rose, given by a friend, in front of

Dorie's portrait and mooned over it. He visited bereaved friends to com-
miserate with news of family losses. He heard, on 10 July, via a letter, that
his brother Michael had been sent to Bermuda, and also that Andries
Meyer's wife was back in Ladybrand after her capture.

The politicking continued in the camp: some officers thought they should
make things more difficult for their captors; others, including Chris, believed they should not stoop to the level of their enemy. It got heated as
loyalties were challenged.

Chris was furious when, on 25 July 1901, the captains of the huts called
them together and demanded they sign a document devised by them, de-
claring they would remain loyal to their governments.

> It was like a sword in my heart to think that a lot of hut captains
> should dare to do something like this – to ask a true Afrikaner, and
> also an officer, to sign a second oath . . . After much discussion the
> document was unanimously rejected, at my suggestion.

But some hut captains and their supporters were not satisfied; the sophistry
of Chris's objection evaded them. As fervour mounted, they demanded a
demonstration of national pride, and began to blame the hold-outs for 'not
doing their duty' by signing this oath of loyalty to the Boer cause.

Chris and his supporters thought that their loyalty was so obvious and
unquestionable that they should not be required to prove it. 'What harm
can it do?' was the response.

It was an impasse. All were, in fact, on the same side, but they turned
on each other instead of their actual enemy: this, the classic politics of
frustration.

The row led to more ructions in the camp, and two days later, at the
Broederlikonderhoud (Mens' Fellowship, a Christian group), General Roux
told Chris that he had been prohibited from preaching due to the unrest.
Chris felt spiritually ill at ease, and tried to calm himself by sitting and
gazing at his wife's portrait (one wonders if that did not make things worse).

On 28 July 1901, it had been a year since they were caught at Slaapkrans, he wrote, and two days later he recalled that it was exactly a year
since they had laid down their arms at Surrender Hill.

A week later, on 6 August, General Roux was removed, along with about ten others, including the ubiquitous Johnny Brink, to Ragama camp just north of the main port city of Colombo. This small camp, with little room for exercise, had opened on 8 January 1901. It had earlier been the plague camp and had advanced security measures: a wire-net fence and a zareba, that zigzag barbed-wire formation, and, an added touch of sophistication, an electric alarm.

Ragama camp was referred to as the 'problem' camp. Five officers who refused to go out on parole for exercise, for example, were sent there, and the threat of being despatched to it hung like a sword of Damocles over everything the men did. Ragama housed 262 men and officers, 'foreigners' from over twenty different nations who had been captured while fighting for the Boers, including Ireland, England and Scotland, as well as the United States, Russia, Scandinavia and elsewhere: they were deemed treasonous, and were treated as criminals rather than POWs.

A short while before, Chris and friends had been teasing Johnny Brink about fancying the 'brown ladies' of the island: now Chris mentioned that he felt disappointed in Johnny, for he had left without saying goodbye to anyone. But, he added, 'I feel sorry for him because he barks with all the hounds and therefore gets into trouble.'

The departure of these men, considered 'irreconcilables', was a divisive jolt. Some, like Chris, felt they had caused unnecessary trouble, while others felt they were heroes and surrounded them as they left, singing national anthems. The whole business left a bad odour.

19

A prisoner in Bermuda – Michael

THE CARGO SHIP on which Michael had endured his unspeakable journey across the Atlantic from Cape Town dropped anchor in Grassy Bay, Bermuda, on 28 June 1901. A crane and a basket, used when there was no quay available, offloaded four men at a time. This, and offloading the cargo on board, took several days, hence the discrepancy between Michael's diarised date (1 July), and their official date of arrival.

He spent the rest of his war – another full year – on Darrell's Island, hardly any distance at all from the Bermuda mainland; it was one of the camps of the *bittereinders*. Quiet Michael may not have been a man who 'made waves' but he was a man of sturdy principles, even when it cost him dearly.

His new home was a small, narrow strip of land less than half a mile in length – not much space for so many prisoners. This cramped island was further divided into two by a high barbed-wire fence, one side for Boer prisoners, the other for their guards. The fence threaded through abundant tall trees, native cypresses and cedars, which provided wood as well as natural shade. Where fence met sea, wooden poles were set in concrete so that the barbed wire extended some way into the water. Between the two sections there was a single, tall iron gate, topped with long angled spikes.

Wooden 'sheds' were used as pontoon latrines on rafts, floating just off-shore and reached by a gangplank. It doesn't bear contemplating what that shoreline was like after a thousand men had completed their morning visit.

Boer prisoners were exiled in their thousands to British colonies: first to the nearest, St Helena (almost 6 000 in April 1900 alone); then to Ceylon;

and later, more than 9 000 to India. Even Portugal entered the fray, owing to the many Boer refugees in then-Portuguese East Africa (today Mozambique) – these 1 500 men, women and children were held in open camps in and around Lisbon, and were treated as parolees.

Bermuda was one of the last colonies to be ordered to accept prisoners; they could hardly refuse, but it was a thorny issue. The 17 000 residents of Bermuda were not exactly thrilled to discover that they were about to have thousands of Boer prisoners foisted on them. This small, pretty cluster of islands relied on tourism as its main revenue then, as now. It has a sub-tropical climate, balmy seas and relatively good weather – apart from the major drawback of it being in the 'hurricane belt'. Water was one of the legitimate concerns of Bermuda residents, just as it had been in Simon's Town, particularly as Bermuda was experiencing its most severe drought in 30 years.

Michael was in the first shipment of Boer POWs to Bermuda. The canny governor made no mention of their imminent arrival during a debate in May 1901; he waited until the ship had actually dropped anchor before passing martial law.

Residents were slightly mollified on hearing that the Boers would not be kept on the mainland of Bermuda, but on the many little coral islands just offshore, within the curve of the Great Sound: Darrell's (not even a mile from the shore, it housed the main telephone exchange connected to all the other islands including the guard-post on the mainland), Burt's (the smallest island camp, set aside for the most resistant *bittereinders*, plus 27 Boer officers, on whom the authorities kept a beady eye), Hawkins', Port's (on which there was a hospital), Morgan's, Tucker's (to where Boers who signed the oath of neutrality were immediately transferred for their own protection; this group eventually numbered 800, and received no special privileges) and Hinson's (for about 200 Boer boys aged, disturbingly, 6 to 16; a school was built here for them but only completed in April 1902, barely a month before the war's end). Some of the islands were so close that if they shouted, men on the next island could hear.

In the year up until the war ended, just over 4 600 Boer POWs were shipped to Bermuda's little water-bound prisons. Thirty-five of them died during their captivity, mostly of infectious diseases such as typhoid or pneumonia.

The spokesman for the Boer POWs on the islands was Commandant Pieter Ferreira of Ladybrand – one of the many Ferreiras from the Free State.

The arrival of Boer 'convicts' – citizens of the Cape Colony who had been convicted of treason against Britain – caused another outcry in Bermuda. Some of these soldiers had been sentenced to death and had their sentences commuted. They had travelled to Bermuda wearing the same prison uniforms they had worn in the Cape, with heart-shaped targets sewn onto the front of their shirts, indicating where the firing squads should aim.

The first of these so-called 'convicts' arrived on the ill-fated *Montrose* in 1901, and then another, much larger batch of 250 more on the *Harlech Castle*. They were forced to work in the quarry on Long Island, to which they were marched across wooden footbridges each day from Hawkins' Island. They were not allowed to receive post or money, and had no access to tobacco. Their clothes and shoes were pitiable, and the food and water they were given was not enough to sustain them in their hard labour, so they tried to find ways of earning a little cash by making and selling handicrafts to the mainland.

Once Bermuda residents got used to the idea of having Boers present, they were treated as something of a spectacle. Sunday-afternoon trippers, the women dressed in white with panama hats and parasols, were rowed over to ogle the newly arrived prisoners. The mood of the residents was on the whole peaceable, and in a few cases actively supportive, for some local families had originally arrived from the United States, which had its own grievances against its former British colonisers.

Michael's simple, sturdy carved Bermuda box.
The lid slides open along the grooved indentations.

The several small islands to which the Boers were allotted were low in the water – in fact, some of them, such as Burt's, disappeared after the war. In a particularly high spring tide or during hurricane weather, they could be swamped, causing panic among the prisoners.

The issue of water was managed by pressing Nelly Island into service: it had a large water catchment with storage tanks, and supplied other islands when their catchments ran out. Each prisoner was given adequate drinking water but it meant that clothes – and themselves – had to be washed in the sea.

Any thoughts of swimming to freedom were countered by armed guards ordered to shoot, as well as the abundant sharks; Royal Navy vessels patrolled, armed and equipped with searchlights. A few succeeded, nonetheless, for the mainland was close. A reward was offered for escaping prisoners.

A youngster was shot dead one night, on 28 April 1902, as he tried to get through the wire. The shooting of this 16-year-old did not provoke the same outrage among the Boers as the deeply controversial death of Philip Cronje in Green Point camp; they seem to have accepted that being shot while escaping was a part of war.

Despite how hard prison is on the human spirit, irrepressible nature will burst out. The men on Darrell's Island, for instance, one night launched a life-size dummy on a raft made of tent floorboards, with the name 'Joe Chamberlain' (the British minister behind the war) attached to it. The searchlight of a patrol boat picked it up. The next morning the Boers spotted the dummy perched on top of one of their tents, without a word having been said – a case of practical joking on both sides.

From Darrell's, Michael could easily see across the narrow stretch of ocean to the mainland of Bermuda, and the sweeping beam from the tall lighthouse on Gibb's Hill which commanded an excellent view of the whole area, as well as of the POWs. And despite the danger from the searchlights and guns and sharks, some young men did take a chance and swim to nearby prison islands at night – to visit their friends.

As in all POW camps, filling the unforgiving hours was a central problem – how to alleviate the endless boredom. Exile is the existential 'now' repeated daily, a length of leaden time. Each day brings anew its burden – the same boring repetition as the day before, and the next.

On Darrell's Island, a large tent was erected for worship; daily devotions and hymn singing was commonplace. That was all very well, but the Boers were active people used to full days of work on their lands, or in their offices and other workplaces. They needed to be *busy*.

Help came promptly from the wealthy and fearless Anna Maria Outerbridge, who lived in Willoughby, an impressive colonial mansion sited on a rise in Bailey's Bay on the main island. She was chief trumpeter among several organisations to aid the Boers and relieve their endless monotony. Within a week of the first POWs' arrival, the Association for Boer Recreation, supported by the governor, had distributed books and magazines, fishing lines and playing cards. Boer relief groups in the United States and the Netherlands collected clothing and money. The POWs particularly appreciated the books, in English and also in Dutch, German and French.

Willoughby was unabashedly a pro-Boer haven, and as Miss Outerbridge's reputation spread among the POWs, escaping prisoners sought refuge there. (Her views enraged many Bermudians; they took revenge on 5 November 1901 by burning her in effigy instead of Guy Fawkes.) The authorities were well aware of this, and if any men went missing, the first thing they did was descend on her house. The exasperated government of Bermuda passed a law with her in mind, making it an offence punishable by up to five years in prison to aid or harbour POWs. It had absolutely no effect.[25]

Luckiest were those POWs skilful in using their ubiquitous pocket knives. The crafts were eventually sold in every curio and tourist shop, earning useful money. Using whatever materials came to hand, they made walking sticks, pipes, boxes of all sorts and sizes, picture frames, napkin rings carved out of bone, and delightful tiny carved 'snake-shoes' – when you slid back a lid on top, a little carved snake popped out. Clever miniature pen knives were made from beaten coins, and playable musical instruments such as violins and bugles were carved out of cedar.

Michael made a small box in rich-coloured wood, likely cedar. He also made frames, one of which has 'Bermuda' carved into it, as well as a date, '14.4.1902'; these items were brought home and inherited by some of his grandchildren.

Exercise was essential to keep the men occupied and fit, for inactivity could lead to depression. There was a rather eccentric croquet court on

Darrell's, while cricket was played on Morgan's (the officers' site), as well as Hawkins', and among the schoolboys on Hinson's; football was played too. Sports days were organised. Tiny Burt's Island had quite a good tennis court.

Darrell's Island boasted a piano, bought by some men who clubbed together to pay for it. Each island had its own choir, and enthusiastic singing could often be heard across the water.

Burt's Island was so small that, except for the tennis court, there was no space to do anything except fish and swim. The inhabitants made up for it by producing a weekly newspaper, *Die Burt's Trompet,* cobbled together from snippets of smuggled information.

Food was, of course, central to the men, as always in prison camps. According to now-settled custom, they took turns cooking over open coal fires, though sometimes a cook was skilled enough to be pressed into service for the duration. It was a monotonous but fairly adequate diet of bread, potatoes, turnips, some beef (carefully weighed out), and canned milk, sugar, tea and coffee, but vegetables were hard to come by. When fresh vegetables were not available, lime juice with sugar was issued, the lessons of scurvy having been learned by the maritime British.

Bacon was issued once a week. Their main meat supply was large (10-pound) tins of mutton, routinely rolled out each week, called 'horse meat' by the prisoners, who quipped that it must have come from the 'biggest sheep' they had ever heard of.

Prisoners were allowed to buy items from the prison canteen – coffee, tobacco, matches, sweets and treats, stationery and stamps, and fresh fruit when it was available – but it was considered expensive.

Liquor was banned in the camps by a majority decision of the men themselves.

A few enterprising prisoners set up coffee shops, a prime example being the Lion's Den on Burt's.

The children on Hinson's were served cooked food, cocoa served up 'morning, noon and night', and their favourite, condensed milk, freely available. A vat of ice cream was donated by residents of Hamilton, Bermuda, who ferried it over to Hinson's and enjoyed seeing the boys from the 'veldt' tasting it.

The POW Ladybranders on Darrell's Island in Bermuda, 1901. Michael is third from the left in the front row, No 14, with his hand on his knee. Each number was rewritten on the back, and signed by that POW. The photo was then sent to their commandant, Chris Muller, captive in Ceylon.

An envelope that contained a letter to Michael on Darrell's Island from his mother (as inscribed on the front); it arrived in 1902.

For Michael, each day brought its burden; the escape of dreams gave way in the dawn's light to the clamour of unfamiliar voices and sights. Never had he thought he would long for Bellevue back in the Cape, but his memory of that roomy camp, with its lovely views of sea and mountain, the daily swim off a pleasant beach, the proximity to the familiar – all these became more precious for their loss. Men who had never seen the sea before the war were now, literally and alarmingly, precisely at sea level; storms swamped the shallow shores and threatened their billets. It was disconcerting, hot and foreign.

Post was the most prized item of all, and news that a ship had come in from South Africa always created a heightened atmosphere. Apart from the poor 'convicts', who were never allowed post, there were no restrictions on the amount of mail a POW could send or receive – subject, of course, to the snip of the censor's scissors. A letter exists from Chris to his brother 'Miki' with much of the page neatly clipped out.

It is fascinating to ponder the resilience of war letters, entrusted to remote postal services, crossing seas, enduring the challenges of weather and the vagaries of war. Yet here they are: little, neat envelopes, careful letters penned on fragile paper, precious words that reached loved ones, and now connect the centuries.

20

Chris struggles with the Boer 'boys'

IN DIYATALAWA CAMP, Chris was told the worrying news on 17 August 1901 that both his father-in-law, Willem, and his brother Pieter were in the hospital, and he rushed to see them. Father Willem was asleep but Pieter looked really ill, he reported, and he feared it was the fever again. He visited them every day.

On 19 August 1901 he received a letter from Bermuda from Michael, though unfortunately he did not record its contents.

The next day, he realised that his eyes were weak and sore from studying, and that he may need to get spectacles; also, some prisoners arrived from St Helena, telling of many deaths there.

Father Willem had improved enough to leave the hospital, and visited Chris on 22 August with a letter from his wife which shattered her son-in-law Chris. She accused him of having said something against her (what, he did not say). He sank into despair.

> During the day it felt as though I had been stabbed through the heart because I am as innocent as a lamb . . . and it is hard to think that Mother can think this of me. I wrote her a letter and laid the case before her and told her of my grief.

It is hard to fathom why such an accusatory letter would be sent to any hapless prisoner of war, so in need of encouragement. Chris reported his heart was so sore that he could not concentrate on anything. Further, the post took many weeks to cross the ocean either way, so there was no quick way of resolving the painful issue.

His health deteriorated under the strain. When, two days later, he went on a walk with his friends Andries Meyer and Fred van Blerk, he felt so weak and had such a bad headache that he did not think he would be able to make it back to the camp.

Later, he received a letter from brother Pieter, and also the news that he had been accepted as a Sunday-school teacher.

His troubled mind continued to seethe. At 3.30 am on 30 August he rose from a painful dream that his Dorie had died, and he could not return to sleep. Instead, he and a friend sat reading and studying in the dining room, and that evening he was relieved when he received a photograph of his wife and their daughter in the post.

The next day Father Willem visited to see the picture of his grand-daughter, while Chris 'ached with longing' for his little girl.

He was still 'sad and heartsore' on 6 September 1901, his birthday, yet certain that his wife would mark the day.

Then the colonel informed them that all officers had to leave the camp on the 18th; the POWs' suspicion was that they were to be sent to Ragama. It was shocking news, and Chris worried about the loss of all the educational opportunities he had had in Diyatalawa that had given him purpose.

He was thrown a lifeline, though it would prove a double-edged sword. There were about 250 'children' in Diyatalawa, most of them post-puberty. These older boys were often well on the way to being men. Not only were they going through the troublesome teens, they were also caught in a masculine environment without normal family constraints. As a result, some had turned into 'incorrigibles', and Cotie van Heerden, a sensible, patient fellow, had been charged with setting up a 'youth hostel'. Cotie suggested to Chris that he remain with him to assist with the often-difficult youngsters.

Chris asked his fellow officers for permission, knowing his motives might cause 'suspicion' (any unusual move was examined for a political motive), but it was granted.

The colonel of the camp agreed that Chris may stay, but without the privileges of an officer. This was hard to swallow, but he did.

Parting with his friends was wrenching, especially Andries and Fred.

> When I said goodbye to Andries I could not speak because we have been together for so long and he has done much for me. Today it is precisely 13 months since we sailed from Simon's Bay.

In fact, these officers, 32 of them, along with 25 men, were not sent to Ragama, but instead to Hambantota, a camp on the much drier, southerly coast of Ceylon, where they were allowed to live on parole, though it was far from idyllic. Andries described the camp in withering terms: an old jail surrounded by a wall, it was located in the middle of the local village. Though they were free to bathe in the sea, he thought the food was very poor.

Still, had Chris known that they were *not* going to Ragama, he may have made a different choice.

Chris (seated third from right) with his 'troublesome youths' in Ceylon, 1901. Several have beards, and some look as if they would have been useful in a college rugby team.

Cotie's desire to set up a youth hostel for these older boys was done out of his Christian charity, an attempt to teach and discipline them in a more formal structure, but first he had to persuade their relatives, who did not want to give them up. Their fathers and guardians were fiercely attached to them.

Chris visited the youngsters to tell them about the intended youth hostel. It was unwelcome news, for they were suspicious of him: was he doing this to get them to join the *English*?

When the boys were first told to report to the youth hostel on 27 September, not all did so; in fact, two refused, saying straight-out that they would rather sit out the rest of their exile in the cells, and were indeed then taken to the prison.

That night, Cotie and Chris and Cornelius van Heerden had 37 youngsters in the hostel hut with them.

An ongoing struggle developed. In an already restless camp, some of the youths left the next day, then returned, but only because they were afraid of prison. The families of the two locked-up lads also arrive to remonstrate, and others came to 'take back' a brother or son.

> Now I feel my lack of power, and insignificance. The children are stubborn and obstreperous – so much so that they sit down at table with their hats on and with cigarettes in their mouths and do all they can to tantalise us. They make as much noise as possible to provoke us and we have to put up with it.

Some asked permission of the colonel (who was aware of the difficult situation) to leave the hostel: he granted it to only one, an 'uncivilised beast' who was already 23 years old and had only one arm, wrote Chris, offering a glimpse of his frustration.

More boys were locked up for bad behaviour, and their friends arrived to cause chaos. Cornelius was hit in the chest by a 'scoundrel', who was jailed.

A youth wanted to go to the nearby 'peace camp' (all *hensoppers* and joiners were immediately sent to this camp for their own protection) and the other lads threatened to beat him up; he laid a charge against the chief culprit, who was put in the cells.

There seemed to be a perpetual uproar. Chris felt slandered and mistrusted, aware that the boys thought he was trying to get them into the hands of the *English*. He begged for 'the Lord's help' in this hard task.

Slowly things improved, for the boys had even less power than Chris. In turn, the adults tried to cut the lads some slack. Cotie asked his assistants what to do about a particular boy who was very obstinate and 'brutal' and also swore a lot, and the decision was that they should wait and give this case some thought.

A couple of days later, tension rose again when a Tommie shot at a boy who had allegedly tried to throw a stone at him. The sentry was replaced.

By the end of October 1901, it was a little better. The boys were treated to a free outing on the train, for a picnic.

Chris continued with his own lessons, particularly those in Dutch and geography, and continued tending the cemetery with Father Willem. He received letters from home, and from Pieter, and from friends elsewhere in Ceylon, but he wrote that the monotony of his days weighed heavily.

Cotie seemed to have the measure of the youths; but when he was away, they gave Chris a hard time. On 3 December 1901, during one of Cotie's absences, all the furniture was taken out of their hut to be disinfected, and one of the boys broke both their table lamps. The next day a youth tore up his bible and another was barely prevented from doing so, an act calculated to cause maximum offence.

Cotie returned on 7 December and, as glad as the youths were to see him, Chris was even more pleased.

A large photograph of all the Ladybranders on Darrell's Island, including Michael, arrived for Chris on 10 December, a present for their commandant, with the men's heartfelt greetings; they had recorded their names on the back. It was a lifesaver that he was still remembered with affection and admiration by 'his men'. How hard it was for him, formerly their commander, to have to do battle daily with boys who cared nothing for his authority or war exploits.

The authorities were not oblivious to the problems in the youth hostel. They decided that the boys should be allowed out more often on parole, under the supervision of a Boer officer, and as a result, on 30 December 1901, Chris took five youths out to spend a day in the veld.

The following day was the last of this unlovely year. Chris again took five youths out (now a daily occurrence) and they enjoyed seeing a review of troops, the younger lads in particular relishing the spectacle. They returned to the camp for dinner at 1 pm, after which he took the boys on another outing and was able to lie on a bank, reading, while they wandered around. The atmosphere was calmer.

As the year closed, Chris felt he was little more than an orderly for thankless boys, a few of whom he had come, unfortunately, to loathe. His short diary entries revealed an unhappy heart, and he often wrote little more than a lacklustre 'everything as usual'.

He could not go on this way.

'I have never begun a New Year like this,' wrote Chris. It was the last year of the war, 1902 – though that was yet unknown.

It is not immediately clear what he meant: he had, after all, been a prisoner for 18 months, and had begun the previous year of 1901 in Ceylon, although an invalid.

This is the last of his eight surviving diaries, and the smallest. The book, bound with a sturdy green cover, could fit in the palm of his hand. He wrote his name on the inside, in copperplate handwriting.

The small pages for each day had narrow lines, and his writing is tiny and neat, to squeeze everything in. His English is good, with few spelling or grammar errors, a tribute to his diligent lessons, and it is possible to see him learning from his mistakes as he self-corrected on subsequent pages. Occasionally, when feeling ill or under stress, he reverted briefly to his mother tongue of Afrikaans-Nederlands, but for the most part, he persisted with English, right to his final entry.

The men rose early at 4.30 am on this first day of 1902, attending an open-air service of about 2 000 POWs. A sports meeting was held outside the camp but it was rainy, and by evening Chris admitted that he did not feel cheerful.

The next day was even more troubling, when he comforted a friend who had heard of the death of his child back home. 'Such news we receive very often.' They all grieved, not only for their friends but also for themselves; such terrible impotence, unable to defend your children, nor bury them.

Though the post was closed for the public holiday, Chris wrote letters in the quiet camp to send as soon as it reopened. There were rumours that the Boers were still 'doing well' in the field, but peace appeared to Chris to be far away.

He continued to take out the boys in his care though it was often raining: on 3 January, the boys had no mackintoshes and were 'as wet as rats' returning to the huts.

Two days later, 5 January, was his brother Pieter's birthday; he remembered too late to visit him in the heavy rain.

On the 12th, there was a more significant birthday.

This day has great meaning for me, this birthday of my first child, now my only one, if she still lives. Oh, my dear child, your father thinks of you this morning. It is a lovely Sunday, the dew shines on the grass stalks like diamonds . . . as a dessert, we had some milk and rice, an 'extra' for my daughter's birthday. My heart feels a little sore today.

A few days later Father Willem brought Chris a little box, a present in honour of Joey.

Suddenly there was a flurry of letters which gave him comfort; the post had opened again and he received four letters from his wife within two days.

His brother Pieter arrived at his hut, bringing a portrait photograph of himself, and a couple of days later handed Chris a letter from their sister Salomina, 'Minnie'. He shared this with Father Willem, and a letter from Dorie reporting that she had lost one of her front teeth. He also mentioned how cold it was – 'it is really winter', and often rainy.

They were also given one of those maddening camp orders that so infuriate prisoners: they were all of a sudden not allowed to keep tables in their huts larger than '18 inches by 24 inches'. There followed a deafening noise of hammering and sawing as they made their tables smaller.

Chris often felt unwell, headachy and tired. The little news they got from South Africa upset them; they had to read between the lines. They worried.

He walked outside the camp to get away from the din, to read and pray.

He was actively engaged in the Christian Endeavour society, and on 24 January was elected vice-chair: many of his entries mentioned this and other religious gatherings, almost on a daily basis. It was a comfort in his most serious grief, which was the separation from his wife.

On Sunday 26 January he walked away from the camp, for 'my heart is very sore. I can't remember a day when I was longing for my dearest like today'. He lay in torment under the bluegums.

The observant Cotie van Heerden, who ran the hostel, had noticed Chris's declining spirits over the preceding months, and wisely decided that it was time to offer him an escape. He told Chris on 27 January that there was a possibility of his returning to the officers' quarters.

Chris asked for time to think about it, but there was little doubt what his decision would be.

Meanwhile, he wrote to his young brother back home – Danie, now aged 11.

At bedtime he informed Cotie that, yes, he had decided to move back to the officers' hut, which he did on 30 January, spending that afternoon reunited with Father Willem and brother Pieter, 'planting some trees at the graveyard'.

Now came a little irony. Chris wrote that the boys were dissatisfied with his 'removal'; also, he felt bad about leaving Cotie to cope with them. So that evening he returned to the place where he had spent so many unhappy weeks and months, to shake hands with all the boys. Then he went back, with relief, to the officers' hut, 'and now I am here for good'.

Yet he found it strange the next morning to have no task, so he kept busy writing at his now-reduced table, and in the evening, brother Pieter and some friends popped in for a visit 'as usual'.

This transition was a mercy for Chris and he admitted he was glad to return to his officer status. He did not have the saintly qualities of Cotie, whose patience enabled him reach the troubled boys. Chris's health had been erratic and he had often mentioned headaches and his troubled stomach, especially after rich food. Now, when his stomach was 'out of order', he was able to tend to his needs without the added strain of worrying about the rowdy youths.

On 1 February, he went for a 'jolly bath', a daily routine made even more pleasant now that he was in no rush, then willingly returned to his lessons in Dutch, English and geography; he sometimes sat at his little table all day. 'I am very thankful for the opportunity to learn,' he noted. He was determined to go on utilising the opportunities.

Chris wrote to his brother Michael on Darrell's Island on 3 February 1902, addressing him as *liewe Broeder* (dear Brother), mentioning it had been a while since he had received a letter from him, and that Pieter and he were well. He explained to Michael that he had left the '*jongenstehuis*' (youth hostel). His handwriting is now beautiful copperplate, a pleasure to the eye – which was his intention.

This letter, like all of those he wrote to Michael, was on a folded piece of paper with neat, precise lettering on the front, then on the back, and finally on the inside. (Michael returned Chris's letters to him after the war.)

On 6 February, Chris diarised a rare description (for him) of the food, bully-beef and biscuits, and also letters from 'my darling, and also from my young brother [Daan]'.

Chris also saw posted on the noticeboard for the first time that all those who had habitually planted vegetables now had to hand in their names on an application form: there seemed to be a tightening of camp discipline as the likelihood of the war's end drew closer.

There was a fuss on 16 February when a man escaped. 'It is a long time since we saw the red flag by the watch houses,' Chris noted about the signal that a prisoner was making a break for it.

Even more shocking to him was the news he recorded on 24 February, of Commandant Stephanus 'Fanie' Vilonel of Senekal, now a joiner, who 'turned against us'. A well educated and affluent lawyer, Vilonel had fallen out with the Boer leadership as early as June 1900, and 18 months later took up arms against his former comrades, assembling more than 300 men in the Orange River Colony Volunteers, an armed and uniformed unit of collaborators within the British army.

Chris added, 'I become every day more convinced that we are going to lose our country and independence.' It was a far-sighted remark, unhappily made.

March arrived. Chris worked increasingly in the camp's library, and continued with his school lessons. He also installed a gymnastic bar on which he exercised every day in the dining room.

His English continued to improve: on the 16th March he wrote that he went to bed and 'was soon in the arms of Morpheus'.

The next day he heard about the capture of Lord Methuen by General de la Rey, but he mistrusted the increasingly polarised political talk in the camp, and said he did not believe it. Yet it was true. In the final large battle of the war, at Tweebosch in the western Transvaal on 7 March 1902, Methuen, the loser of Magersfontein, was again defeated by De la Rey, and this time taken captive, along with 870 of his soldiers. De la Rey gave his personal cart to carry Methuen, whose leg was broken, to the nearest hospital at Klerksdorp. By all accounts, the two generals became quite friendly.

Chris read a book about the ill-treatment of families at home, and alternated between anger and dismay; yet he disliked his comrades' attitude towards the *English*, which he described as 'narrowmindedness'.

Then, on 25 March, there was significant news that the war may be winding down.

> The governments of the [Boer] republics are allowed to communicate with the President [Steyn] and De Wet, for treaties of peace. It is something hopeful. [He adds the prayer] that the Lord will give us our land.

This happened just before the Easter weekend, which passed quietly. The first day of the following week, 31 March, was Easter Monday, and Chris did not know what that meant, and whether he should work on a religious day. After asking around, he discovered that it was just a 'bank holiday' (public holiday), and he returned to his studies.

The month of April passed. Chris added algebra and Latin to his already bulging curriculum, though after several weeks he decided that taking them on had been over-ambitious.

He was still often unwell, with ongoing stomach problems and many headaches, often severe. The doctor visited him in his cot in the crowded officers' hut and prescribed bed rest and a milk diet again. It had been a year and a half since he had contracted typhoid fever, yet his health still plagued him, as did the daily monotony, so he tried to fill every unforgiving minute with work, devotional services and walks.

Now came a loss that shook him: a friend, Mannie Hartman, was dying in hospital. Chris was ordered to take 30 men out on parole the following day, 17 April, and on returning at 4 pm, was aghast to see the funeral of Mannie, of whom he was very fond: 'Oh, he is very dear to my heart.'

This intensified his longing for his wife; it became a litany in his diary, with petitions to the Lord for help in coping. He was, thankfully, getting letters from her, as well as from his parents, sisters, Michael and cousins. They took about five weeks to arrive; but to his distress Dorie (he now referred to her as Dorothy) wrote that she was not getting post from him, though he wrote frequently. She had, however, received a box of curios, including brooches and trinkets, that he had posted to her.

Peace, peace, was on everyone's minds, not just those of the Boers: public opinion in Britain had swung against the war, and even senior politicians such as Lloyd George and Sir Henry Campbell-Bannerman, both future prime ministers, were speaking out about its deadly effects on the Boer civilian population.

Chris's friend, 'Adjudant' Loets (also spelled in his diary as Lutz), received a telegram on 24 April informing him that the Boers would get their independence but had to give up the mines, and that they would get 'Zululand', that portion of modern-day KwaZulu-Natal that had been annexed by the British in 1897.

But the following day Chris received a letter from a friend from home saying that 'our cause is hopeless and the Boers ruin it by carrying on'.

Rumours and conspiracy theories abounded. Chris increasingly felt sceptical of any news, while 'street mobs' in the camp attacked anyone who did not share their opinions.

In May the pattern continued: he worked hard at studying, reading in the library and attending devotions, sometimes several a day. He was annoyed on the 4th when two of his fellow officers involved him in a little roughhouse play, and he ended up on the floor, hurting his knee – he was cross with such nonsense, he declared, his dignity impaired. The bounce had gone out of him; long gone were the days when, despite the bloody, recent battle of Magersfontein, he could join in with fun on the veld, and wrote in his diary, 'I laughed myself silly.'

On 14 May, letters arrived about peace negotiations and the Boer delegation in Pretoria. 'Almost all in the camp say we will get our independence back, but I do not think so, but if we do, nobody will be more glad than I.' He was emotional, feeling that the camp was 'full of lies'; that evening, beautiful band music brought him close to tears.

On the 19 May public holiday, he took a long walk with Father Willem and his brother, Pieter. 'When will the day dawn when we can go home to our loved ones?' he wrote.

On the last day of May, he made a short list of books he had bought, including *Architects of Fate, or, Steps to Success and Power* by Orison Swett Marden, a pioneer of positive thinking.

On 1 June, oblivious to the momentous events taking place in his homeland that ended the war, Chris wandered out of camp alone; his diary entry that day was an impressive feat of his mastery of fine handwriting and idiomatic English. He sat on a hillock

> whence I have a beautiful view. Oh! Nature here is so picturesque. The ridges of the mountains, the jungles in the glens, the tea plantations, and the quietness of the morning. My heart goes out to my country and loved ones. God grant that peace comes soon!

His prayer was answered the very next day. But it was a very mixed blessing.

21

Linked by letters –
Michael on Darrell's Island

MICHAEL, LIVING ON cramped Darrell's Island in Bermuda, was more cut off from news in this last year of the war than was Chris, who was an officer and allowed out freely on parole, and who had far more access to both news and rumour. But two letters written by Michael to his wife, Nelie, still exist, and reveal his state of mind, and his longing for release.

The first he penned in March 1902.

> *Lief Vrouw* [Dear Wife]
> It gave me great joy to receive again from you a very recent letter, of 10 February, and to discover from it that all of you are still doing well, through the love of the Lord. With me and Oubaas and all those known to you, things are still fine, for which we can never thank Him enough.
>
> I feel so unworthy when I hear, every day, so many death notices from all sides and places, and that the Lord has spared us so wonderfully. I hope and I trust, dearest, that you will not take this time of 'proving' lightly nor carelessly, in the knowledge that the Lord is never closer to us than when He sends us suffering. And while we are suffering, let us bow before the Lord who created us.
>
> In connection with these words, I am going to send you a little tract. Read it carefully and give it thought and ask the Lord continually to make you aware of what is still wrong within you. This is the desire of our dear Lord, to make known to us our defects, if we really, from the heart, want to distance ourselves from that.
>
> My love, write to let me know whether you and your little household, mornings and evenings, gather around God's word. Where there is a heaviness in your heart, share it with me, even though we

are so far removed from one another. We can give one another coun-
sel and pray for one another. I am not implying that you do not
already do this, but it is still my duty to verify it.

After this rather sober beginning, Michael referred to some family news
and asked after people he knew. Only then, near the end of the second page,
did he write the words she must have been longing for – though something of a mixed compliment.

My darling, thank you also for the photograph. I almost did not
recognise you, for it looks as if you have become so darkly burned
by the sun. You may be overtiring yourself. [Nelie and other Boer
women had to take on the outdoor labour, once their men's task.]

. . .

Is the cart that was made from a wooden chest still there?
I have almost forgotten where you got the big dog that is next to
you in the portrait.
Don't hold it against me that I ask these questions. There is no
news here and therefore I'm letting you know what I long to hear
and see, from your perspective.
My longing is always for South Africa. It is my fatherland. We
hear many things from there, perhaps more than you may think.
Nothing about the war, but about other things, a lot.
I am sorry for [POW] Jacobis van Wyk. He is on St Helena. That
he should, in his exile, hear the heavy news of what has happened
to his people – a death notice.
Many such notices come here, and I am very glad to hear that it
is still going well with Oupa's oxen. I want to believe that he will be
able to keep his wagon.
And I see . . . that A Fourie also arrived from Bloemfontein. Has
he seen the women who are in the camps? He will surely have much
to say about the life of the women there, in the tents. [This was a
veiled reference to let Nelie know that the POWs were very aware
of what was happening to the women and children in the camps.]
The latest news from Pieter and Chris is that it is still going well.
Give my greetings to Pa and Ma, and all the family and friends,
too many to name. And you, my love, are heartily kissed by me in
spirit.
From your longing husband, MA Muller.

(PS) Don't forget me in your prayers. Tomorrow we are having a day of prayer outside the camp on the 'school' island [Hinson's]. We will pray for our nation. On 1 February we held a day of prayer for the sick and for the women in the camps.

A letter dated 8 April 1902 received from Chris (written across the bottom left corner of the envelope, at an acute angle, are the words 'From his brother') was stamped with a Diyatalawa POW censor mark in Ceylon, and arrived in Hamilton, Bermuda on 10 May 1902. It was written in ink, in a beautiful, fluent and extremely neat hand.

> With great joy I received a letter from you last night, dated 11 January [1902], with a cedarwood twig and a sliver inside it. Your letter was very pleasant – when I read it, it is as if Bermuda comes closer to me . . .
> With us, it is going well. Pieter is going to school . . .

He then asked Michael to send him a leaf from the same tree from which he had plucked the twig, so that he would have a clearer idea of what it looked like, to find out whether there were any similar to those in Ceylon. These farmer-brothers were interested in botany; Michael was always a keen *tuinbouer* (gardener) and, as mentioned, Chris collected saplings in Ceylon which he propagated in tins.

An important letter from Chris was penned on 17 June 1902. It told Michael not only that his brothers had fully recovered from their typhoid but also that Chris had received a letter written on 12 April from their *liewe Moeder* (beloved Mother).

> The Peace has been announced here, on 2 June. There was a huge cheer of joy from 'Boer and Brit', but I could not cheer, because I did not know the 'result' and since our capture I have expected the worst. But we want to accept God's will. We hope that the Lord spares us to meet again soon.
> [Fellow POW] Oom Piet Grobler is very sick and weak: it looks to me as if the cause is longing and *aantreklykheid* [stress]. He is completely emaciated.

He asked that his brother give his greetings to all who knew him – for in his mind, and theirs, he remained their war commandant – and finished with, 'You are heartily greeted, I wish for everything to happen that you wish for. Your brother, Chris.'

The brothers' fervent wish to go home was soon to be granted; but it would be to a captured land.

PART V

GOING HOME
1902

22

'The Peace' and unrest in Ceylon

NEWS OF THE peace had arrived – the Treaty of Vereeniging signed on 31 May 1902 – but the way in which it happened turned out to be a *mislukking* (fiasco), and caused riots and divisions between the men for many weeks to come.

Chris outlined his diary entry on 2 June 1902 in red ink, as he did the word 'Peace' at the top of the page; he must have done this later. It was indeed a red-letter day, at first. A cable had arrived at 9am with the long-awaited news. In his haste, he wrote, 'It is peas,' a rare and rather charming error.

> Oh! it is a glad tiding, the whole camp is in joy, the Boers, Tommies, Coolies [sic] and officers rejoice together. *English* and Boer bands play till late, cheering goes on.

(And where was Chris? Working in the library till late, and writing to his 'darling'.)

This cable caused enormous trouble, however; it did not give the outcome of the peace agreement, and many burgers believed that they had either won the war, or, at the very least, had not lost their independence. Difficult as this may be to understand with hindsight, the fact is that these Boers had been living for months and years on a toxic mix of censored letters, stolen shreds of news, and rumours. It was a mistake to cut them off so entirely from events dragging to a bitter end in South Africa. When victory for Britain was told to men who had been POWs for nearly two years, they were not prepared to believe their captors, nor to accept that their sacrifices had been 'for nothing'.

When another cable arrived the next day with news of the general surrender of the Boers, and the loss of their independence, there was a great
sadness in the camp, wrote Chris, and great resistance to believing it.

> The camp Commander calls the Boer senior officers in to explain
> that our country is conquered, and to hand in our names to arrange
> for going home.

The uproar was not helped when another cable arrived with slight altera-
tions, leading the nay-sayers to claim that it was all a hoax. Chris was
consulted and said he had not expected to retain independence (he had
long been bracing himself for this). His words were repeated in camp, 'and
many slanders were passed on me'. He responded that this was his opinion and he couldn't help it, but he felt stung. His diary noted:

> We have received the terms of the Peace. Ach! the people can't
> believe it, they cannot grasp this. I hope when the mail arrives then
> they will believe it, when informed people write to them.

The turmoil continued, for not just days but weeks. On the 10th, General
Roux sent a letter confirming they had lost their country. 'I expected it and
yet my heart breaks and I shed tears,' wrote Chris. Others remained defiant.

In the midst of this, he received a photo of Dorie and Nelie, Michael's
wife; pretty young sisters-in-law. 'Oh! It nearly kills me when I see my
darling.'

On 16 June the Peace Agreement was posted in camp for all to read, but
was ripped down by a Boer officer. The camp was in a bad state, some
attacking those who, like Chris, had accepted the facts; he resolved to exercise patience but was sorely tested.

His last letter to his brother Michael, still in Bermuda, was written on
17 June 1902, in which he mentioned the turmoil in his camp.

General Olivier arrived from his private quarters on the 20th – he lived
outside the camp, on permanent parole – and told Chris that the camp
commander had given him permission to cable whomever he wished, for
information to assuage his scepticism about the bad news. Chris, not one
to mince his words even with a superior, told him he was just being foolish
and also that his 'broad language' did not suit a general.

Nelie (left) and Dorie. The sisters-in-law each
sent a copy of this photo to their husbands.

Later, two officers were allowed by the camp censors to read the Dutch
newspapers, which of course contained the dreaded but undeniable terms
of the peace.

By 28 June, four weeks after the signing of the treaty at Vereeniging, actual
fights were breaking out in the camp, 'Boer against Boer, *English* against
Boer', so seriously that a Boer's arm was broken and an *English* sergeant's
head badly wounded. Soldiers with weapons had to intervene. 'God deliver
us soon,' wrote a troubled Chris.

Finally, on 1 July, the *English* and Boer officers got together to 'restart the
Peace'. After a quarrel, they met again in the afternoon and decided to
cooperate so that order could be restored. The Boers agreed to hand over
offenders, on condition that the police did not enter their huts.

Chris also recorded that during the same evening a full concert was successful in raising funds for widows and orphans of the war – a calm evening
at last.

The following day Chris was asked by a burger if he should take the oath of loyalty to the British king, that bitterest of pills that was now required of every prisoner. 'I said yes, because everyone shall have to do it sooner or later,' was his resigned response.

A telegram confirming the official terms of the peace agreement arrived from the generals, Botha, De la Rey and De Wet – heroes in the eyes of the Boers, so surely their word would carry weight. But when General Olivier tried to read it out on Sunday 6 July, he was drowned out and had to give up 'because he fears the mob'. Andries Meyer's diary confirms Olivier was threatened.

Chris and others read the telegram for themselves the next day. When they, too, confirmed the terms, the intimidation increased and some of them were physically attacked. They were as shocked at the terms as anyone else, but Meyer, Chris and Fred van Blerk resolved to step into the crisis, for these instructions had, after all, been sent by their most revered war leaders.

One of the hardest and bitterest moments of their entire war happened on Monday 14 July. Chris, Andries and a few friends signed the declaration, the oath. In reading Chris's signed copy of the oath, it was self-evident how much this act cost them, for they had to swear fealty to the king and all his heirs and successors. Other foes had fought the British (and would do so again in the twentieth century), yet retained their lands after losing. This mercy was not offered the Boers.

> It is hard to do it, but circumstances bring me to do it, thus I must be satisfied with God.

On his return to camp, Chris was challenged about having signed the oath; he told them 'straight out' that he had done so, and that if they did not, he was not responsible for their having to remain behind. For there was really no option – they had to sign the declaration to claim their free passage home. So others began to follow suit.

'Foreigners', including Irish and Dutch POWs, were not allowed to return to South Africa at all unless they could prove they were naturalised citizens: they had to make their way back to their original nations, or anywhere else that would have them.

Now that home beckoned, the POWs' return could not come soon enough. Only Boers who had the funds were able to leave immediately, however; this included Paul Kruger's son.

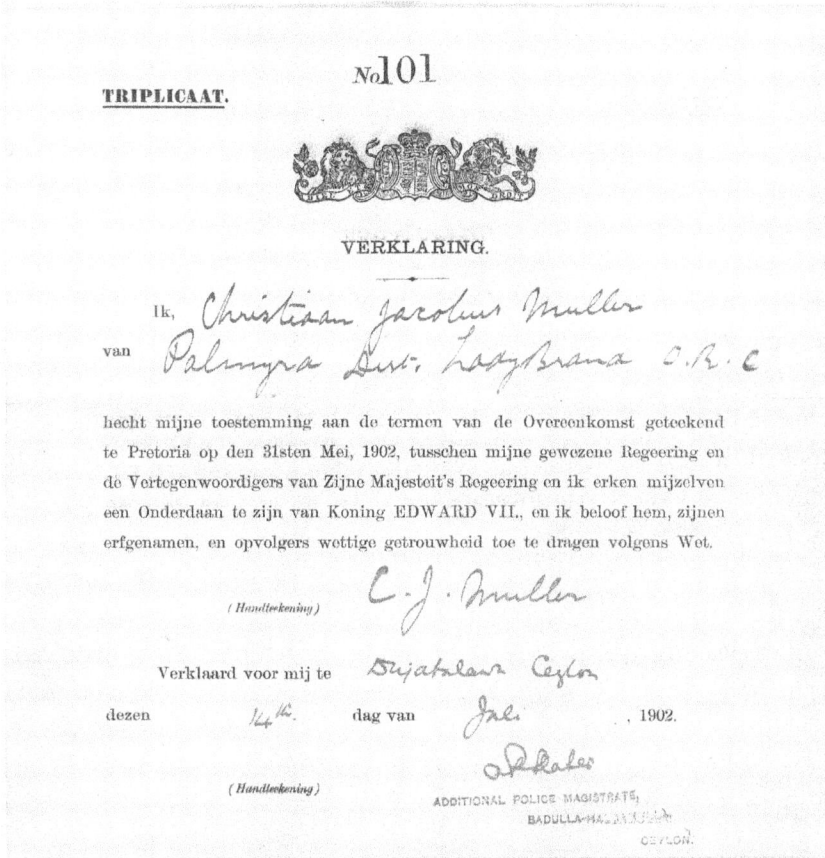

TRIPLICAAT.

N⁰101

VERKLARING.

Ik, *Christiaan Jacobus Muller*
van *Palmyra Dist., Ladybrand O.R.C.*

hecht mijne toestemming aan de termen van de Overeenkomst geteekend te Pretoria op den 31sten Mei, 1902, tusschen mijne gewezene Regeering en de Vertegenwoordigers van Zijne Majesteit's Regeering en ik erken mijzelven een Onderdaan te zijn van Koning EDWARD VII., en ik beloof hem, zijnen erfgenamen, en opvolgers wettige getrouwheid toe te dragen volgens Wet.

(*Handteekening*)   *C. J. Muller*

Verklaard voor mij te   *Bujatalawa Ceylon*

dezen   *14th.*   dag van   *Julie*   , 1902.

(*Handteekening*)   *[signature]*

ADDITIONAL POLICE MAGISTRATE,
BADULLA-MA...
CEYLON.

Commandant Chris Muller's oath of loyalty to the British king, signed with deep reluctance on 14 July 1902, as the condition for his being sent home from exile in Ceylon.

23

Chris's long trek home

CHRIS WAS RELATIVELY lucky to be included in the second home-bound contingent, carrying 400 men, which they were told would leave early in August. He began to pack his things.

Some burgers in camp continued to ask for his advice, while others mocked him: it was bruising, for he had been a trusted and respected leader for so long, both in war and in exile. Still, he did not waver, for he was now a seasoned realist.

They were taken to the 'segregation camp' designated for those who had signed the oath, which he found filthy and cold.

After cleaning their hut the next morning, he returned to the main camp, for he had business to settle, and was shouted at, while others refused to greet him.

On 28 July 1902 – two years since the Ladybranders had surrendered at Slaapkrans – he wrote:

> This morning at 11am we signed parole and they fetched our luggage . . . at 3 pm the trains started. We waved our handkerchiefs.

Many had come to say farewell, and Chris saw how sad they looked.

The officers travelled in a first-class carriage to Colombo, in which they slept overnight – his last privilege of rank.

Their arrival in the capital was not auspicious; they were housed in dirty huts at Cosaba station, forced to submit to this 'third-class' accommodation. 'Some of my friends are angry about that, but I kept quiet.' He coped by making a tent on his cot with a sheet to shut out the grubbiness, and asked for parole to sightsee in Colombo, while they waited several days for their berth.

He discovered that first class berths, to which he was entitled, were full. He submitted to third class, rather than waiting for better accommodation on a later ship, for nothing would halt his haste to get home. There were 26 officers due to board, among them General Crowther of Ladybrand; the vessel carried POWs mainly from the Free State.

On 2 August he and Loets took a train from their transit camp into Colombo. They reported first to the police station, then hired a rickshaw to see the city as free men for the first and only time. They enjoyed a hotel lunch and visited the jetty, before catching a crammed train back. They prayed it would be their last weekend in Ceylon, and it was.

On the 5th they were told to send in their heavy luggage for stowing, and at 3am the following day they rose to prepare for the walk of three and a half miles to the station. They had breakfast, and an hour later they commenced marching.

At the station, the train was not ready to leave because 'the steam was not in yet'. They slept on the stationary train; it was noisy for much of the night, the local people singing and dancing and keeping them awake.

At long last, on 7 August, after a morning swim in the sea, they boarded the single-funnel four-masted ship that would take them home, named, with supreme irony, the SS *Englishman* (Meyer recorded this with some humour).

There was one last, heart-stopping moment. Leaving the harbour after 4 pm for 'dear South Africa', the ship suddenly stopped, did an about-turn and steamed back to Colombo. This caused a terrific fright on board, until they were placated with the news that the mail had been forgotten and needed to be fetched.

Seasickness set in almost immediately, for Chris as well as many others. But their hearts were glad, for now they were definitely headed home, as Pieter soon would be, too.

The two Boer generals, Roux and Olivier, left later, on 22 October, on the SS *Lake Manitoba*, packed with more than a thousand men.

The last two ships bearing POWs sailed in December 1902; five refuse-niks remained. One of them said he would not sign the declaration and never did, right up to his death in 1922 – Ceylon's last Boer POW.

Another Boer who refused to sign was Deneys Reitz of the distinguished Free State family, whose celebrated book of his war on commando is still in print. He, along with his father, Francis William Reitz, the fifth president of the Free State, and his brother were deported into exile, eventually moving to Madagascar, where they stayed for four years. While there, Reitz received a letter from Isie, wife of Jan Smuts, saying that what was good enough for her husband, who was trying to rebuild the country, should be good enough for him. He accepted her rebuke and returned in 1906: in turn, she nursed him through his severe malaria, which he had contracted on the island.

For the first couple of days, Chris and the others lay in their hammocks, seasick.

On the 9th there was another little irony: a concert was held on board to mark the coronation of King Edward, and most of the performers were Boers. Chris attended for a while before returning to bed.

So the voyage passed, rough days when seasickness returned, then calmer ones. On 16 August they saw Mauritius, and the next day a couple of whales, and they sang on board; Chris recorded that they were happy. It had been a while since he had last used that word.

On 19 August, in the roughest seas yet, they passed Madagascar, and on the 22nd men began to crowd the decks, looking out for their homeland, not quite on the horizon.

When Chris woke on the morning of the 23rd he saw through his porthole that they were already in Durban harbour.

They were entrained to Umbilo camp, where he separated from his fellow officers to take care of Oom Piet Grobler, who was again poorly.

Women and children came from their own camp to join them for divine service the next day. Glad as he was to see them, he was now 'face to face' with the reality of their suffering. 'Oh, now I see the deep humiliation of my nation.' Hearing their high voices singing, he was deeply moved, writing that his heart went out to his darling wife, as it had done every day and every night during this final year of waiting. 'My heart burns for my darling.' His blessing was that he had a wife and a child to return to, knowing that many of his suffering fellow soldiers did not.

He washed clothes for Grobler and himself, and packed for the train trip ahead.

On the afternoon of the 26th they boarded the train to the Free State, and passed many pineapple and banana fields on the way. It was a full train, and not a fast one. They arrived in Estcourt the next day, and Chris was interested to see views of the battlefields. As they approached home, their mood changed, however, for they saw a 'bare country' with everything destroyed, he wrote. The full disaster of the scorched-earth war was now terribly manifest.

Two days later, on the 29th, a month and a day since they had left Diyatalawa Camp in Ceylon, they arrived at Elandslaagte. They were put in what Andries Meyer described as coal carriages, bound for Brandfort. Chris could see on either side a long line of open carriages filled with men; it was winter and very cold, which had a serious affect on his febrile health.

The last of all Chris's entries was on Saturday 30 August: 'Some people get down . . .' Here, his final diary abruptly ended but we know what happened next from the memoir of his friend, Andries Meyer.

Chris was again extremely ill. At their own cost, Andries and he were able to travel by train to Sannaspos, arriving on 2 September, and from there they had to walk to Thaba'Nchu, overnighting in homes that offered them hospitality (a common experience for returning soldiers, for the *English* were not obliged to drop them near their homes, and didn't).

Early the next morning, before sunrise, they were back on the road but now Chris could walk no further. Andries trudged on to Tweespruit and was relieved to discover a cart sent there by Chris's father to fetch him; he returned with it to collect Chris. Andries stayed with Chris all the way to his father's farm, Palmyra. Andries's brother-in-law was waiting there with a horse for him, and after saying farewell to the Mullers, these two relatives left together.

If ever there had been a good companion in war, it was Andries Meyer. Their close friendship had begun even before Meyer had been elected Ladybrand's veldkornet under Chris's command, and continued through all their battles and skirmishes, their capture, the voyages to Ceylon, the trials of the camp, and their repatriation. He was at Chris's side during his severe illness in Diyatalawa, and stayed with him until he could deposit the invalid Chris right on the doorstep of the Muller family farm in the far eastern former Free State.

Andries had literally walked the extra mile for his friend. The affection with which Chris referred to him in his war diaries showed that he was well aware of his value, and perhaps his own survival: their descendants recalled that this war comradeship lived on through their families.

There is no record of the reunion between Chris and his relieved parents. They would have been dismayed at the poor health of their usually strong son, yet overjoyed that he had survived, unlike Lool, their youngest soldier-son, who would never return. They were still waiting for the safe return of Michael and Pieter, for Chris was the first home of those close-knit brothers who had ridden off to war.

Nor do we know of the reunion between Chris and his 'darling little wife', Dorie, but it is not hard to imagine. Safe in her arms now, after the long hard years apart, there was no more waiting.

24

Back from Bermuda – Michael's return

FOR MICHAEL, the wait to get home was somewhat longer, and more nerve-wracking. As an ordinary soldier-prisoner without rank, he was not part of discussions about repatriation nor given priority, as Chris had been. Also, the Boer POWs on the various little Bermuda islands had less agency and ongoing information than did their comrades in Ceylon, which had been a more accommodating and expansive place to have spent months and years in exile.

Michael simply had to wait, fretting, while home beckoned – the goal they had longed for, hardly daring to wonder when it would happen. Now it was in their grasp: they would surely be home for Christmas by the end of 1902 – as indeed, all three surviving brothers were. How fast, and then how slowly, the last exiled months had passed.

A letter written by Michael to his wife on 7 July 1902 from Bermuda, dated after the peace agreement, is written on both sides of a single page, in black ink.

> I am taking just a moment to let you know that I am still alive and fresh through the love of the Lord, and I hope that it also is well with you, my love.
>
> Last week I answered your letter of 11 May, and I mentioned in it that I received the portrait of you and Dorie. When I see your image so clearly I long even more for you. It jogged my memory; believe me, I could not stop my thoughts from returning to the past, and to transpose me, in spirit, back to 11 May 1900, the day I saw your eyes for the last time. It never occurred to me then that it would be more than two long years that I would have to endure without

seeing your eyes. When I was still at home, in a time of peace, it would have been bitter for me to be separated from you for just a month, but such is the will of the Lord . . .

I said in my last letter that there was talk here that some of our people might leave on the fourth, but it was all lies. Now everything is unsure. We do not know when we are going back.

Further, with Oubaas and all the others, things are fine . . .

Further, love, I have no particular news. Little to write but lots to tell you. Be satisfied with this little bit.

Give my greetings to Pa and Ma, sisters and little brother [Daan] . . . also to Sannie.

For you and the children, my heartfelt love,

Your longing husband, MA Muller.

PS Reply to this when you receive it. I do not know how long this duration will be. Everything is uncertain. A Mara lies before us.

Mara, meaning 'bitterness', was one of the places identified in the bible as having been travelled through by the Israelites during the Exodus, and it would be a Mara indeed, though fortunately Michael did not know how hard the years after the war would be for him. In reality, his Mara journey would never quite end.

First they had to cross the agonising hurdle of signing the oath, to recognise their enemy's victory and ownership of their two republics, as well as pledging their fealty. There was no way around this; if they did not, they would not be given free passage home and they could not afford to pay for one – and the call of their families was the strongest pull.

So, like the other two Muller brothers, Michael signed the oath, as tens of thousands of Boers did, choking back the pain of it. It enabled them to travel, though the arrangements for repatriation were slower than they had hoped.

Before he returned home, there was one more episode in his personal life to record, as it would have life-altering consequences for him and his family: he changed his church.

At last, on 8 October 1902, after a nerve-stretching four-month wait, Michael boarded the *Aurinia*. It was one of three large ships each carrying over a thousand POWs back to Cape Town. He brought his Bermuda carvings with him, as well as a large, brown-freckled conch shell. (His grandchildren remember him playing with the conch shell and, when no one was watching, putting it to his ear 'to hear the sea').

From Cape Town, Michael was sent by train to Bloemfontein and made his own long way back to Bankfontein farm, in what was now the British-held Orange River Colony.

At the farm, Nelie was setting out the children's clothes for the eventful day of their father's return. While struggling to untie a knot in his shoe-laces, young Pieter recklessly used a table fork; he lost his grip on it and it plunged into his right eye, destroying its vision and placing something of a cloud over the reunion. Yet even that startling accident could not reduce the joy and relief they felt when reunited.

Michael's religious change of heart was no insignificant event for a Boer. Alongside their country and their families, their church, the NGK, was the kernel of their community existence – where they were baptised, married and buried, and where they met every three months for *nagmaal* and tra-ditional *toenadering* (coming together) between families and old friends, some trekking in especially for this event from far afield.

This tightly knit church had been established in the 1800s in the Free State and, due to a shortage of dominees, was stocked with many Scottish Presbyterian ministers, who were first sent to the Netherlands to learn Dutch. The influential Rev Andrew Murray and his family were a product of this scheme; many of Scottish descent in the Free State (and elsewhere) became Afrikaans-Nederlands speakers and considered themselves pro-Boer, hence the many local place names with Scottish antecedents, includ-ing Commandant Diederichs' farm, Haltwhistle.

But this war had challenged the faith of some; had their God forsaken them? There are records of Boers tearing up their bibles when the peace was announced.

It was not his faith that Michael rejected, but rather the manner in which he observed it. A deeply religious and pious man all his life, he began, along with a few other fellow prisoners, to question *how* they expressed and acted out their faith. He became part of a faith and prayer group in Bermuda that would later have significant influence in South Africa; on his return, he left the NGK.

Why such a quiet, mild-mannered man came to make this life-changing decision is not recorded; his nervous anxiety while on board the prison ship in the Cape may have triggered the process, which continued during his difficult days on Darrell's Island. In 1908, he and his wife Nelie were founder-members of the Apostolic Faith Mission, a central tenet of which is adult baptism, and for the rest of his life Michael would be active in this church, considered 'charismatic' by the staid, disapproving NGK. Its origins lay in the United States, and it is possible that the random chance that Michael was sent to Bermuda, where such charismatic churches were already known, may have had some influence.

His decision would shock his extended family, friends and neighbours after his return home, perhaps one of the reasons why, during the time of *helpmekaar* after the war, he was seen as an outlier and did not prosper (another being that he was not as entrepreneurial as Chris).

Being 'different' was hard going, not helped by the fact that their new church was interracial (the term 'non-racial' was not used then). The Faith Mission appealed to the poorer, dispossessed communities, many of whom literally came from the wrong side of the tracks; Michael and his congregants did mission work among impoverished coloured railway workers – this too, carried social disapproval. It did not deter Michael, who never owned a car, nor much else, and who rode his bicycle miles around the district to visit anyone who would welcome him.

Michael's sons Pieter and Chrisjan, born before the war, were brought up in the NGK and remained members. (Pieter was teased by his schoolfriends because his father's church had invited a black preacher from Basutoland to address them – an unimaginable act for many Boer churchgoers then and later.) But their parents and their three post-war siblings remained part of the charismatic Christian movement, perhaps the most unanticipated and longest-lasting consequence of Michael's unwanted war.

Michael's terror throughout his years as soldier, and then prisoner, had been not the danger to himself, but that he might never again see his beloved wife and two little sons. Nelie's courage in dodging between the conflict's frontlines, and at times taking refuge in Basutoland, meant they managed to survive a war in which women and children were the main casualties. Her resourcefulness saved them.

Here, home at last with his dear family among these verdant fields and golden hills, Michael would spend the rest of his long, poor and loving life.

PART VI

AFTERWARDS

25

The ugly consequences

ALL WARS EVENTUALLY END, and seldom well; this one was no exception. Rudyard Kipling later commented that the Boers had given Britain 'no end of a lesson'. It is a strange way to describe a win, though he was not wrong.

The Empire had eventually struggled to its drawn-out victory by sending out its largest army ever overseas, almost half a million men in number, and by spending unprecedented sums of money – £1 250 000 every week – in their costliest war ever until the Second World War.

In contrast to this, when the Free State government was captured at Reitz in July 1901 (President Steyn, in pyjamas, managed to escape on his trusted horse, Scot), their whole treasury was only £11 500, mostly in Free State notes – useless to the captors. This may be one of the more incredible aspects of this conflict: that the determined Boers were fighting on little more than a wing and a prayer.

Afterwards, many in Britain, including Winston Churchill and the royal family, viewed the Boers in a different light. Churchill, who had served in many military campaigns, reckoned that the Boers were his finest foes ever. He developed a mutual admiration society of two with General Louis Botha. He also picked up a few Afrikaans phrases that appealed to him: he enjoyed using '*Alles sal regkom*' ('Everything will be alright'), if slightly inaccurately.

The brilliant, Cambridge-educated Boer general Jan Smuts later became Churchill's favourite Commonwealth prime minister, trusted adviser and life-long friend, and ensured that South Africa joined the Allies in both world wars.

From the moment he signed the Peace of Vereeniging in 1902, Smuts devoted his long life to the daunting task of reuniting Boer and Brit, and regaining the shattered South Africa. (The whataboutism of why Smuts didn't resolve the 'colour question' is self-evident: he recognised that the black population, some of whom had been comrades during battle,[26] had been badly treated; but, gifted as he was, he was not a miracle worker. That would take a new freedom struggle.)

Under his guidance, less than eight years later, the Union of South Africa was formed, with Louis Botha as the first prime minister, followed by Smuts. These two admired Boer leaders had continued to the bitter end of the war; their stalwart persistence in no small measure contributed to their now controlling not only the two former Boer republics of the Transvaal and Free State, but also the large former British colonies of the Cape and Natal – a breathtaking political finesse, perhaps the most unanticipated outcome of the war.

When the guns fell silent in 1902, the Boers had had to face their future as British subjects in a land that had been vacuumed up by the mighty Empire.

What is more, the Boers were threadbare. In the worst cases – and this was quite widespread – they faced a literal wasteland. At least 30 000 farms, along with livestock and crops, had been deliberately destroyed by fire or dynamite. And not only were their buildings burned down and/or vandalised, but the very fields were often salted, creating soil conditions unsuitable for growing crops for some time to come.

Some of the worst war recollections came at its very end: those thousands of returning Boer exiles, streaming along the roads towards a terrible silence, dreading what they would find, or not find. More than forty small towns had been utterly demolished; many returning Boers had no family left at all. When men go to war, they assume that it will be them, not their women and children, who will be most at risk of dying. Never had the Boers imagined the opposite might become true.

The iconic short poem 'Dis al' ('That Is All') by the poet Jan FE Celliers (with whom Lool fought at Colesberg) hung on the wall of virtually every Boer home for generations to come. The second and last stanza (translated) reads, 'An exile came home from over the sea / A grave in the grass, a tear breaking free. / That is all.' In the original language, it has devastating power, and evokes the plight of those homecoming soldiers who had lost everyone. This was the Boer take-away from the war: that in order to win, their enemy had been prepared to oversee the deaths of their women and children. In the years immediately after the war, empty classrooms testified to a whole generation that had been lost.

The surviving Muller brothers had loved ones to return to, but they were not unscathed. Lool's grave was 700 miles away in Cape Town; Chris had lost two infant sons in the war; and Nelie's younger half-brother and half-sister were buried in the Bethulie concentration camp's cemetery for children. Their homesteads were lost too, burned to the ground, as well as their possessions, including livestock, destroyed.

Their comrade Jan Diederichs' two teenaged brothers, Roelfie and Albert, non-combatants, had been captured and taken to St Helena without their mother ('Three Ms', the widow of Commandant Diederichs) knowing what had happened to them – the ultimate nightmare of missing children. Only one returned; Roelfie's grave is still in St Helena. Their mother, greeting a gaunt stranger at the door of her lean-to on the burned-out ruin of Haltwhistle, did not recognise Albert, now aged 17, until he spoke her name: '*Moeder.*' He suffered from traumatic survivors' guilt for the rest of his life.

Like so many warriors returning home, the men seldom spoke of their war. It remained for women to talk of it in muted tones, while children played at their feet, little ears flapping – the way war stories are often preserved.

Returning to their farms was not an enshrined right: Britain considered itself the rightful government of the two former Boer republics, so could (and did) revoke bonds because the soldier-farmers had been unable to repay anything during the war years. These were the years before the *Landbank* (a later state-financed cooperative to fund agriculture), and actual cash or loans were terribly difficult to secure for returning Boers; some were helped by sympathetic friends and even distant neighbours who stood surety for loans, but very many lost their farms. Most valuables, except for those buried at the beginning of the war (such as Nelie Muller's china and big kettle) were gone for good.

Painful Boer 'piano stories' crop up frequently in the literature of the war: a family's prized piano, treated with such tenderness that only the *Moeder* was allowed to dust it, was roughly hauled out of their home and often chopped up before being set on fire. There were people on both sides who had not imagined a conflict so bereft of ordinary decencies.

Other valuables 'went missing', taken by none-too-honest neighbours and not always returned after the war: *hensoppers* went from farm to farm and simply helped themselves to goods belonging to Boers who had fled or been captured.

The Mullers were among the many who confronted new poverty: often merely the clothes they stood up in. It was the beginning of something the self-sufficient Boers could never have foreseen, that large numbers of their people would have no way of sustaining themselves.

The Transvaal, at least, had their mines to offer work. But the majority of Free State farmers came home to an unrecognisable world. Even those in professions found it difficult to sustain a living, due to a lack of ready money within their much-diminished population.

So began the era of 'poor whites' on an unprecedented scale; untold conflict lay ahead, as they began competing for jobs with black South Africans.

This war, founded and fostered in Britain, had the result of binding two separate and defeated Boer nations into a common destiny. Theologian Dr John Daniel Kestell ('*Vader*' Kestell) recognised this: 'God has formed the Africander nation in this great struggle,' he wrote in 1903.

It would have ugly consequences.

Professor Pumla Gobodo-Madikizela, recorder of apartheid atrocities, wrote in 2012: 'Without any attempt to compare the evil of the British concentration camps to the evil of the Nazi camps in Germany and Poland, I wonder why [this] atrocity on South African soil has not been addressed with equal force?'

British statesman Sir Henry Campbell-Bannerman, prime minister after the war, was equally emphatic in a speech on 14 June 1901 when the war was still in full swing: 'When is a war not a war? When it is carried on by methods of barbarism in South Africa.'

Campbell-Bannerman's opinion was far from isolated. There had been almost universal condemnation of Britain's war of aggression in South Africa. Influential voices in neutral countries such as France, Russia and the United States, and in British colonies such as Australia and Canada, and in particular Ireland, felt that the war on the Boers had been deeply unjust, based on the thinnest of pretexts.

But the Boers had learned that even their traditional allies, the Netherlands and Germany, had not come to their aid. Their fight for their freedom – including their language – had not been won, despite all the sympathies offered. Journalist Max du Preez commented in the *Cape Times* in April 2004 that 'the Anglo-Boer War had a massive impact on the Afrikaner psyche, and on their ethnic nationalism in the decades after. The war and its aftermath, involuntary urbanisation on a large scale, extreme poverty for many, and an overwhelming sense of insecurity and inferiority, influenced Afrikaner thinking.' He also recalled his grandfather repeating the old adage: 'The sun never sets on the British Empire *want God kan nie die Engelse in die donker vertrou nie*' (because God cannot trust the *English* in the dark). It was a dark quip borne out of painful experience, one that is unforgotten.

This war had become a bullet lodged in the hearts of Boer survivors, boring into their lack of security. This resulted in a deep mistrust of others, leading to both mental and emotional isolation. Their destiny would never be allowed to lie in anyone else's hands again.

When the moderate government of Smuts lost power in 1948, populist nationalism formalised an existing racialised system. Apartheid was a cruel but not unforeseeable offspring of this war: the Boer descendants were not the first, nor would they be the last, to make bad choices based on fear, so that it would *never happen again* – amplified in later decades as generational trauma. To grasp this tragedy, we need to understand how close the Boers believed they as a people and a culture had come to the edge of deliberate annihilation: at least a sixth of their population died in the war, though the actual figure is likely to have been higher.[27]

The war's aftermath led to a new *broedertwis* in families, between those Afrikaners who supported reconciliation between Boer and Brit, and those who would never accept it.

Later, during the apartheid years, these families were further torn; some of the most effective dissidents were Afrikaners, less easy to dismiss than English-speaking activists. These included the Oxford-educated advocate Bram Fischer from the politically prominent Free State family, whose grandfather Abraham Fischer was a prime minister of the post-war Orange River

Colony; Bram defended Nelson Mandela and other anti-apartheid activists in the Rivonia Trial, before being imprisoned until the end of his life.

This *broedertwis* affected the Muller descendants and relatives too. Apartheid-era president Nico Diederichs was the son of Jan Diederichs, whose grandsons Ampie and Piet Muller (also Michael Muller's grandsons), while maintaining civil and even close family relations, chose to take an active part in the progressive Afrikaner movement known, not always kindly, as the *verligtes* (enlightened).

Wars end, but their impact may last much longer. From this turn-of-the-century invasive war, another freedom struggle was born, on these same bloodied fields, on the bones of so much grief.

26

The war's aftermath for the Mullers

FOUR MULLER BROTHERS rode to war, and three returned.

Michael, the first-born of the ten Muller siblings, never fully recovered from the war's effects. He had come from a quite prosperous family, and before the war had rented the farm Bankfontein; the hardship caused by the war's destruction meant he never made enough to buy his own place – he rented and worked on farms (as did many son-rich Boer families), though he was never a *bywoner*, a 'hired hand' – a very low status for the self-reliant Boers. In addition, as a director of a 'Boer co-op' at Commissie-poort, the stock of which was commandeered after the outbreak of the war, he shouldered his share of the debt. Thus, he and his family became 'genteel poor', that awkward place of struggling to keep up appearances.

He and Nelie worked incredibly hard all their lives; both were physically slender, even thin – particularly in old age – yet they bent their backs to all that was needed. It proved not to be enough.

Another issue was his new religious faith, forged on Darrell's Island. Having seen the worst of what men can do to each other, his faith held that all God's children, regardless of race, were one, and indivisible. This made him and his young family a target.

His son Pieter, he of the '*vurkoog*' (the fork-damaged eye), captured something of their struggle in a long letter he wrote to his own youngest son, Piet, two years before his death in 1982 at the age of 87. He described their post-war years, first on the farm Pleasant View, on the Caledon River, which they shared with four or five other families. Here, the war-broken stone house had to be rebuilt.

'How many times in my lifetime did I not have the experience of hail, or droughts, or locusts destroying everything that we had to live off, and Father had to pay the rent. And then there would have to be new loans taken out ... Then Father again would have to make vegetable gardens, buy sheep and slaughter them, and take them every week with the cart and two horses to supply his customers.'

When his father drove the heavy plough, they had to use a cow and calves because he could not afford *trekbeeste* (oxen). 'I had to lift it up, turn it and push it back into the ground again.' He would have been no more than 9 years old. 'Every time, we had to start over again. A farmer's courage is without limit.'

Later, Michael and a relation by marriage hired a much-prized farm of 700 morgen, Hexrivier. Michael lived there and worked the land, and of all the farms he lived on during his lifetime, this was the one he loved the most. It was here that the three post-war children were raised: Corrie (Cornelia), the first post-war baby born in 1905, Michael, born in 1910, and Martha, the *laatlammetjie*, born in 1914.

'On this farm,' Pieter recalled in his letter, 'there was a huge heap of bones, of sheep and cattle, about a foot deep and covering a large area, a whole erf. These were the remains of the poor dumb animals that were shot and also stabbed to death by the *English* during the war, so that the Boers would not be able to find food.'

Schooling became the Boers' burning grievance after the war, for the despised Alfred Milner, now in charge, had decreed that all school teaching had to be in English, allegedly to 'unite' the country, though (as all historians know) nothing could have been more calculated to produce the opposite effect. It is not widely known that even the greatest Afrikaans poet, NP van Wyk Louw, born four years after the war's end in 1906 (who later became the father-in-law of Michael Muller's grandson Ampie), was taught entirely in English. If children reverted to Afrikaans, a 'Dutch plank' on string was hung around their necks, which had to be worn along with a cap with long donkey-like ears as punishment. This gave impetus to the creation of the private 'farm schools' system.

Despite the chronic shortage of money, Michael ensured that his children were properly schooled, even if it meant that his eldest son Pieter had to board during the week with a woman in town, wearing his mother's cut-down shoes – 'We had to endure the cruel teasing of the other children because of our old and patched clothes, and naturally it led to fist-fights,' Pieter recalled.

Pieter became headmaster of the school in Warden, Free State at a young age; here he remained for the rest of his working life – his own four children were schooled there. All three of his sons would obtain their doctorates, and his daughter, Rina, became a qualified midwife who later attended Stellenbosch University. What had been taken to heart after the war was the realisation that the best method to both survival and dignity was through education – a view shared decades later, in a different era, by Nelson Mandela.

Michael died in Ladybrand in 1945. Nelie died in Bloemfontein in 1970, aged 92. Cherished and supported by their family, neither of them left enough for a *boedel* (estate); their children, organised by Pieter, had cared for their needs in their old age. 'My Oupa and Ouma Muller were two incredibly lovely people,' said their grandson Ampie, who had known them well.

Their twin graves lie together in Ladybrand.

Michael and Nelie Muller in retirement in Ladybrand (date unknown).

Chris Muller recovered from his war illness and remained active on his lovely farm, Fortuin, near Commissiepoort. He and Dorie had five children after the war: Tommie (named because he looked like a 'real *Tommie*'), Pieter, and daughters Willie, Mimmie and Dollie.

Men who were able to scratch together ox- or horse-wagons went into the transport-and-trading business while keeping their farms running. Chris built a lucrative trade in Basutoland, which he plied for many years. An ever-resourceful man, he became prosperous enough to send all his children to good schools in Bloemfontein – the boys to St Andrews, and the girls to Eunice.

Years after the war, Chris penned a long, heartfelt and reconciliatory ode titled 'Magersfontein'. Though it reflects on a time when he was a young soldier being tested in battle for the first time and features the deaths of his commandant, Diederichs, and Veldkornet Jan de Wet, it also offers his maturity, forged in hardship. The last stanza reads:

> From the graves across this land,
> From the Cape to the Transvaal,
> Boer and Brit reach out their hands –
> The debt of justice has been paid.
> Afrikaners, sisters, mothers,
> In unity, each other trust –
> Now all work like one, as brothers,
> To nurture freedom, build the future, we must.

Chris remained involved in political affairs, occasionally with his former brother-in-arms, Jan Diederichs. He was an active ally of Louis Botha, and remained a 'Smuts man', under whom he served as a major in both world wars; his reconciliatory attitude was not shared by all, even within his family.

Chris died in 1947, aged 77. After his death, Dorie, who was very ample in her later years, took to her bed and ruled the farm with a rod of iron – an old matriarchal Boer custom.

After burying her husband, Dorie ordered that all his war material should be destroyed. Her view was that it was a bad time, now over and best forgotten. Fortunately, her Irish daughter-in-law Patricia disobeyed her, and kept it safe – her defiance ensured that this story of Chris's war has survived.

Dorie died in 1958 and lies alongside her husband in the grassy grave-yard. Here, too, lies Joey, buried in 1936, their only child to survive the war.

Chris Muller in 1929.

Pieter Muller married Diena Taljaard in Ladybrand in 1903 and had four daughters. He farmed in Dewetsdorp until his death in 1960 at the impressive age of 87. War photographs reveal his damaged eye, and in his last years he was quite blind, though active in his community, including the Ladybrand church, where he served on their board.

Pieter married Diena Taljaard shortly after the war, in 1903.

Lool Muller had died as a young POW, leaving no descendants, and for years the location of his grave was a puzzle for the current Muller family. Then, in 2012, a memorial wall within Fort Wynyard in Green Point, commemorating Boers who had died in the nearby camp, was unveiled. Among the hundred-odd names listed is Ludwig [actually Lodewyk] Theodorus Muller.

The bodies of dead Boer prisoners had been transported from Green Point to Fort Knokke for burial. Knokke was demolished in 1927 to make way for the new large Salt River rail junction, so the remains of Lool and his dead comrades were transferred to Wolraad Woltemade Cemetery in Maitland (near what is now Gate 4).

Yet this was *still* not the final resting place of Lool. In the 1960s, authorities decided that 'other arrangements' must be made for these Boer dead, and Lool's last resting place is revealed in an oasis of clean, clipped order in the otherwise overgrown and extended Maitland Cemetery accessed through Gate 10. Here, the Commonwealth War Graves Commission has taken honourable care of the war dead, including those not its own.

In the far right corner of this neat section of the cemetery lies a flat granite stone on which rests a long metal plaque: 'Members of the Republican Forces [Boers] who died and were buried in Fort Knokke cemetery, transferred to the Military Allotment, Woltemade No 4 in November 1927.' There are 50 names on the plaque, including Lool's (although wrongly listed as 'LJ' rather than 'LT'), and that of Philip Cronje, shot in Green Point.

Former foes lie silently united here, for cemeteries are the ultimate levellers of conflict.

The fifth and youngest brother, Daan, had been too young to join the battle – he was barely 9 years old when his elder brothers left to fight. A friendly, sociable individual, liked by all, he married a Dutch woman, *Tant* Ans. He was firm friends with Michael's son, Pieter, even though Daan was technically his uncle, for they were much the same age.

When Michael's first-born son Pieter married Martha, daughter of the Mullers' war comrade Jan Diederichs, in 1923, these two families were fully united. Martha had survived the war as an infant solely because she was born in Tsolo, Basutoland, in 1901, under the protection of the local chief,

'*Die Drie Adriaans*' (the three Adriaans) on their farm Juistzoo, 1933:
Oupa Jan (APJ) Diederichs, who fought at Magersfontein; his son
Adriaan; and Ampie (Adriaan Diederichs Muller) as a little boy.

after the Diederichs farm Haltwhistle was burned down – it was less than
ten miles from the Basutoland border.

Jan Diederichs bought Juistzoo, the neighbouring Jan de Wet's farm,
which had also been burned down, after which almost the entire family had
perished. On this rebuilt, prosperous farm that incorporated the former
Haltwhistle farm, many of Michael Muller's grandchildren spent childhood holidays, playing near the twin-stone grave of their ancestor, Commandant APJ Diederichs, who had died at Magersfontein.

The sacrifice of the Ladybranders in the Boer War is memorialised on
a painted *In Memoria* board inside that town's civic building, built in 1905

for war orphans. The 64 names in gothic script include those of Commandant Diederichs, his son Roelfie, who died on St Helena, and Lool Muller.

The nearby village of Hobhouse, named after the pro-Boer campaigner Emily Hobhouse, still marks the tight link between these two Free State families; its main road, running off the R26 to Ladybrand, is Muller Street, while the parallel road is Diederichs Street.

EPILOGUE

The enigma of Magersfontein

THERE IS A great field in the heart of South Africa that carries a majestic name. Baking in summer and freezing on winter nights, it lies at the foot of the koppie for which it is named. Remnants of trenches can still be found, and gravestones and memorials on its veld. Once, this red soil was thickened with the blood of men, and the overhead cries of raptors were drowned by the thundering boom of cannons.

Visitors to Magersfontein may puzzle at this isolated place, once so fiercely contested. But on a day, 11 December 1899, it was the centre of the universe for two small republics and an Empire. During that long evening, wounded soldiers cried for water, and their mothers. Those who heard them wept with exhaustion and pity. For the dying, it matters little whose side you are on.

It shaped and altered, in unforeseen ways, the history of this land well into the next century. Like the fields of all wars, its import now seems hard to fathom. Standing here, we ponder on what to take away.

Notes

1   It was official education policy not to teach the Boer War in schools as it was felt it would be too divisive, historian Prof Albert Grundlingh told the author in 2021.
2   More than 100 Boer sympathisers from Norway, Sweden, Denmark and Finland joined the Boer army as volunteers. Of those 60 or so who fought at Magersfontein, 23 died in the battle or immediately after of wounds; the rest (all wounded) were taken prisoner. Only seven, all but one wounded, made it back to the Boer lines. Their dead were buried with the Boer casualties and are honoured at the Burgers' Memorial in Magersfontein. Their own countries honoured them later with specially minted medals.
3   Sir Arthur Conan Doyle, there as a medic, was horrified at the results: 'It may be doubted if any single battle has ever put so many families of high and low into mourning from the Tweed to the Caithness shore,' he would later write. All dances and festivities were cancelled in Scotland, as the country went into mourning.
4   This 'promise', which developed mythological status, was made by President Martinus Steyn at Bloemfontein in November 1899: 'I promise you, I will not put my hand to any paper that will destroy our independence,' he assured Diederichs and Jan de Wet (all three men were close cousins). And he never did (partly due to his wasting illness). Days later, the two older men were dead.
5   The wife of Commandant APJ Diederichs, Martha Maria Magdalena née Wolmarans, was always referred to as 'Three Ms'.
6   After the Cape Dutch farmhouse Zeekoegat had been built, the second prominent Muller family residence in the Cape was the farm Kleinberg, 13 miles before Mossel Bay; its white gateposts featuring the Muller crest are still easily seen from the N2. All 'Mullerfees' gatherings have been held there, the last, in 2010, featuring more than 800 Mullers.
7   Milner promptly reinstated Transvaal's former policies immediately after the end of the war, first by increasing the requirement for citizenship in the new colony from five to ten years. 'How ironic, considering this was the [very] issue which, four years before, Milner had pushed to the point of war,' points out Diane Cammack in her 1990 book *The Rand at War 1899-1902*.
8   These telegrams were sent in February 1899 on behalf of the Colonial Office. The Royal Commission, under the Crown's authority, held its first hearing on 8 October

1902 and its last on 10 June 1903. It sat for 55 days, and heard 114 witnesses, including all the most senior British officers, replying to 22 000 questions, to try to establish how and why so many mistakes had been made on their side (freely admitted by the senior officers called to testify). Steyn's struggle with Milner to avert the war was therefore undermined from the start of 1899; Milner had knowingly acted in bad faith during the mid-year conference in Bloemfontein called by Steyn, and Rhodes was an integral participant of those back-room plans.

9   The confusing similarity between these two names has often been remarked on. In Methuen's first despatch from Magersfontein, he uses a compilation of the two names, as 'Majersfontein' (UK National Archives). Logan banked on this, when persuading Lady Wauchope in Scotland to agree to a 'proper' military funeral, though in Matjiesfontein. The family spokesperson, General Sir Arthur Grenfell Wauchope, later confirmed it was a mistake. After the war, Lady Wauchope visited the large memorial about ten kilometres south of Matjiesfontein which had been a huge remount station; it is now easily spotted from the N1 national highway. Although she regretted that her husband had not been buried at the battlefield where he died, due to the name confusion, she felt she could not have him moved again.

10 Methuen claimed afterwards not to have known about the trenches or wires, which is false. His original despatch, not the later, revised version, includes the following line: 'The guns on Sunday [the day before the big battle] fired with accuracy and effect *on the kopje and the trenches* at the foot of the kopje.' He attached his order for this bombardment. The Mullers and their Boer comrades at Magersfontein won the great battle not only because of Methuen's blunders but because they were far better prepared, thanks to De la Rey's forward planning.

11 Butler was admonished by his political masters as 'running counter to what Her Majesty's government wished', an admission of the war lust of Conservative Prime Minister Lord Salisbury, and Joseph Chamberlain, who was in close contact with Rhodes. Butler was recalled to Britain within a month of the war: although he had held the information-rich position of Commander-in-Chief in South Africa, neither the Prime Minister nor the Colonial Secretary would agree to see him on his return and the Secretary of War gave him ten whole minutes.

12 The Free State's economy was primarily agricultural and needed to be sustained during the war. It was commonplace and accepted for sons, brothers or close male relatives to swop places within their commandos so that essential farming and harvesting could continue on their farms.

13 Royal Commission of 1903, ref. statement 161. Colonel GFR Henderson, Director of Military Intelligence, had discovered on arrival in South Africa that there were *no war maps* suitable for military purposes – not even of the Cape Colony. To prepare for this anticipated war, Sir John Ardagh had asked for an initial £18,000 for map-making, and been offered a paltry £100. Kitchener had arrived in South Africa as second-in-command to Field Marshal Lord Roberts (who arrived after him), with massive British reinforcements, and would later succeed him.

14 Steyn's courage in continuing to the very last day of the war he had never wanted became the stuff of legend, and enabled him to keep his sacred promise, made to Diederichs, that he would never sign a surrender; admittedly, his illness, perhaps a form of early-onset myasthenia gravis – (botulism has also been suggested, by family members) – rendered him unable to do so. His wife Tibby, who had been

very shabbily treated during the war, afterwards took him to the Netherlands for treatment, though he was never well again.

15 Properly used, no percentage given should exceed 100 per cent, but percentages are relative to context. The British army calculated the rate at which mounts 'usually' were used up, but the sorry death rate during the Boer War far exceeded even their highest calculations. By the end of the war, British mounts were lasting on average three months – a far higher rate than any previous war.

16 The term 'Hottentotten' was commonly used at that time, particularly for brown Capetonians who later became racially classified as 'coloureds' and were regarded as distinct from the darker Sotho people so familiar to the Free Staters.

17 Boers who lived in the Cape Colony and who were active Boer sympathisers were deemed to be criminals, ie, traitors liable to be shot; if caught, they were dressed in convict clothes with a yellow patch over their hearts where the firing squad should aim, and received no POW benefits such as post. Some were reprieved from the death sentence and sent to POW camps overseas, but were kept separately.

18 News of their dexterity spread: local townswomen came to view the handicrafts and, according to Michael, on 6 October 1900 an exhibition was held of all types of crafts made by the prisoners. This selling of the Boer POW handicrafts, some of them made with great skill, also happened in all the overseas POW camps, and today are collectibles.

19 This has been amplified by historians Bill Nasson and Albert Grundlingh: also, in discussion with Albert Grundlingh, Cape Town, 11 August 2021.

20 British soldiers appeared to suffer even more from typhoid fever, possibly because they had a lower immunity to local conditions. This fever killed about 60 per cent of British casualties, far more than all the battles put together.

21 The only visible remains of this large POW camp – or indeed, any structure built for the war in the area – exists in the form of a red corrugated-iron house in Grant Avenue, just off Bellevue Road, where the camp's main entrance was. In private hands now, this house was an office for British staff; the Mullers would have noted it as they were marched in. There is no signage whatever that this golf course once held thousands of Boer prisoners.

22 Nelie and Sannie's ancestors included Verenigde Oos-Indiese Kompanjie (VOC, Dutch East India Company) slaves Catharina van Malabar, Lijsbet Sanders van de Kaap, and Trijntje Harmensz, likely the daughter of an Angolan slave. (Van de Kaap, or Caap, was a suffix applied to the Cape-born offspring of slaves and free blacks.)

23 This entry of Michael is the 'missing page' from his diary that had been separated many decades earlier, for unknown reasons, and which was fortuitously rediscovered while preparing this book: it adds much to the richness of his story.

24 After Jan de Wet's farm Juistzoo was burnt down, seven of his family died in concentration camps, including his wife Leseja (a cousin of Paul Kruger), youngest son Pieter (10), daughter Cecilia Erasmus (34) and her son, JM Erasmus (14), daughter Leseja (18), granddaughter Magel (7 months) and grandson Johannes (5), whose father Johannes died as a POW on St Helena. Three other sons were sent to that island too, and one to Ceylon, but they survived. One of them, Casparus Jan Hendrik de Wet, was a 13-year-old POW.

25 At the end of the war, a number of Boers on Bermuda refused to sign the required oath of allegiance in order to receive free passage home, at which point Bermuda washed its hands of any support for them, leaving them standing on the quay. Miss Outerbridge promptly employed ten of them as 'gardeners'; some Boers

remained on the island for years, one of them running a curio shop selling Boer POW handicrafts.

26 The notion that this was a 'white man's war' is patently false – there was extensive use of armed black men on both sides throughout the war (sometimes disguised as police, or 'scouts' so heavily armed for combat that their horses must have struggled to carry the extra weight! There were some woman combatants as well). Smuts, a brilliant lawyer, conceded that it was not contrary to the rules of international law to employ blacks under white officers in combat (see Warwick, p 17). He was personally opposed to this practice, yet recorded in his autobiography the brave deeds of his two good and faithful 'boys' [sic] Charlie and Kleinbooi, half brothers, the former who lost both his legs and the latter who died 'by my side that fearful night at Paardekop' (Smuts autobiography). The notion that blacks were merely 'agterryers', there solely to load guns and do menial work, is unsustainable; see Warwick, pp 17-27. On a lighter note, Charles Lucan of the Colonial Office suggested that "Many of the Boers are very dark, and might perhaps be mistaken for natives' (see Warwick, p 19). Just a week later he acknowledged 'the use of natives by the Boers is beyond anything we have done...' though the British forces had no scruples in doing exactly the same thing. There were black combatants, held at Bellevue at the same time as Michael, who resented being acknowledged as mere servants.

27 Milner had pontificated in a letter on 20 April 1898 that any Boer government was 'too great a curse' to be allowed to exist, and that war alone could pull it down. The deliberate policy had been not only to wage the war as brutally as possible, in order (so he stated) to ensure a swift end (which failed), but also in his mind that any remnants of Boer influence would be gone forever. This inevitably and foreseeably meant that any such war would include Boer civilians.

References, resources and further reading

Benbow, C. 1994. *Boer Prisoners of War in Bermuda*. Bermuda: The Bermuda Historical Society.

Bosch, JA. 1967. *Ladybrand 1867-1967*. Bloemfontein: NG Sendingspers.

Breytenbach, JH. 1971. *Geskiedenis van die Tweede Vryheidsoorlog 1899-1902*. Pretoria: Staatsdrukkers.

Cammack, D. 1990. *The Rand at War 1899-1902: The Witwatersrand & the Anglo-Boer War*. Pietermaritzburg: University of Natal Press.

Conan Doyle, A. 1999. *The Great Boer War*. Alberton: Galago Publishing.

Dommisse, E. 2011. *Sir David Pieter De Villiers Graaff: First baronet of De Grendel*. Cape Town: Tafelberg.

De Villiers, B. 1998. '"De Emigratie", 30 Mei 1901' in *Boereoorlogstories: 34 verhale oor die oorlog van 1899-1902* (ed. Jeanette Ferreira). Pretoria: JL van Schaik.

De Villiers, JC (Kay). 2008. *Healers, Helpers and Hospitals: A history of military medicine in the Anglo-Boer War* (two volumes). Protea.

De Wet, CR. 1902. *Three Years' War*. New York: Charles Scribner's Sons.

Du Preez, M. 'Two cultures that need to understand each other better' in *Cape Times*, 5 April 2004.

Du Preez, M. 'Die Joiner en die General' in *Die Burger*, 7 May 2005.

Field, K. 2007. *Soldier Boy: A young New Zealander writes home from the Boer War*. Auckland: New Holland Publishers.

Gobodo-Madikizela, P. 'What we must remember' in *Sunday Times*, 25 March 2012.

Gray, A. 2004. *Vocal music of the Anglo-Boer War (1899-1902): Insights into processes of affect and meaning in music*. Doctoral thesis, University of Pretoria.

Grundlingh, AM. 2006, *The Dynamics of Treason: Boer collaboration in the South African War of 1899-1902*. Pretoria: Protea.

Harrison, D. 1981. *The White Tribe of Africa: South Africa in perspective*. London: BBC.

Heese, HF. 1985. *Groep sonder grense: Die rol en status van die gemengde bevolking aan die Kaap 1654-1795*. The University of the Western Cape Institute for Historical Research, Bellville.

Iklé, F. 1971. *Every War Must End*. New York: Columbia University Press.

Jenkins, R. 2002. *Churchill.* London: Macmillan.

Kestell, JD. 1903. *Through Shot and Flame: The adventures and experiences of JD Kestell, chaplain to President Steyn and General Christian de Wet.* London: Methuen & Co.

Lategan, FV and Potgieter, L. 1982. *Die Boer se roer tot vandag: Die ontwikkeling van die vuurwapen in Suider-Afrika.* Cape Town: Tafelberg.

Lee, E. 1985. *To the Bitter End.* Viking.

Lewis, HE. 2016. *Apartheid: Britain's bastard child.* Reach Publishers.

Marquard, L (ed). 1967. *Letters from a Boer Parsonage: Letters of Margaret Marquard during the Boer War.* Cape Town: Purnell.

Meredith, M. 2007. *Diamonds, Gold and War: The making of South Africa.* London: Simon & Schuster.

Meyer, IA. 1952. *Die ervarings van 'n veldkornet in die Engelse Oorlog 1899-1902.* Ladybrand: G. Balharrie & Kie.

Muller, A and Roos-Muller, B. 2020. *Vuur in sy vingers: Die verreikende invloed van NP van Wyk Louw.* Cape Town: Hemel & See Boeke.

Nasson, B. 2010. *The War for South Africa: The Anglo-Boer War 1899-1902.* Cape Town: Tafelberg.

Nasson, B and Grundlingh, A. 2013. *The War at Home: Women and families in the Anglo-Boer War.* Cape Town: Tafelberg.

Pakenham, T. 1979. *The Boer War.* Johannesburg: Jonathan Ball Publishers.

Paterson, AB. 1980. *Happy Dispatches: Journalistic pieces from a war correspondent.* Sydney: Lansdowne Press.

Phillips, H. 2012. *Plague, Pox and Pandemics.* Johannesburg: Jacana.

Plaatje, ST. 1999. *The Mafeking Diary.* Centenary edition (eds. John Comaroff and Brian Willan) Cape Town: David Philip Publishers.

Pohl, V. 1944. *Adventures of a Boer Family.* London: Faber and Faber.

Polk, M and Tiegreen, M. 2001. *Women of Discovery.* London: Scriptum Editions.

Pretorius, F. 1998. *The Anglo-Boer War 1899-1902.* Cape Town: Struik Publishers.

Pretorius, F. 1999. *Life on Commando during the Anglo-Boer War 1899-1902.* Cape Town: Human & Rousseau.

Raal, S. 2000. *The Lady who Fought: A young woman's account of the Anglo-Boer War.* Cape Town: Stormberg Publishers.

Read, AE. 1998. *Simon's Town and the Anglo-Boer War 1899-1902.* Cape Town: Simon's Town Historical Society.

Reitz, D. 1999. *Adrift on the Open Veld: The Anglo-Boer War and its aftermath 1899-1943.* Cape Town: Stormberg Publishers.

Saks, D. 2010. *Jews in the Boer Armed Forces 1899-1902.* Cape Town: Charlie Fine Printers.

Schoeman, C. 2010. *Boer Boy: Memoirs of an Anglo-Boer War youth.* Cape Town: Zebra Press.

Schoeman, C. 2011. *Brothers in Arms: Hollanders in the Anglo-Boer War.* Cape Town: Zebra Press.

Schoeman, C. 2013. *Vegter en balling: Boereoorlog-ervarings van Veldkornet Charles von Maltitz.* Cape Town: Tafelberg.

Schrøder-Nielsen, I. 2012. *Among the Boers in Peace and War* (ed. Ione Rudner and Bill Nasson). Cape Town: Africana Publishers.

Shubin, GV. 2001. "'I'd like to go to South Africa": The participation of Russian volunteer officers in the Boer War, 1899–1902' in *Voenno-Istoricheskiĭ Zhurnal*, Issue 1.

Spies, SB and Nattrass, G. 1994. *Jan Smuts: Memoirs of the Boer War*. Johannesburg: Jonathan Ball Publishers.

Stead, TW. November 1903. 'How Britain Goes to War: A digest and an analysis of evidence taken by the Royal Commission on the War in South Africa' in *Review of Reviews*. London.

Steenkamp, W. 2012. *Assegaais, Drums & Dragoons*. Cape Town: Jonathan Ball Publishers.

Steyn, R. 2015. *Jan Smuts: Unafraid of greatness*. Cape Town: Jonathan Ball Publishers.

Steyn, W. 2015. *Die Groot Boere-ontsnapping*. Cape Town: Cederberg Uitgewers.

Swart, S. 2010. *Riding High: Horses, humans and history in South Africa*. Johannesburg: Wits University Press.

Van der Merwe, FJ. 2000. *Horses of the Anglo Boer War*. Stellenbosch: US Printers.

Van der Merwe, NJ. 1921. *Marthinus Theunis Steyn: 'n Lewensbeskrywing*. (Two volumes.) Cape Town: De Nationale Pers.

Van der Wall, EH. January 1929. 'The Boers at Diyatalawa' in *Journal of the Dutch Burger Union of Ceylon*, Vol XVIII, No 3.

Van Dyk, CP. 1987. *Boer Prisoners of War at Simon's Town 1899-1903*. BAHons Thesis, University of Cape Town.

Van Rensburg, T. 1977. *Oorlogsjoernaal van SJ Burger*. Pretoria: RGN Publikasie.

Van Warmelo, D. 1977. *On Commando*. Johannesburg: AD Donker.

Walker, M. 2010. *Simon's Town: An historical review with early postcard illustrations*. Cape Town: Shumani.

Warwick, P. 1983. *Black People and the South African War 1899-1902*. Johannesburg: Ravan Press.

Watt, A. June 1989. 'Harrismith: A Military Town During the Anglo-Boer War, and After, Part I' in *Military History Journal*, Vol 8, No 1.

Weinberg, P. 2012. *Dear Edward*. Cape Town: Jacana.

Wessels, E. 2001. *They Fought on Foreign Soil*. Bloemfontein: Anglo Boer War Museum.

Wulfsohn, L. 1992. *Rustenburg at War*. Cape Town: CTP Book Printers.

Original letters and documents

MULLERS

Muller, CJ. War diaries 1899-1902. (Privately owned; copies of five of these diaries are in the National Archives, Pretoria, A1027.)

Muller, LT. War diary 1900. (Privately owned.)

Muller, MA. War diary 1900-1901. (Privately owned.)

Muller, Chrisjan. Memoir. (Privately owned.)

Muller, N. 1952. Joernal, a memoir. (Privately owned.)

Letters written by Oupa Michael Muller; letters written by Chris Muller in Ceylon, and his 'veld' documents, as well as photographs, other documents and artefacts from his war experience; letters written by Lool Muller; letters written by Pieter Muller, son of Michael; documents from Nella Muller Coetzee, Anneke Muller, Meril Muller, Colleen Muller Loesch, and other Muller cousins and descendants.

DIEDERICHS

Documents of Jan Diederichs from Marie Diederichs, his daughter-in-law, including her letters and maps; documents of President Nico Diederichs, from his daughters Lente and Marga née Diederichs; also from other Diederichs cousins and descendants.

ARCHIVE DOCUMENTS

British Army documents, including despatches and letters written from the Magersfontein battlefield, December 1899, in the British National Archives, London, WO|32/|16; letters, hand-drawn maps of Bellevue POW camp, photographs, illustrated cards and assorted original documents, Simon's Town Museum; war records from the War Museum of the Boer Republics, Bloemfontein; diary of GJ van Riet written on board *Montrose* to Bermuda, A252/1, War Museum of the Boer Republics, Bloemfontein.

Acknowledgements

ARCHBISHOP EMERITUS DESMOND TUTU made the remark in the Introduction to me in 2006, when discussing modern pilgrimages, about the need to understand each other's stories. He made similar comments, in slightly different versions, to others over the years. I am grateful for his wise insights, and to his biographer, John Allen, for his recollection.

My grateful thanks to the families of my late husband Professor Ampie Muller, for their trust, generosity and patience over so many years.

Ampie's daughter Anneke Muller (the family genealogist) and brother Dr Piet Muller have caringly offered much support and assistance, and were also careful readers of my many drafts. To them, my deep and heartfelt thanks.

Cousin Colleen Muller Loesch (granddaughter of Commandant Chris Muller) trusted me with her precious cache of war material, including all eight war diaries of her grandfather, and many other documents, photographs and memorabilia; posthumous gratitude to her mother, Patricia O'Connor Muller, who saved Chris's diaries from destruction.

The little box and the wooden frames carved by Michael Muller in Bermuda are owned by cousins Helgaard Raubenheimer and Maurien Muller, respectively.

My particular thanks to family members Rina Muller, Simon Muller, Nico Muller, Meril Muller, Dave Muller, Chris Wiggett, Eugen von Maltitz and Stephan Pretorius. *Tant* Marie Diederichs wrote down for me all she could remember of the Diederichs history at the farm Juiszoo, including hand-drawn maps, and spent hours telling of her memories. Marga Diederichs kindly lent me her father President Nico Diederichs' bible.

Professor Albert Grundlingh generously read and commented on the manuscript, and offered diplomatic suggestions. Max du Preez was an inspiration, as always. Professor David and Virginia Welsh offered continued support and advice, and many reminders to get a move on. Peter Joubert lent me his rare copy of the Royal Commission of 1903 on the South African War. Martin Meredith, in 2011, offered pointers, including from his book, *Diamonds, Gold and War* (an excellent record of the lead-up to the war). Professor Fransjohan Pretorius graciously helped with my enquiries.

Thanks to the useful War Museum of the Boer Republics/Oorlogs-museum in Bloemfontein, and to Elria Wessels and Dr Arnold van Dyk.

The staff of the National Archives of the United Kingdom were friendly and helpful; also, my thanks to the British Library and the Imperial War Museum: all of these invaluable resources are freely offered to accredited researchers. The Simon's Town Museum was also a much valued resource; my gratitude to CEO Cathy Salter-Jansen and staff for repeated access to their archives. Basia Hitchcock, who lived in the only remaining British Command wood-and-iron house in Simon's Town (off Bellevue Road), graciously allowed access. Thanks to Harry Croome (retired), SA Navy. Kevin Ashton showed us the Cape Garrison Artillery at Fort Wynyard. The University of the Free State, and their Archive for Contemporary Affairs (INCH) and Institutional Repository, were generous in sharing material. 'The Mapmaker' Peter Slingsby patiently answered my queries.

Thanks to professors Hugh Corder, Boet Heese, Douw G Steyn, Bernard Lategan and Kay de Villiers; to Willem Steenkamp, JA Bosch, Dalene Dommisse, Biebie van der Merwe, Bernard du Plessis, Peter Louw, Merle Martin and the South African St Helenian Heritage Association, Damian Samuels, Petrovna Metelerkamp, Helga Steyn, Dirk van Zyl Smit, Myra Shackley, Neil Berens and Heather MacAlister.

My family and friends have been enduringly supportive: special thanks and loving gratitude to my daughter Nandi Roos, cousin Moira Duck-worth and stalwart friend Shelagh Gastrow.

My good fortune in having Jonathan Ball Publishers as my publisher began when the then CEO Jeremy Boraine read my manuscript and judged that, despite its enormous size, it might be something worth considering. Tracey Hawthorne assessed it and agreed, for which I am more than thankful – her insistence as editor that it be reduced to the core story of the Mullers was a key factor in its being the concentrated and manageable story it is today; my particular thanks for her heavy work. Thanks also to the rest of the Jonathan Ball team, including Annie Olivier and Gill Moodie, and all their publicists and team members who work hard to bring quality reading to the public, and with whom I have happily transacted for decades (wearing my other longtime hat as a reviewer/interviewer).

This book would not have existed had it not been for a lucky day in 1997, when Ampie and I met on his Rosebank doorstep and instantly fell in love – there is no other way to describe it. He placed complete trust and confidence in my recovering his family's war, starting with the diary he inherited from his grandfather, Michael Muller – the sole document with which this long journey began. He assisted in translating the ten Muller diaries and was endlessly encouraging. It is amazing to have someone believe in you. I realise I'm biased, but that doesn't make it less true.

Index

Note: Page numbers in italics indicate a photograph

About the author

DR BEVERLEY ROOS-MULLER is a veteran journalist and broad-caster, and former academic lecturing in humanities at the University of Cape Town. She was an anti-apartheid activist in the 1980s, including spokesperson for the multi-organisational *Open City* campaign opposing the Group Areas Act. She is the co-author, with her late husband, Prof Ampie Muller, of *Vuur in sy vingers*, about his father-in-law, the poet NP Van Wyk Louw.

www.ingramcontent.com/pod-product-compliance
Lightning Source LLC
Chambersburg PA
CBHW072135090426
42739CB00013B/3199